Not So with You

Not So with You

Power and Leadership for the Church

EDITED BY
MARK STIRLING AND
MARK MEYNELL

WIPF & STOCK · Eugene, Oregon

NOT SO WITH YOU
Power and Leadership for the Church

Copyright © 2023 Wipf and Stock Publishers. All rights reserved. Except for brief quotations in critical publications or reviews, no part of this book may be reproduced in any manner without prior written permission from the publisher. Write: Permissions, Wipf and Stock Publishers, 199 W. 8th Ave., Suite 3, Eugene, OR 97401.

Wipf & Stock
An Imprint of Wipf and Stock Publishers
199 W. 8th Ave., Suite 3
Eugene, OR 97401

www.wipfandstock.com

PAPERBACK ISBN: 978-1-6667-6016-3
HARDCOVER ISBN: 978-1-6667-6017-0
EBOOK ISBN: 978-1-6667-6018-7

06/22/23

Scripture quotations marked NIV® or NIV 2011 are taken from The Holy Bible, New International Version®, NIV®. Copyright © 1973, 1978, 1984, 2011 by Biblica, Inc.® Used by permission of Zondervan. All rights reserved worldwide. www.zondervan.com. The "NIV" and "New International Version" are trademarks registered in the United States Patent and Trademark Office by Biblica, Inc.®

Scripture quotations marked ESV are taken from the ESV® Bible (The Holy Bible, English Standard Version®). Copyright © 2001 by Crossway, a publishing ministry of Good News Publishers. Used by permission. All rights reserved.

Scripture quotations marked NLT are taken from the Holy Bible, New Living Translation. © 1996. 2004, 2015 by Tyndale House Foundation. Used by permission of Tyndale House Publishers, Inc., Carol Stream, Illinois 60188. All rights reserved.

For Jerram Barrs, kind and gentle friend, mentor and example of everything good I hope this book might achieve.
(AMS)

For Bishop Edward Muhima, dear friend, mentor and prayer partner.
(MJHM)

But Jesus called them to him and said, "You know that the rulers of the Gentiles lord it over them, and their great ones exercise authority over them. It shall not be so among you. But whoever would be great among you must be your servant, and whoever would be first among you must be your slave, even as the Son of Man came not to be served but to serve, and to give his life as a ransom for many."

(MATT 20:25–28 ESV)

Contents

List of Contributors ... ix
Acknowledgments ... xi
Introduction: Why Another Book on Power and Why Now? ... xiii
Mark Stirling

PART 1: BIBLICAL AND THEOLOGICAL FOUNDATIONS

1   Imitating the Mindset of Christ ... 3
Mark Stirling

2   Confessions of a Potential Authoritarian: Knowing the Trinity as Antidote to Pastoral Authoritarianism ... 17
Jared Michelson

3   "You must not do as they do . . ." Old Testament Israel's Distinctive Patterns of Leadership ... 32
Chris Wright

4   Sin and Why We Need to Take It More Seriously ... 47
Nick Mackison

5   The Power of the Imago Dei and the Imago Dei in Power ... 61
Mark Meynell

6   Symbolic Capital and the Dynamics of Leadership: The Gospel and the Idolatry of Status ... 83
Grant Macaskill

7   Use, Not Abuse: An Augustinian Approach to Loving People ... 101
Graham Shearer

PART 2: PRACTICAL AND PASTORAL REFLECTIONS

8	When a Church Becomes a Cult: Twenty-Five Years On *Steve Wookey*	115
9	The Cost of Brokenness *Blythe Sizemore*	128
10	Authoritative, *Not* Authoritarian *Sam Allberry*	138
11	When Our First Love Is Loving to Be First *Chris Green*	147
12	Mentors, Not Masters *Marcus Honeysett*	158
13	Of God and God-Men *Sushila Ailawadi*	173
14	Pastors Empowering Women to Flourish *Tasha Chapman*	185
15	Signs and Symptoms of Unhealthy Leaders and Their Systems *Mark Stirling*	200
	Conclusion: That No Bruised Reed Is Ever Broken *Mark Meynell*	218
	Author Index	237
	Subject Index	241
	Scripture Index	257

List of Contributors
(in chapter order)

MARK STIRLING directs Chalmers Institute and teaches at Highland Theological College, Scotland. He is a former medical doctor and pastor and has a PhD in New Testament from St Andrews University.

JARED MICHELSON is pastor of Cornerstone Church, St Andrews, Scotland, and has a PhD in theology from St Andrews University.

CHRISTOPHER J. H. WRIGHT is a missiologist and Old Testament scholar who, after twenty years as international ministries director, is now global ambassador for Langham Partnership.

NICK MACKISON pastored in the Free Church of Scotland and is currently completing PhD studies at Aberdeen University as a Chalmers Fellow.

MARK MEYNELL serves as director (Europe & Caribbean) for Langham Preaching (a program of Langham Partnership), is ordained in the Church of England, and has a DMin in cultural apologetics from Covenant Theological Seminary, St. Louis.

GRANT MACASKILL was appointed to the Kirby Laing Chair of New Testament Exegesis at Aberdeen University in 2015, having completed doctoral and postdoctoral projects in St Andrews. His research focuses on both the historical dimensions of the New Testament and its significance to contemporary theological and ethical issues

GRAHAM SHEARER formerly worked with UCCF and was a pastor. He is currently working on a PhD with Union Theological College in Belfast and is a Chalmers Fellow.

STEVE WOOKEY is a retired Church of England minister, serving ten years at All Souls Langham Place in London, and twenty-four years as Rector of St David's Moreton in the Marsh.

BLYTHE SIZEMORE is director of children's ministry at Covenant Life Church, Sarasota, Florida and is a DMin candidate at Covenant Theological Seminary, St Louis.

SAM ALLBERRY is a writer and teacher, and associate pastor at Immanuel Church, Nashville.

CHRIS GREEN is vicar of St James' Muswell Hill, London and formerly vice principal of Oak Hill Theological College.

MARCUS HONEYSETT is executive director of living leadership in the United Kingdom, having spent thirteen years in campus ministry with UCCF.

SUSHILA AILAWADI is actively involved in the ministries of The Hub church, New Delhi in India.

TASHA D. CHAPMAN is professor of educational ministries at Covenant Theological Seminary. Her research focuses on the teaching/learning process and ministry sustainability.

Acknowledgments

Mark Meynell

This book is the fruit of years of conversations. In particular, I need to thank the scores of survivors who have trusted me with their stories of hurt and devastation. They are the brave ones. This is but a small response to their suffering in the hope that others may not be forced to endure what they did. Thanks to all those who have helped with getting this book together, including the friends who wrote short pieces for it at a point when this anthology was initially shaping up to be something slightly different. My coeditor and all the contributors have been very kind and patient especially at points when I was the one holding things back. I'm thrilled with the variety and breadth of experience captured in these essays. Thank you all. Rachel, my wife, has of course endured the most and yet has been supportive and patient to the nth degree, so she certainly deserves much credit.

    My dedication is to my friend and former mentor, Edward Muhima. Soon after we moved to Uganda in 2001, Edward kindly agreed to meet once a month or so with me. I was acutely conscious of being a young, inexperienced and naive foreigner bumbling around in East Africa, and so knew I needed an older hand to help me. I had little idea how precious our friendship would become and I owe him so much, not least because he walked a very different leadership road than many around him. It was a privilege and joy to be present at his installation as Bishop of North Kigezi in Rukungiri in 2004. We both wept when our time in Kampala came to an end in 2005. I still thank God for Edward and his dear wife Vasta.

Mark Stirling

I am grateful for my companions on this road. We have wrestled through much together as we lamented and longed for church to be different. I am grateful for the community of Cornerstone Church, St Andrews, who were infinitely patient with me as I sought to lead them faithfully. "We loved you so much, we were delighted to share not only the Gospel of God, but our very lives" (1 Thess 2:8). I think also of all the tragic testimonies I have heard over the years and long that these brothers and sisters would find comfort in the One True God, while rejecting the distorted image they have seen demonstrated. My time at Covenant Theological Seminary was formative for me; I thank God for the godly examples of wise leadership I encountered there. I have mentioned Jerram Barrs in my dedication, but I must also credit Dr. Hans Bayer. His example of humility (and humor!) while teaching people like me who knew so much less than he did, remains an inspiring example.

My wife Jenny has put up with me for many years and has endured this project and all the conversations surrounding it. Her resilience and strength, combined with unflinching truth-speaking in love, especially in the face of opposition or criticism, have inspired me to keep walking with God and keep loving his people.

Introduction

Why Another Book on Power and Why Now?

Mark Stirling

You Can't Do Jesus' Work in Non-Jesus Ways

IN ALL THE RECENT leadership scandals on both sides of the Atlantic, the consistent factor is Christian leaders trying to do Jesus' work in ways that are inconsistent with Jesus' example and teaching.

The widespread misuse or abuse of power amongst "christian" leaders is traceable to a misunderstanding, and consequently a misrepresentation, of God and the gospel. This is bad for everyone and a tragic compromise of the church's witness. We cannot afford to treat this lightly and simply tweak our leadership structures or practices; we need to start with the theological and biblical issues at the root of this disease that infects so many of our churches and organizations.

Any critique must start with ourselves; we need to remove our log before our brother's speck. This is not a problem "out there," but "in here." The problems we are diagnosing are widespread and are not limited to any one theological or cultural perspective. This is why our contributors represent a wide range of denominations and traditions.

Our sincere prayer is that this book is not used primarily as a resource for judging others, so much as an aid to prayerful self-examination. That said, many readers will have to wrestle prayerfully (but, we hope, not alone) with the question of when bad character should be exposed publicly for the protection of others. This is a complex and challenging question to which there is no formulaic answer, but we can say confidently that coverup and lies are not the Jesus way. He does not need us to lie to protect his reputation; rather, when we speak the truth, we demonstrate that we trust him. Such truth speaking in this book will also be an affirmation that what many have experienced is indeed wrong. We hope bringing sin into the light will also be a step on the way to healing for many.

The overall message of this book constitutes a call to repentance that starts with a recognition of the severity of the diagnosis. The first section of the book therefore addresses the theological and biblical roots of the problem before proceeding to pastoral and practical reflections in Section 2.

SECTION 1: BIBLICAL AND THEOLOGICAL FOUNDATIONS

We start with an exploration of Jesus' pattern of self-giving love in Phil 2:5–11 as the attitude to be imitated by all believers. Power is for self-giving, not for selfish gain. In chapter 2, Jared Michelson reflects on the theological (and specifically trinitarian) misunderstandings that may underly harmful leadership. More robust theology is required. Chris Wright then summarizes Old Testament teaching on characteristics of godly leadership. This leads us to the key issue of what has gone wrong. In chapter 4, Nick Mackison addresses the fact that leadership abuse often flourishes because of evangelical naivete about the depth and extent of sin. We must be willing to face the awfulness of sin if we are to guard against its most damaging effects in the life of the church. Mark Meynell then explores the implications for leadership that all humans are divine image bearers and therefore infinitely precious. In chapter 6, Grant Macaskill argues that symbolic capital and the social status we gain by accruing it is the "rubbish" Paul rejects in Phil 3. The implications of this for how we think about and practice leadership are far-reaching. The final essay in this section is Graham Shearer's provocative reflection on Augustine's idea of never allowing a human person to become the ultimate object of our love, but being led through those we love to God himself.

Section 2: Practical and Pastoral Reflections

Section 2 starts with Steve Wookey's sad reflection on cultish behavior in churches twenty-five years on from the book he wrote warning about exactly that. In chapter 9, Blythe Sizemore shares some of her own experience of harmful leadership and reflects on the process of healing from it. Sam Allbury then provides a careful nuance that authoritarian abuses do not argue *against* the use of authority, but *for* the right use of it. Chris Green's chapter is then a helpful exploration of competitiveness and pride in ministry leadership, drawing on the example of Diotrophes in 3 John. We then move to very practical advice and pointers towards best practice in mentoring. Marcus Honeysett warns against mentors ever becoming masters. This then leads us to what is one of the most disturbing chapters in the book. Sushila Ailawadi details heartbreaking examples of abuse of women in her home Indian culture. Tragically, what is true in the culture is also true in the church. It is a sober warning to Western readers who may be quick to see what's wrong in another culture, but blind to the faults in their own. Tasha Chapman in chapter 14 addresses the fact that many women in our churches are not treated with dignity and respect as partners in God's kingdom work. She suggests multiple ways church leadership can honor women. Chapter 15 is Mark Stirling's extended reflection on the often-subtle signs and symptoms of unhealthy church leadership, arguing that, though none of these is necessarily diagnostic of abuse, they should all cause us to ask good questions. Mark Meynell's conclusion suggests ways to apply all of this as well as guarding us against some of the pitfalls along the way.

This book is offered with the prayer that in some way it may help shape leadership culture and practice so that God's people may be served by their leaders to flourish individually and collectively, and may then demonstrate in their love for one another the presence and character of the God who is in their midst.

We pray that "many will see and fear, and put their trust in the Lord" (Ps 40:3 ESV).

PART 1

Biblical and Theological Foundations

1

Imitating the Mindset of Christ

Mark Stirling

INTRODUCTION AND AIMS

THE IDEA AT THE heart of this chapter (and of this book) is simple: power and leadership are the means of giving oneself *to* others, not the means of getting something for oneself *from* others. Simple to understand, harder to apply.

Believers are commanded in Phil 2:5 to imitate Jesus' attitude to his equality with God. The articulation of Christ's attitude to rights and power in Phil 2:6–11 is radically at odds with popular conceptions, not just in the world, but also, sadly, in the church. Leadership must never be the means of self-advancement, self-assertion, or selfish gain. Rather, it is for the service and blessing of others. Consequently, any reversal of the direction from self-giving to self-gain is, by definition, a misuse or an abuse of power. This is the central theological and practical burden of this book.[1]

Our approach in this volume is to address misuse of power by leaders in explicitly biblical and theological, rather than exclusively psychological, terms, so as to avoid reduction of the diagnosis to bad behavior by a few bad leaders. How we understand power and its misuse depends on our understanding of God himself—who he is, what he is like, and what he wants

---

1. In view of this, it is interesting to see some recent academic writing from Africa arguing for a reform of understanding and practice of leadership based upon Phil 2:5–11. See Kgatle, "Servant Leadership"; Ottuh, "Concept of κένωσις"; Mdingi, "Kenosis of Leadership."

from us. Paul's articulation of Jesus' model in Philippians and how it is to be imitated will help us address these questions. We will then observe a couple of biblical examples of application of the pattern found in Phil 2 before concluding with the challenge that misuse of power by leaders misrepresents God's character and, in bearing his name in vain, breaks the third commandment.

PHILIPPIANS 2:1–12: THE PARADIGM OF POWER

The heart of Phil 2:1–11 is a command to disciples to have a mindset patterned after Christ's attitude to his "equality with God." The passage raises multiple interpretive questions which go beyond the scope of this project.[2] Here, rather than proceeding verse-by-verse, we will first consider the wider contextual picture, then examine the use of Isa 45 in Phil 2:9–11, before going backwards to the exegetical details of Phil 2:5–8.

It is worth setting out a literal translation of the text of Phil 2:5–11 in order to highlight the interpretive issues:

> Think this way, which is also in Christ Jesus, who [though being or precisely because he was] in the form of God did not consider [his] equality with God as [something he already had and needed to hold tight to or something he did not have to which he aspired], but [emptied himself or poured himself out] (by) taking the form of a servant, (by) being born as a man, and (by) being found in appearance as a man, he humbled himself by becoming obedient right up to death, even death of the cross. For this very reason, God hyper-exalted him and gave him the Name that is above every name, in order that at the name of Jesus, every knee should bow, in heaven and on earth and under the earth and every tongue should confess that Jesus Christ is Lord to the glory of God the Father.

The context and flow of thought of the passage is crucial in resolving these exegetical issues. However, it seems to me that Paul's use of Isa 45—the name above all names given to Christ because of his humble self-giving—is the key to right interpretation.

---

2. For good surveys of scholarship, see Bockmuehl, *Philippians*; Hawthorne, *Philippians*; Silva, *Philippians*; Hansen, *Philippians*.

Context

Paul's concern for unity in the church of Philippi is widely noted (see, for example, his exhortation to Euodia and Syntyche in 4:2 to get on with each other). Unity for Paul is not a matter of an optional extra—a luxury if you can manage it. Rather, unity of believers is directly related to their union with Christ. Thus, Phil 2:1–2 is an exhortation to unity ("complete my joy by being of the same mind, having the same love, being in full accord and of one mind" [Phil 2:2 ESV]) based on the believers' gracious union with Christ in verse 1: "So if there is any encouragement in Christ, any comfort from love, any participation in the Spirit" (Phil 2:1 ESV). In other words, if they are united to Christ, unity will follow.

This relationship between union and unity is key; to be united with Christ is inevitably to be united with other believers in the "one new humanity" (Eph 2:15) that is created as a result of Christ's peacemaking work on the Cross (Eph 2:13–14). Unity of believers is therefore a demonstration of the efficacy of the cross, reconciling us to God vertically and to each other horizontally.[3]

Here in Philippians, Paul's concern is with the attitudes and the relational qualities that foster and maintain unity and are expressive of union with Christ. The famous passage from Phil 2:5–11 in which Paul encourages the imitation of Christ's mindset or thinking is bracketed on both sides with reference to union with Christ. It is those who have encouragement in Christ and participation in the Spirit (Phil 2:1) and who are practically outworking their salvation (Phil 2:12–18) who are to take on a set of attitudes and relational approaches that are supremely demonstrated in Christ (Phil 2:5). Imitation of these attitudes that promote unity is thus a fruit of being united to Christ, it does not unite to Christ.

The context of Phil 2 thus suggests that its purpose is to inculcate a particular way of thinking or attitude that is supremely demonstrated in Christ, and will be most conducive to unity in the church.

Flow of Thought

The flow of thought may be summarized as follows:

- Paul appeals to his readers to be united on the basis of their union with Christ (vv. 1–2).

---

3. This unity also has important missional implications in that this united new humanity becomes the "dwelling place for God" (Eph 2:22) by means of which God's presence and character is manifested.

- Unity among believers is expressed and fostered by a set of attitudes towards others—doing nothing out of selfish ambition or "vainglory," in humility considering others more important, and looking out for others' interests (vv. 3–4).
- This set of attitudes (the fruit of union with Christ) is commanded and is patterned after Christ's supreme example (v. 5).
- Christ's attitude is explained in verses 6–8—his way of thinking about his equality with God and the actions which flowed from that attitude.
- Because of this attitude of Christ's and the actions that follow, he is "hyperexalted" and given the "name above every name," citing Isa 45 (vv. 9–11)
- Therefore live out this salvation (vv. 12–18)

Paul's Use of Isaiah 45

Much debate on Phil 2 has centered on what it means for Christ to "empty" himself (the theological term "kenosis" is derived from this Greek verb) or not to consider his equality with God "a thing to be grasped," but we will look first at Phil 2:9–11 as the key to understanding verses 6–8.[4]

The flow of thought above clarifies the logic of the passage; God's "hyper-exalting" of Christ in Phil 2:9 is introduced with a strong causal "for this very reason." The exalting of Christ is therefore not despite the attitude and actions of 2:6–8, but because of them. Furthermore, God not only "hyper-exalts," but also gives Christ "the name above every name," applying Isa 45 to him in a bold and shocking move.

> Therefore God has highly exalted him and bestowed on him the name that is above every name, so that at the name of Jesus every knee should bow, in heaven and on earth and under the earth, and every tongue confess that Jesus Christ is Lord, to the glory of God the Father. (Phil 2:9–11 ESV)

Isaiah 45 is punctuated with the refrain that Yahweh alone is God and there is no other (Isa 45:5, 6, 14, 18, 21), culminating in the declaration that Yahweh alone saves:

> Turn to me and be saved, all the ends of the earth! For I am God, and there is no other. By myself I have sworn; from my mouth

---

4. For two recent treatments of kenosis, see, e.g., Evans, *Kenotic Christology*; Pardue, "Kenosis and Its Discontents."

has gone out in righteousness a word that shall not return: "To me every knee shall bow, every tongue shall swear allegiance." Only in the LORD, it shall be said of me, are righteousness and strength; to him shall come and be ashamed all who were incensed against him. In the LORD all the offspring of Israel shall be justified and shall glory. (Isa 45:22–25 ESV)

The nations are to turn to Yahweh alone for salvation. He will rule and reign and in Yahweh the seed (lit.) of Israel will be justified. Paul applies this text to Christ with the introduction "for this very reason." Yahweh is the only God and only Savior who will rule supreme over the nations, and this, says Paul, is affirmed as the identity of Jesus demonstrated in the attitude and actions described in verses 6–8.[5]

Paul thus identifies Christ with Yahweh in the highest possible christological move. More than that, it is Christ, whose attitude towards his equality with God led him to "empty himself," become human, become a servant and become obedient to the point of death on the cross, who is identified with Yahweh. The logic is that Christ did these things and "for this very reason" (v. 9), he is exalted and given the divine name of Yahweh.

The significance of this cannot be overstated; the giving of the divine name is not in spite of Christ's course of self-giving self-sacrifice, but precisely because of it. To put it another way, Christ's attitude and course of action is not a temporary departure from the divine character, but rather is the supreme demonstration of it, a demonstration that must be endorsed using Isa 45—"This is Yahweh and this is what he is like."

God's Fullness in Himself and the Incarnation of the Son

How does this then fit with an understanding of God? How might the character of God be consistent with this humble, self-giving sacrifice? Since doctrine of God is addressed in greater depth by the contributions of both Jared Michelson and Graham Shearer, I am merely introducing the topic here. The idea of God's fullness in himself illumines Paul's argument: God is eternally full and eternally satisfied in himself in Triune fellowship.[6] He

---

5. Discussion of whether this is applied to Christ in his divinity or humanity seems to me to miss the point. It is the single acting subject and his attitude towards equality with God who is affirmed with the divine name. See especially Cyril of Alexandria, *On the Unity of Christ*, 95.

6. "Divine aseity lies at the heart of this doctrine of God. It is an attribute that signifies that God is not dependent on anything or anyone else to be the God that he is but instead has life in and of himself. This is a life eternally fulfilled in the fellowship of the Father, Son and Holy Spirit." Duby, *Jesus and the God of Classical Theism*, 22.

lacks nothing, needs nothing, wants nothing. God in himself needs nothing outside of himself to make himself complete or to realize his identity. This means, for example, that when God created the heavens and the earth, he did so not out of any need, certainly not out of loneliness and needing some creatures to relate to. Rather, the act of creation, is pure lavish gift—the outpouring from the fullness of his being. This has huge pastoral implications. We do not relate to a God who needs something from us. He does not depend upon us for anything. He will not throw a tantrum or sulk if we don't give him what he wants.[7] It is this God who becomes incarnate. Church fathers such as Cyril of Alexandria or John of Damascus reflected deeply on the nature of the incarnation, carefully articulating what it means for the divine and human to be united in the person of Christ, with no loss or diminishment of the divine nature. Cyril comments:

> We must not think that he who descended into the limitation of manhood for our sake lost his inherent radiance and that transcendence that comes from his nature. No, he had this divine fullness even in the emptiness of our condition, and he enjoyed the highest eminence in humility, and held what belongs to him by nature (that is, to be worshipped by all) as a gift because of his humanity.[8]

Or, more simply, "And the Word became flesh, without incurring change."[9]

From this perspective, Christ in the incarnation is fully God and loses nothing of the divine nature, which, being full and complete in itself, required nothing outside of itself for completion, fullness or to realize its identity. This means that whatever "emptying" (or "kenosis") is in Phil 2:7, it does not represent any loss or diminution of the divine nature in the person of Christ.[10]

The logic of the passage is illuminated by considering these theological categories of fullness and incarnation without loss of divinity—the One who is full in eternal Triune fellowship needs nothing outside himself and therefore does not consider his equality with God "a thing to be grasped," but by contrast "empties himself" and serves to the point of death.

---

7. God is therefore not "like us, but bigger." This is one of the core mistakes that results in leadership that misrepresents God's character. See Michelson's chapter in this volume as well as my discussion in chapter 15.

8. Cyril of Alexandria, *On the Unity of Christ*, 123.

9. John of Damascus, *On the Orthodox Faith*, 163.

10. For recent discussion of theological interpretation of Scripture, see Jamieson and Wittman, *Biblical Reasoning*.

What we see in Christ's pattern of self-giving in his incarnation and passion is not a temporary diminution of his deity, nor a suspension of divine attributes. his course of action could not receive the application of Isa 45 were that the case.[11] Rather, when we look at the incarnation and the passion, we see the character of God himself in the supreme expression of image bearing. It seems to me that we are consistently tripped up in our considerations of this by our assumptions that power is the means to gain something and that for Jesus to humble himself must necessarily mean the suspension of the use of power that could avoid servanthood and the cross. When the logic of our assumptions is explored, we can see that it rests on denial at some level of the Son's divine fullness in the incarnation. But, if God is full in himself and thus lacks nothing, then his posture towards his creation can be neither one of need nor of self-protection. It is one of lavish generosity and self-giving grace. The incarnation and passion, therefore, are expressions, transcriptions in flesh if you will, of the divine nature. Fullness is poured out towards and on behalf of others, needing neither to receive any return as though lacking something, nor to protect against harm, as though something could be taken away. We thus see in the "kenosis" of Phil 2 that divine fullness means a generous, self-giving love that needs nothing and withholds nothing precisely because it is already full and lacks nothing. This then means that Paul's command to think in a way patterned after Christ's self-understanding of his equality with God principally concerns giving in love out of fullness and never using power to gain what is lacked or to protect against perceived threat. If this is what it means to be restored in his image, the ethical implications are revolutionary.

Christ's Mindset and Actions

This passage hinges at v. 5 as already noted, literally "Think this among you which is also in Christ Jesus." "This" points backwards to the previous verses, in which certain attitudes (doing nothing out of selfish ambition or conceit, considering others more important than self and looking out also for the interests of others, vv. 2–4) that are expressive of union with Christ (v. 1) are to be emulated (the imperative "Think this . . ." in v. 5).[12] The argument pivots at this point to introduce and expand upon the example of Christ Jesus as the one who supremely demonstrates this way of thinking (vv. 6–8).

---

11. See, for example, Duby, *God in Himself*, 158–61. Duby discusses this passage, noting that the Son's divine fullness is not compromised or threatened by the incarnation.

12. Hawthorne, *Philippians*, 80.

Verses 6–7 are the subject of a great deal of discussion and contention. It seems to me that keeping in mind the bigger picture as discussed above is vital, not least to guard us against needless speculation. Part of the problem in these verses is the difficulty of rendering the concepts into easy English. I will discuss it phrase by phrase—

- "who being in the form of God" (Phil 2:6)—the ESV at this point translates the participle concessively ("though he was in the form of God") which we should note, is an interpretive move, rather than being demanded by the text. In view of the discussion above on the use of Isa 45, I think this is unjustified[13] and should either be translated neutrally ("being in the form . . ." cf. NIV) or even causally ("because he was in the form . . ."). The point is that Paul's exposition of Christ's attitude emphasizes Christ's divinity and his attitude towards it. Being in the form of God, he had all the rights, prerogatives, and power of deity.[14] It is from this perspective that Paul's argument proceeds. How does One who has equality with God use such equality and all that comes with it?

- "did not consider being equal with God '*harpagmon*'" (Phil 2:6)—I'll leave the last word untranslated for now.[15] Paul is exploring Christ's attitude towards his equality with God. He did not consider it "*harpagmon*," but by contrast, followed the course of action described in the following verses; that is, incarnation, humble service, and sacrificial suffering to the point of death on the cross. Christ's attitude towards his divinity and all the power and rights that accompany it is one of humility leading to service, suffering, and sacrificial death. These stand in opposition to "*harpagmon*," which is therefore a way of thinking about power and rights that was the opposite of that exemplified by Christ. The NIV (2011) reflects this, translating "did not consider equality with God something to be used to his own advantage." "*Harpagmon*" is therefore something that belongs to a person by right and is theirs to use as they wish for their own benefit.[16] This understanding of the concept of

---

13. The concessive translation of the participle in Phil 2:6 ("though being . . .") cannot be justified on the basis that this course of action is inconsistent with the character of God, otherwise Isa 45 would not be used in verses 9–11. The only justification for this translation would be if it indicates surprise from the human perspective that One in the form of God with equality with God would choose to use such power for the sake of humble, self-giving love.

14. See, e.g., Hawthorne, *Philippians*, 84; Hansen, *Philippians*, 136–37

15. This word occurs only here in the New Testament.

16. Hoover, "Harpagmos Enigma"; O'Neill, "Hoover on Harpagmos Reviewed, with a Modest Proposal Concerning Philippians 2:6." In addition, all the major commentaries

"*harpagmon*" receives support in the considerations above of divine fullness. Christ, being full in himself, did not need to use his equality with God to get anything for himself, nor to protect himself from anything. He did not consider his divinity "an advantage to exploit."[17]

- This brings us to the discussion of verse 7. He did not consider equality with God "an advantage to exploit," but "emptied himself" (ESV) or "made himself nothing" (NIV). I don't think either of these quite gets what Paul is saying here. Cyril points out that this "emptying" is given content by what follows;[18] Christ's "emptying" is expressed in taking the form of a servant, being in the likeness and appearance of man and humbling himself to death on the cross. Given the flow of argument of this passage, it seems to me that a much more fitting rendering in English would be "poured himself out."[19] The problem with "emptied himself" is that it simply invites the question "of what?" which seems to me not to be what Paul is concerned with here. If, however, the Son loses nothing of his deity in the incarnation—he undergoes no change with respect to his divine identity—then the logic of the passage pushes us towards the much more helpful "poured himself out." The argument can be summarized—

    a. The overall purpose of the passage is to encourage attitudes expressive of union with Christ that foster unity in Christ's people.

    b. These attitudes are described as humble consideration of others as more important than self, attention to the interests of others and doing nothing from selfish ambition.

    c. These attitudes are supremely demonstrated in Christ's attitude towards and use of his own equality with God.

    d. He did not use this equality with God, which was his by right, as the means to gain something for himself as though he lacked anything, or to defend himself against the loss of anything.

    e. Rather he used his equality with God and all the power and privilege associated with it to pursue the course of pouring himself out in humble service of others, to the point of death on the cross.

---

discuss this at length. More recently, Hansen translates the term "an advantage to exploit." Hansen, *Philippians*, 142.

17. Bockmuehl concludes that "Christ did not consider his existing divine status as a possession to be exploited for selfish interests." Bockmuehl, *Philippians*, 130.

18. Cyril of Alexandria, *On the Unity of Christ*, 86.

19. This is the interpretation proposed by Hawthorne. See Hawthorne, *Philippians*, 85.

This seems to me to make sense of the particulars of this passage, the point of which is to show us the supreme example of One who had all the power in the universe at his command and chose to use it in humble, painful, costly, and loving service. Paul is effectively saying, "Here is Christ with all the power of the universe at his disposal and he did not use it to get something for himself but used it to persevere on the road of self-giving love to the point of death. You are to do the same with whatever rights, power or privileges you have been given."

The parallel between this passage and John 13 is often observed. Jesus' washing of the disciples' feet is prefaced by the comment that he knew all things had been given into his hands (John 13:3). With all authority available to him, he served humbly—and when he had finished, instructed his disciples that he had just set them an example that they were to follow in their relationships with others (John 13:12–17). The point is the same—power is given not to enable personal gain, but to empower personal giving for the sake of others.

Reflection on his "obedience to death" (v. 8) further reinforces this. It is tempting to think of Christ as a helpless and innocent victim as he goes to the cross. Innocent he certainly is, but the biblical account seems at pains to disabuse us of the notion that he was helpless. In Gethsemane the night before when he is arrested, he rebukes the disciple who uses the sword to attempt to resist arrest, reminding the disciples that he could call twelve legions of angels to his side should he wish (Matt 26:53). Jesus is stressing that we must not think this course of action is forced upon him against his will. Rather, it is freely, willingly chosen. Thus, when Christ is tempted—"If you are the Son of God, prove it and come down from the cross"—it is infinitely sobering to realize he not only had the right but also the power to do so. All he had to do was issue the command, but he did not. He did not consider his equality with God "advantage to be exploited," but instead poured himself out in obedience to the point of death, resisting the temptation to stop the pain, until he could cry out "It is finished!" and thereby secure redemption and eternal blessing. The cross itself is the triumph of humble service over selfish self-interest.

SUMMARY: WHAT IS POWER FOR?

This overview of Phil 2:5–11 allows us to draw some conclusions. Believers are to have a way of thinking that understands all they are and all they have been given (their rights, power, and privileges) are for the purpose of enabling them to give themselves to others, not to enable them to get something from others. This is the pattern we see in Christ and it demonstrates God's character. Though it is commanded of all believers, I am applying it here particularly to leaders as their temptation to violate this pattern is exacerbated by their positional power and authority.

DEFINITION: USE AND MISUSE OF POWER

One of the things this passage is not teaching us is that the answer to misuse or abuse of power is nonuse of power. Rather, it is showing us how power is to be used rightly as those who are united with Christ and being restored in his image. The passage does not call for the renunciation of power, but for its legitimate use. It is a common mistake to allow abuse to argue against right use and, instead of reforming or redeeming the use of power, simply run away from it, which solves nothing.

So, I propose a definition: Power is granted to empower humble, self-giving service of others for the sake of their growth and flourishing as creatures in God's image. Any use of power to get something from others or to defend oneself against the cost of loving others is, by definition, misuse of power.

FULLNESS IN CHRIST: HOW CHRIST'S PATTERN IS IMITATED

For us to imitate this pattern depends on receiving from God in order to give to others, instead of exploiting others to gain what we feel we lack. This takes us to the heart of what is paradigmatic for all believers, not just Christian leaders.

For if fellowship with the Triune God is not enough to make you content and secure, then nothing will be. And if you are not content and secure in that Triune fellowship, then you will inevitably use the power available to you (whether formally from office or position, or informally from personal influence, relationships, time, money, career, etc.) to get from others what you perceive you lack or to defend yourself against perceived threat. And the problem with either of those is that they are the exact opposite of a biblical understanding of love and a violation of the pattern we observe in Phil 2.

Ephesians 2:18 is a beautiful one-sentence summary of communion with God enjoyed by believers: "Through him (that is, through Christ), we both have access to the Father by the One Spirit." In the context of the rest of Eph 2, Paul is saying that those who are formerly "dead in sins and transgressions" (Eph 2:1-3) and are enemies of God and each other (Eph 2:12) are now, by God's gracious intervention and through the peacemaking work of Christ on the cross (Eph 2:14-15), united to God and to each other in "one new humanity" (Eph 2:15). This is expressed in Eph 2:18 as access to the Father, through Christ by the Spirit—communion with the Triune God. This is, if you like, the *sine qua non* of Christian living.

Jumping forward to Eph 5:1-2, we can see the practical implications of this fellowship in Paul's command to be imitators of God. There is a recapitulation here of the pattern we have already observed in Phil 2. In Eph 5:1-2, Paul commands that believers are to be imitators of God, but carefully defines the conditions of that imitation.

> Therefore be imitators of God, as beloved children. And walk in love, as Christ loved us and gave himself up for us, a fragrant offering and sacrifice to God. (Eph 5:1-2 ESV)

Imitation is "as beloved children," flowing from the condition of already being beloved children as a result of God's grace. But imitation is not of God in an undefined or comprehensive manner. Rather, it is defined as "walking in love as Christ loved us and gave himself as a sacrifice for us." Creaturely imitation of God is therefore expressed in following the pattern of Christ's self-giving and self-sacrificial love.

Imitation in Eph 5:1-2 involves receiving from God (as beloved children) and giving to others (following Christ's demonstration of love). This pattern of receiving and giving is a helpful rubric that can be applied to leaders. Any leader can ask whether they are receiving from God so that they are secure and content enough to love people and not use them. Receiving and giving stands in sharp contrast to what can be observed every time leadership in the body of Christ goes wrong—grasping and getting. To the extent that a spiritual leader is not content and secure in their relationship with Father, Son, and Spirit, they will use their leadership to try to get something from those whom they are leading. Here is the taproot of spiritual abuse. They will, in Ezekiel's words, feed themselves upon God's sheep instead of feeding God's sheep (Ezek 34).

Leaders must engage in prolonged and prayerful examination of their own hearts to assess the extent to which they are indeed serving and loving others out of security and contentment in God himself. Of course, it is obvious that on this side of the eschaton there will be insecurity and discontent in all of us, which is why, if they are to lead and serve faithfully, leaders must continuously prioritize attention to their own spiritual growth. Application to spiritual practices that deepen their experience of God is crucial. No leader ever outgrows the need for this to be their daily priority.

THE PATTERN APPLIED: PAUL AND THE THESSALONIANS

There is space only for the briefest biblical example of this pattern, though it may be widely observed in Scripture. In 1 Thess 2:3–8, Paul gives us a window into his own ministry and specifically his use of apostolic authority. In a fascinating passage, he explicitly renounces manipulation, flattery, or seeking glory from those to whom he was ministering. Most striking is verse 6 which is literally "though we could have been weighty among you as apostles of Christ." Paul is saying that he could have "thrown his weight around" as an apostle, but this is precisely what he did not do. Instead, Paul was, "gentle among you, like a nursing mother taking care of her own children" (v. 7). It is a startling contrast; the apostle does not manipulate, flatter, or use people in any way, but rather exercises his apostolic authority like a breastfeeding mother nursing her child. He continues that he loved the Thessalonians so much he shared not just the gospel but his very soul.

This is Paul's application of the pattern we have observed in Philippians, John, and Ephesians; he does not use his apostolic authority to get anything for himself, he does not throw his weight around. Rather, he gives himself to these people in love and concern for their well-being and growth. Paul is a shepherd who feeds God's sheep (Ezek 34).

BEARING THE NAME? ABUSE OF POWER AS BREAKING THE THIRD COMMANDMENT

A concluding and sobering point is necessary here. If the life of those who are united to Christ is patterned after Christ's humble self-giving love, then a life that consistently fails to demonstrate that pattern, but nevertheless professes or claims his name, bears his name in vain; it misrepresents the character of God. This lies much closer to the heart of the Third Commandment than mere use of offensive vocabulary. Far more offensive are leaders who, operating in the name of Jesus and claiming Jesus' authority for what they do, lead in such a way as to violate Jesus' pattern by using power for selfish ends. This is not only an abuse of power; it bears his name in vain.

A PRACTICAL, PASTORAL PROBLEM WITH A THEOLOGICAL ROOT

Abuse of power by those leading in the name of Jesus is a serious concern. It is not the problem merely of some bad characters occasionally behaving badly. It is, at root, a theological problem: a misunderstanding of who Jesus is and how we are called to live in union with him and in obedience to his commands. Our attitude must be the same as Christ Jesus who considered his equality with God the means for humble service all the way to death on the cross. This is Jesus' Way. And we cannot and must not do Jesus' work in non-Jesus ways.

BIBLIOGRAPHY

Bockmuehl, Markus N. A. *A Commentary on the Epistle to the Philippians*. London: Black, 1997.

Cyril of Alexandria. *On the Unity of Christ*. Translated and with an introduction by John Anthony McGuckin. Crestwood, NY: St. Vladimir's Seminary Press, 2000.

Duby, Steven J. *God in Himself: Scripture, Metaphysics, and the Task of Christian Theology*. Downers Grove, IL: IVP Academic, 2019.

———. *Jesus and the God of Classical Theism: Biblical Christology in Light of the Doctrine of God*. Grand Rapids, MI: Baker Academic, 2022.

Evans, C. Stephen, ed. *Exploring Kenotic Christology: The Self-Emptying of God*. Vancouver: Regent College, 2010.

Hansen, G. Walter. *The Letter to the Philippians*. Nottingham, UK: Apollos, 2009.

Hawthorne, Gerald F. *Philippians*. Waco, TX: Word Books, 1983.

Hoover, Roy W. "Harpagmos Enigma: A Philological Solution." *Harvard Theological Review* 64 (1971) 95–119.

Jamieson, R. B., and Tyler Wittman. *Biblical Reasoning: Christological and Trinitarian Rules for Exegesis*. Grand Rapids, MI: Baker Academic, 2022.

John of Damascus. *On the Orthodox Faith: A New Translation of an Exact Exposition of the Orthodox Faith*. Translated by Norman Russell. Yonkers, NY: St Vladimir's Seminary Press, 2022.

Kgatle, Mookgo S. "Servant Leadership: An Urgent Style for the Current Political Leadership in South Africa." *Verbum et Ecclesia* 39 (2018) 1–9.

Mdingi, Hlulani. "Who, Being in the Form of God, Did not Consider It Robbery to Be Equal with God: Kenosis of Leadership." *HTS: Theological Studies* 76 (2020) 1–8.

O'Neill, John Cochrane. "Hoover on Harpagmos Reviewed, with a Modest Proposal Concerning Philippians 2:6." *Harvard Theological Review* 81 (1988) 445–49.

Ottuh, John A. "The Concept of κένωσις in Philippians 2:6–7 and Its Contextual Application in Africa." *Verbum et Ecclesia* 41 (2020) 1–13.

Pardue, Stephen. "Kenosis and Its Discontents: Towards an Augustinian Account of Divine Humility." *Scottish Journal of Theology* 65 (2012) 271–88.

Silva, Moises. *Philippians*. Grand Rapids, MI: Baker Academic, 2005.

2

Confessions of a Potential Authoritarian

Knowing the Trinity as Antidote to Pastoral Authoritarianism

Jared Michelson

YOUNG, RESTLESS AND REFORMED: THE APPEAL OF CHRIST THE CONFRONTER

> Some emergent types [want] to recast Jesus as a limp-wrist hippie in a dress with a lot of product in his hair, who drank decaf and made pithy Zen statements about life while shopping for the perfect pair of shoes. In Revelation, Jesus is a pride fighter with a tattoo down His leg, a sword in His hand and the commitment to make someone bleed. That is a guy I can worship. I cannot worship the hippie, diaper, halo Christ because I cannot worship a guy I can beat up.[1]

I GOT THE APPEAL of Driscoll. It is easy to underestimate the depths of anxiety and angst which secularization generates in believers. During the early

---

1. Mark Driscoll in "From the Mag: 7 Big Questions," para. 19. This essay was originally published in "Mere Orthodoxy" and is adapted and used here with permission.

2000s, evangelicals like me were caught amongst three different movements, each promising to restore Christian vitality: the seeker-friendly movement, the emergent church, and the "young restless and Reformed" or what Brits might call the keen "Banner of Truth" types. Emergent churches saw themselves as an antidote to the commodified, milquetoast gospel of the seeker movement but to many of us, the emergent church seemed like a natural extension of the seeker-friendly trajectory. Whereas seeker-friendly churches believed in things like final judgment or distinctive Christian sexual ethics but never mentioned them, emergent churches dropped them altogether. To those less than optimistic about softening orthodoxy as an evangelistic strategy, strong "call it as I see it" leaders who would not just talk about, but positively revel in, the sharp edges of Christian doctrine were appealing.

The key to Driscoll's ministry was a particular vision of Christ which was the way—as Driscoll liked to say—to "get the men." While emergent liberals highlighted the meek Jesus, the "reformed" (by which Driscoll means the "young restless Reformed" movement rather than the historic Reformed tradition) accented the exalted, kingly, warrior Christ of Revelation. He went on to say that this "Ultimate Fighter Jesus" is "perhaps my favorite picture [of Jesus] (and that of my young sons)."[2] This confrontational, hypermasculine christological vision of Christ the warrior king offered young men someone on whom to model themselves.

Driscoll, as is well known, particularly in view of *Christianity Today*'s *The Rise and Fall of Mars Hill* podcast, stepped down from Mars Hill, the church he planted, and Acts 29, the network he helped found. He was accused of a domineering, abusive leadership style, as well as bullying, micromanagement, the suppression of dissent, and the use of a marketing ploy to place a book on bestseller lists. Driscoll's fall is paradigmatic of a number of similar, alleged cases of authoritarian abuses of power within Reformed evangelicalism. When I look at the path Driscoll took, and his one-time influence upon me, his road is one that at times I felt I was on. In my own ministry to this very day, I continue to see the same dark potential. Attending to Driscoll's particular example allows us, therefore, to see where things often go wrong in cases of pastoral abuse and authoritarianism, and how we ourselves might seek to avoid the same dangers.

In what follows, I want to suggest an antidote to the toxic potential of every Christian leader to abuse their power and office. While Driscoll spoke a great deal about theological truth and error, the irony is that his ministry was theologically deficient with regards to the doctrine of God—and this is just as true for many evangelicals across the theological spectrum. The wife

---

2. Driscoll, "Supremacy of Christ," 132.

CONFESSIONS OF A POTENTIAL AUTHORITARIAN

of one of Mars Hill's first elders, in a heart-wrenching account of her family's tragic experience, said this:

> The church began committed to certain distinctives . . . and then one driven, talented individual . . . turned the church into a "City within a City" where he functions like a king because he believes this is the best way to "grow the numbers." . . . A Christianity which perpetuates the exaltation of mere men to god-like status . . . is completely antithetical to what Jesus taught.[3]

What starts with a myopic vision of Christ the warrior king whom men emulate, easily engenders a ministry led by a man of "godlike" status reigning as "king." We might think this can be easily rectified by emphasizing instead the gentleness and humility of Christ. This is not altogether incorrect but is nonetheless inadequate. The dangers of authoritarianism can be just as present—or at least nearly so—when pastors model themselves upon Jesus's self-giving love. My suggestion instead is this: despite their passion for "sound doctrine," Driscoll and many evangelicals *implicitly and unintentionally* articulate an insufficiently exalted view of God and correspondingly of Jesus Christ. To put it plainly, the problem is not—or at least not *merely*—that their Jesus is not "nice" enough. The problem is that their vision of God is too small. A transcendent vision of the triune God is an indispensable component in avoiding king-like figures who model their ministry upon Jesus in the *wrong* sorts of ways.

A RICHER ACCOUNT OF DOCTRINAL TRUTH AND ERROR

Evangelicalism has tended to view orthodoxy as what John Webster calls "mute subscription to dogmas."[4] We can mistakenly think that to have a "solid" doctrine of the Trinity is merely a question of affirmation. We declare "there is one God in three persons," or something along those lines. The problem is that this renders doctrine dispensable. Once I can offer a definition of "the Trinity" that is not clearly erroneous, I can dispense with it and move on. I've ticked the correct box and now can get on with the real work.

What is needed instead is a recovery of a richer, more contemplative and formative approach to doctrine. Theology is an ongoing spiritual exercise through which we are brought from death to life, as our minds and

---

3. Petry, "My Story," 13–14.
4. Webster, *Culture of Theology*, 146.

hearts are turned towards God. Augustine is an obvious example of this approach. Countless readers of his conversion story, *Confessions*, run aground in the final chapters. After a number of pages detailing exciting matters related to love, crime, sex, identity, the meaning of life, and more, Augustine turns—or at least *appears* to turn—from talking about his own personal story, to considering at length the nature of God, creation, and time. Surely such esoteric, *theological* matters have no place in a personal testimony? Yet one finds a similar dynamic in Augustine's greatest theological treatise, *De Trinitate*, only working in the opposite direction. This supposedly *theological* text, apparently focused on the nature of the triune God, strangely moves in its final chapters to an extended reflection upon the *human* mind and salvation. As Edmund Hill states, "Augustine is proposing the quest for, or the exploration of, the mystery of the Trinity as a complete program for the Christian spiritual life, a program of conversion and renewal and discovery of self in God and God in self."[5] In coming to know the triune God, we delight in him and lovingly gaze upon his beauty. In turn, we come to know ourselves, grasping who we are meant to be in this life and the next.

What this implies is that, even if one's doctrine is formally correct, it can still be defective if we misapprehend what a doctrine is meant to *do*. John Webster often referred to this as a question of dogmatic scope, proportion and order.[6] Many of the most important theological disagreements concern what role a given doctrine is asked to play in one's wider theology or how a given doctrine is meant to reshape the moral space in which we act and understand ourselves. In other words, if we misconstrue how a doctrine is meant to reform us, how can we claim to have understood the doctrine?

IMITATING GOD *AS CREATURES*

The way the doctrine of the Trinity is applied to ministry and the Christian life is flawed in the theology of Driscoll and a large swath of evangelicalism.

Driscoll develops an account of pastoral leadership which makes the novel claim that Christ's three offices of prophet, priest, and king map on to different pastoral leadership styles. Some pastors are more prophet-like, focused on the proclamation of truth and rejection of error, others are more king-like, excelling at "maximizing resources to accomplish measurable results," whereas still others are more priest-like, emphasizing pastoral care.[7] This is a rather straightforward error of doctrinal "proportion and scope."

---

5. Augustine of Hippo, "Trinity," 19.
6. E.g. Webster, *God without Measure*, 7, 30, 45, 144, 215.
7. Driscoll, *Book You'll Actually Read*, 67.

The *munus triplex* is a christological doctrine demonstrating the unique way in which the various threads of the Old Testament are brought together in Christ. There is little (no?) biblical indication that these three offices denote personality or ministry types, and many Old Testament examples do not fit within the personality/ministry types Driscoll and other evangelicals propose. Moses is the paradigmatic prophet and yet he institutes one of Scripture's clearest instances of "maximizing efficiency" (Exod 18). Priests were linked with preaching and proclaiming the truth more consistently than prophets (e.g., Lev 10:11; 2 Chr 15:3; 17:7; Ezra 7:6, 10; Neh 8:7–9; Jer 18:18; Ezek 7:26; Mic 3:11). And when Paul refers to the "priestly duty" he had been given, he refers not to a calling to pastoral care, but to his task to "proclaim the gospel of God" (Rom 15:16).[8] Driscoll seems to make an overly quick movement from a claim about the nature of Christ as king, to the assumption that because we are remade in Christ's image, the kingly identity of Christ may be applied to us straightforwardly.[9]

This too-quick identification of Jesus the kingly judge with church leaders fits with a trend within the thinking of Driscoll and evangelicalism more broadly, in which one moves too quickly between supposedly "divine" characteristics, to a call for humans to emulate them straightforwardly. (Think for example of the evangelical defenses of the novel doctrine of the eternal functional subordination of the Son to the Father, often articulated as a means of defending the authority of husbands and pastors.[10]) Driscoll straightforwardly and without nuance suggests that "The Trinity is the first community and the *ideal* for all communities."[11] He proceeds to note various aspects of the triune life which humans more or less directly emulate in their relations. According to Driscoll, the hierarchical yet ontologically equal relationship of Father, Son, and Spirit, is the foundation for the

---

8. For a more thoroughgoing critique, see: Jones, "Prophets, Priests, and Kings Today?" 63–85.

9. There are places where God's people are said to share in his rule such as Dan 7 or in some interpretations of the *imago Dei*, but in such settings the emphasis is upon the fact that divine rule is a *humane* one. The Son of Man in Daniel is contrasted with the beastly, violent rule of the kings of the world, and we don't replace him, but somehow represent his rule under his kingship. We serve as his representatives on earth, not as co-regents per se. Cf. Wright, *Hearing the Message of Daniel*, 156–58.

10. E.g., Bruce Ware's influential article, published by the *Council for Biblical Manhood and Womanhood*, argues that there *must* be eternal subordination of the Son to the Father in the Trinity, for otherwise the Trinity is not practical, since it would then have no implications for the "superiority of what is masculine over feminine." Ware, "Tampering with the Trinity," 4. Throughout the article, one finds an assumption that what is true of God should be imitated by human persons, with little nuance or reflection upon the difference the creator-creature distinction implies.

11. Driscoll and Breshears, *Doctrine*, 12.

relation between parents and children, husbands and wives, and pastors and parishioners.[12] Likewise, he suggests we should love one another with the same perfect, complete, and total love that the triune persons have for one another, holding nothing back and being completely transparent to the other. Throughout, there is an assumption that whatever is true of the triune God should serve as a straightforward model for our own life and, more specifically, for pastoral ministry.

Scripture presents a much more complex picture. Yes, we are to be perfect as our Father in heaven is perfect (Matt 5:48), but humanity's first sin is wanting to be "like God" (Gen 3:5). The vision of the "Day Star, son of the Dawn" in Isa 14, often associated in the Christian tradition with the fall of Satan, speaks of one who proudly said: "I will make myself like the Most High" (Isa 14:14). The task of Christian discipleship is to be *like God* in the *right* way, i.e., in a creaturely way, while refraining from being *like God* in the wrong ways. As Miroslav Volf suggests: "There is a duty prior to the duty of imitating God, and that is the duty of not wanting to be God, of letting God be God and humans be humans."[13]

Might it be that in highlighting the combative, kingly dimension of Jesus, and being insufficiently attentive to the ways in which imitating God can be a temptation rather than a virtue, Driscoll has subtly encouraged pastors to be *like God* in the wrong ways? For example, to imitate God rightly involves loving "your enemies and pray[ing] for those who persecute you. . . . For [God] makes his sun rise on the evil and on the good, and sends rain on the just and on the unjust" (Matt 5:43–45). Christ instructs us that as creatures, i.e., through the uniquely creaturely act of prayer, we are to imitate in a creaturely mode God's benevolent kindness and generosity even to those who hate us. On the other hand, Paul states: "Beloved, never avenge yourselves, but leave it to the wrath of God, for it is written, 'Vengeance is mine, I will repay, says the Lord'" (Rom 12:19–20). Christ instructs us to be benevolent in a creaturely way *because* God is benevolent, but Paul says *not* to be wrathful, precisely because God *is*. God's exercise of wrathful judgment frees us from the burden, obligation, and right of taking vengeance into our own hands.[14] What this implies is that, although there is a necessary place for confrontation in the Christian life, one should not simply assume that Christ's confrontational style should be our own, for he is God and we are not. More pointedly, Jesus' overturning of temple tables does not license pastoral pugnaciousness. Rather than following Driscoll in thinking

---

12. Driscoll, "Trinity God Is."
13. Volf, *Exclusion & Embrace*, 301.
14. This is a major theme of Volf's work. Cf. Volf, *Exclusion & Embrace*, 34.

that ministry needs confrontational kings who "maximize" efficiency for the sake of "results," my own tradition (in line with other reformed denominations) asks of ministers seeking ordination: "Do you believe, as this church in her historic testimony has constantly affirmed, that the Lord Jesus Christ is the *only* King and Head of the church."[15]

The solution then is not *merely* to have a "nicer" picture of God, for, as Karen Kilby and Kathryn Tanner have compellingly argued,[16] when human relational models are *first* used to clarify God's triune nature, it is difficult to think that *then* those triune relations can serve as a peculiarly insightful model for how humans should act. In short, if we model God's trinitarian relations on human ones and then turn round and model human relations on these newly understood trinitarian ones, we have in effect modeled human relations on human relations with a short divine detour for justification in the middle. First, Driscoll tries to make sense of God by depicting him using images of human warriors, kings, MMA fighters,[17] and so on, but then second, he appeals to this newly constructed, all-too-human vision of God to tell us how men and male church leaders should act. Why not just skip the middle man—or in this case the middle God—altogether, for the ultimate model for pastors here is *human* warriors and MMA fighters? Of course, it is inevitable that we employ analogies drawn from creatures to make sense of God, but to avoid this viciously circular reasoning and the danger of projection, these analogies must be disciplined by constant attention to "the distinction"[18] between Creator and creatures.

This is why simply affirming a "kinder" or more gentle vision of God, a God that doesn't judge sin or is not a ruling king, will not solve the problem of circularity, and further, has nearly as much potential to engender pastoral abuse. To demonstrate why this might be, we turn to a discussion of the classical doctrine of the Trinity.

THE INIMITABLE TRIUNE GOD

While yes, we imitate the triune God insofar as we are creatures restored according to the image of the Son, the doctrine of the Trinity serves primarily to highlight the *unlikeness* of Creator and creature. It protects us from

---

15. Ordination vows of the United Free Church of Scotland. This reflects the language of *The Westminster Confession* 30.1.

16. Kilby, "Perichoresis and Projection," 432–45; Tanner, *Christ the Key*, 207–46.

17. Eds. MMA = Mixed Martial Arts, a particularly violent sport.

18. On "the distinction," see Sokolowski, *God of Faith and Reason*; Burrell, "Christian Distinction," 191–206; Burrell, *Faith and Freedom*, 3–19.

seeking to imitate God in the wrong ways which fail to account for our creatureliness.[19] Let us therefore retrieve a few of the things the doctrine of the Trinity is meant to *do*.

One of the classical dogmatic functions of the doctrine was to secure simultaneously absolute divine aseity and perfect goodness. By goodness, we mean something like God's generosity. As the puritan Stephen Charnock explains: "goodness is . . . a strong inclination to do good . . . it is an inclination towards communicating itself, not for its own interest, but for the good of the object."[20] Part of what makes God's goodness uniquely *divine* is that it is rooted in God's aseity, which defines God as totally independent and without need. God is so superlatively happy and consummately perfect, that his life cannot be enhanced. When you put aseity and goodness together, we see that every act of God towards creatures is a unilateral, one-way gift, solely for the good of creatures.[21] It is ontologically impossible for God to try to *use* you or to get something from you. This is God's *perfect* goodness: "He is too rich to have any cause to envy, and too good to have any will to."[22]

A question will immediately occur to the sharp observer. If God is necessarily generous, it is an aspect of God's perfect nature to do good to others. Does this then imply that God *needs* to create in order to be the good God he is, since a giver needs a recipient? Yet if God *needs* the world in order to be good, then his very unilateral, one-way, perfect goodness is undermined. He is not creating now because he is *already* good, but *to become* good. Theologically speaking, a great deal hangs on this, not least of which is that God is now using creatures to become perfect. Fortunately, Charnock hints at an answer: "Goodness is his nature. Hence were there internal communications of himself from eternity."[23] In referring to these "internal communications" Charnock draws upon a venerable medieval discussion

---

19. I am contending that the doctrine of the Trinity is *practical*. This might come as a surprise to many who have emphasized that because God is the final end of all things, he is not merely a means for the attainment of some other good. Yet one can recognize the practical implications of a doctrine like the Trinity without reducing God to a mere utilitarian means to some other good. Hopefully my wife appreciates my labor in our garden, but noting some practical benefits which I render her, however meager they may be(!), need not imply she treats me merely as a means to those practical benefits.

20. Charnock, *Works*, 2.278.

21. This means that even acts like divine judgement or even final judgment must ultimately be for the benefit of creatures, not God. Charnock goes on in this very discourse to seek to explain how this can be the case.

22. Charnock, *Works*, 2.288.

23. Charnock, *Works*, 2.288. See for example his discussion of the necessary Triune processions which are the ground of the voluntary and contingent missions of the Son and Spirit in time. Charnock, *Works*, 3.410–11.

which speaks of the inner relations of Father, Son, and Holy Spirit as perfect acts of giving within God himself.[24] It is only because God is Trinity that he can be perfectly good.

If God is Trinity, he *is* a relation of perfect, total self-giving, prior to and before any action outside himself.[25] The great medieval theologian Richard of St Victor says, "What is more magnificent than the desire to allow others to participate in everything that one possesses?"[26] Richard argues that since the more perfect the more giving one is, it must be that the Father perfectly and totally gives himself over into the Son. This is called the Father's begetting of the Son. This means that the only thing that makes the Son different from the Father, as Thomas Aquinas says, is "the very relation, which is to have one's nature from another, so that the very relation of sonship in the son takes the place of all the individuating sources in created things."[27] Stated more simply, because the Father gives the Son all that he has, i.e., all of his being and perfections, the only difference between the Son and the Father is that the Father is the giver and the Son the recipient. The Son has the same nature as the Father—it is what he receives from him—but he has this perfect nature in the mode of sonship or reception. Likewise, the Father has all the Son has, but he has it in the mode of fatherhood or donation. This further implies that the Father is not Father, he is not himself and thus in a very real sense is *nothing*, apart from the Son, since what it means *to be* the Father is to be the one who gives to the Son. Correspondingly, the Son is not Son apart from the Father. The entirety of who these persons are *as persons* is these perfect relations or acts of giving and receiving. Finally, as Aquinas goes on to stress, a perfect act of self-giving might still remain a selfish act, if the joy in giving and loving is not shared with another.[28] The perfection of God's inner love, therefore, requires someone to share in the joy which rebounds from this perfect giving and receiving and this person is called the Holy Spirit. To summarize, the Trinity shows God to be *already* perfectly

24. See Gilles Emery's summary: Emery, *Aquinas*, 23–25. According to Emery, something like the view of the Trinity I outline in this paragraph was widely shared by the Medievals. Where disagreements arose, they concerned the extent to which this conception of the Trinity could be known according to natural reason, as well as fine grained questions about whether the triune persons are distinguished solely in terms of their relations or also in terms of their acts of generation.

25. In what follows, I try to outline a line of scholastic thinking on the Trinity in simple, plain language. All sorts of caveats could be introduced of course and, as is often the case, simple language, like the language of "person" for example, has the capacity to mislead us.

26. Angelici, *Trin.* 3.4 (p. 119).

27. Aquinas, *Pot. dei.* 2.1 (p. 24).

28. Aquinas, *Pot. dei.* 9.9 (p. 274–75).

generous in himself, because he is three persons who are exhaustively who they are in the act of giving, receiving, and joyfully loving one another. God then needs creation for nothing, not even to become good, and thus towards us he is always perfectly generous, needing nothing in return.

This understanding of the Trinity was fairly standard in the medieval, reformation, and post-reformation eras, yet for many of us today, it all might seem strange or abstract. We are not used to speaking in these terms.[29] This is a pastoral problem.

---

29. To tell the story of how this occurred would take us too far afield, but in brief: Pre-modern modes of reading Scripture as a set of signs which as a canonical whole reveal their divine source were undermined by the effects of post-enlightenment, historical criticism beginning with figures like Spinoza and reaching their apogee in Strauss and others like him. One of the decisive impacts of this sort of criticism was to restrict the meaning of Scripture to what was in the mind(s) of the "original" biblical author, redactor, sources, or authorial communities or to what stood behind those written traditions in historical events and figures. This resulted in a naturalizing of Scripture. In response, intellectually serious evangelicals resorted to "biblical theology," which they thought could recover the classical doctrines undermined by historical criticism, without needing to make recourse to the classical modes of reading biblical texts which had undergirded those very doctrines. Although there was a focus on the unfolding storyline of Scripture, at each moment in that story, the focus of the biblical theologian could remain on what God had revealed to each individual biblical author's mind within their "grammatical-historical" context. This approach perceived itself as more "biblical," and was often contrasted with what was derisively seen as overly "Greek," "metaphysical," "philosophical," and/or "abstract" categories which had supposedly invaded theology in the patristic or medieval era. However, rather than a mere return to the "Bible" over-against false impositions of "philosophy" upon the text, such evangelical thinkers were largely unknowingly and implicitly merely adhering to a *different* philosophical tradition. They were following what became known as the "Hellenization thesis," associated with Protestant liberals like Adolf von Harnack and Albrecht Ritschl, which posited a sharp distinction between Hellenistic, metaphysical philosophy and the teaching of Jesus and his followers. The claims of this thesis have been progressively undermined by a generation of scholars, yet the thesis itself was in many ways a product of the early modern, largely German, philosophical milieu in which it originated. Is it a coincidence that this rejection of metaphysics just so happened to follow upon the devastating critiques of metaphysical thinking leveled in early modernity by *philosophers* like Hume and Kant? Kant in particular rejected that we could have knowledge of the natures of things in themselves, and likewise, labeled claims to knowledge of the divine nature as pure speculation. Is it really merely because of attention to the Bible that, post-Kant, talk about the nature or metaphysical attributes of God was deemed "speculative" or "abstract"? Further, is it mere happenstance, that the focus upon the progressive unfolding of salvation history as the key to understanding God in a concrete, non-abstract manner, developed shortly after the philosophy of Hegel? Hegel himself had insisted that rather than accepting the abstract metaphysical views of the ancients, one needed a dynamic approach which focused on the unfolding of the absolute (i.e., Hegel's "God") in Hegel's version of salvation history. In sum, the reason modern evangelicals might assume that the modes of trinitarian reflection outlined above are "abstract," is not because we simply read the Bible "better" than the

How so? It means that our love for one another is utterly unlike God's, both in terms of his inner-triune love and his love for creatures. If the triune persons were not God, their love would be, almost by definition, grossly codependent. All that each person *is*, is rooted in what they are for the other. As persons they are *nothing* else. If any pastor or church leader demands this sort of devotion from you, run. Similarly, some members of my congregation want precisely that sort of love from their pastor. They want to offer me complete and total affection and perhaps in some cases even obedience, so long as I am willing to sacrifice everything I am, including my time, my family, and even at times my integrity, to ensure the growth of our church and the security and well-being of each of them. It's a Faustian bargain, one which replaces God with the pastor, and likewise, remakes the congregation (strangely enough) in another deformed image of God. Both pastor and congregation become codependent. Pastors are rarely criticized and are often rewarded for acting in this codependent manner, for it can enhance a church's outward "success."

When we realize we do not merely need a "nicer" portrait of God, but a more transcendent One who lives and loves in a mode totally beyond us, we gain a more realistic way of identifying the roots of pastoral authoritarianism. For me, the temptation to pastoral abuse is knocking at the door, precisely when the good things which both I and my congregation long for seem just out of reach. It's not because I am a megalomaniac drunk on authority, it's because I want people to meet Jesus, home groups to flourish, our services to be winsome and well-crafted and people to hold one another accountable to what Jesus asks of us. It is when we fear those good things are slipping through our fingers, that we, like Israel so long ago, cry out to God, saying: "Give us a king." "Give us a strong man who will secure our flourishing." At the same time, we pastors then say to our congregations, "give more, obey more, sacrifice more, and I can give you what your heart desires." When this happens, we fall into the profoundly subtle trap of thinking that we can give and love like gods.

A classical view of the Trinity, with its strong emphasis on how unlike God we are, makes a real difference when facing the subtle slide towards pastoral authoritarianism. It does so by undercutting some of our most common assumptions about church. For example, consider the frequent proclamation that "The church does not have a mission, rather the mission has a church," or similarly, the church "does not exist for herself but for

---

ancients (although of course in some cases that might be true!), but because our biblical theological and grammatical historical assumptions tend to read the Bible in light of a different philosophical and intellectual tradition.

the world."[30] This might seem like a mere hyperbolic ways of saying mission is *really* important, but it is not the case that the end of the church or the reason she exists, is as a means for accomplishing tasks on this earth. In the eschaton, Christ will have his bride. He will call her "my beloved." He will call her "the church," but mission will no longer be her task. Thus, while I appreciate the need to shake Christians out of insularity, selfishness or lethargy, *mission* exists for the sake of the church, not vice versa.[31] And this has crucial consequences for pastoral abuse. The tendency of pastoral abusers is to *use* the members of the congregation for the end of advancing what they see as "the kingdom" or "the mission." Pastors become kings, as the testimonial from Driscoll's church suggests, because this is the way to "grow the numbers."

If the church is ultimately a means to some other end, even the best of possible ends like people meeting Jesus, then it is easy to convince ourselves that we are actually working for the kingdom when we push people to "get with the program," or to obey, or to do more.[32] But what if God's program is that creatures would know and love and be known and loved by him? What if his agenda is that they might become all they were created to be and enjoy as much bliss as is possible for a creature, since there just is nothing better than enjoying God? What if God's plan for us can only and ever be for *our good*, not what he can get us to do *for him*, because he already has all he needs as Father, Son, and Holy Spirit? This means that while mission, discipleship, and church growth are important, they are themselves only the means to the greater end of God unceasingly giving good gifts to his children (Jas 1:17). If God does not really need us, then pastors must utterly refute the lie which insists either that congregants are instruments through

---

30. You can find affirmations similar to these in a huge diversity of different thinkers including: Christopher Wright, Rob Bell, John MacArthur, Ed Stetzer, Stanley Hauerwas, and more.

31. To be fair to those who make such statements, there is an important conversation to be had about the way forms of mission or Christian service can be undermined, curtailed, or criticized by a requirement that all Christian service immediately contribute to the growth of specific institutional forms of the church. Mission *does not exist* merely so our denomination, tribe, local congregation, or parachurch organization sees a boost in the numbers.

32. Even if the final or ultimate end of the church is not mission, nonetheless part of the reason for the church's earthly existence *is* mission. Mission is a subsidiary aspect of God's purposes in election. Thus, it is right to say there is no earthly church which is not participating in God's mission, or that any church which fails to participate in mission is unfaithful to its very calling and identity as a church since mission is one part of God's rationale for the church. However, it is wrong to suggest that the sole end or ultimate purpose for the church is mission or that "church" is derivative of God's ultimate end of mission.

which kingdom work can be accomplished, or conversely, that the kingdom cannot grow without them. No, they are beloved children of God. It is true, the best thing for them in this life is to participate sacrificially in what God is doing on this earth and thus in God's mission. But because God's ultimate end is never what he can *get from us* but what he can *give to us*, pastors and church leaders must be rigorously self-critical when appealing for sacrifices for the sake of the mission. We must root out the ways we are tempted to use people for the sake of some other end, recognizing that *they are the end.*

This view of the Trinity also undermines the equally simplistic approach to pastoral authoritarianism which simply tells pastors "you are there to serve your congregation, not to benefit from them." This is just another way of asking your pastor to be a god. Creatures have needs: physical, emotional, spiritual, and more. Every time we do anything, whether caring for another person or pursuing a professional vocation, we form and create our *own* identity. In all we do, we actualize our potential or enact our nature (to use more traditional terms). It is impossible for a creature *only* to meet the needs of another while not simultaneously and subtly to be meeting their own. Only God can love in a one-way, unilateral mode.

Therefore, the task before us pastors, or rather, the task before us as redeemed *creatures,* is to emulate the self-giving of God, but in a necessarily imperfect, creaturely mode. It is to benefit from one another without becoming codependent. Pastoral authoritarianism often begins with a pastor who not only asks too much of his or her congregation—too much time, too much obedience, or worse—but who asks too much of him or herself (or a congregation that does the same). The first step in addressing pastoral abuse is telling one another: "you don't need to be the triune God! We already have one!"

CONCLUSION: WHY THE TRINITY MAKES ALL THE DIFFERENCE?

When Hannah Arendt wrote about the trial of Nazi war criminal Adolf Eichmann, she initiated an international scandal regarding the "banality of evil."[33] Arendt suggested that what was most noteworthy about Eichmann was not his malevolence or cruelty, but his desire to please others and get ahead. She provocatively concluded that the traits that made Eichmann capable of performing acts of heinous terror were unremarkable and normal.

---

33. Nearly every aspect of Arendt's work has been the subject of significant controversy and criticism, but many of her most controversial arguments, particularly those on the broad theme of the banality of evil, have become more rather than less widely influential as time has gone on.

In an essay written during the Second World War, she suggested that the unique flaw in Germany during the Third Reich was not that it was more nationalistic or racist than other nations. It was that Germany idolized middle-class values like financial and professional security. Despite their best efforts, the Nazis were not able to turn "normal" mainstream Germans against the Jews until they made the careers and livelihoods of middle-class German bureaucrats and administrators depend upon "following orders" related to the final solution.[34] For Arendt, the same vices we see playing out in our workplaces, neighborhoods, homes, and churches were the foundation of the most heinous moment of the twentieth century.

Might it be that the potential for pastoral abuse is much closer to home than we might want to admit—that it begins, not with monsters bent on dominating others, but with good intentions going wrong? All of us have this dark potential, and part of the solution is a willingness to admit our innate and irrepressible desire to take the place of God.

God's perfect, triune giving and receiving is not a straightforward model for pastoral ministry, but it has significant implications for it. The first and most profound implication is that pastors are not God. The good news is that they don't need to be. Pastoral abuse is less about moral monsters, and more about codependent people who think they can love like the Trinity. It's about a symbiotic, codependent relationship in which pastors demand *everything*—total respect, total obedience, total submission—and congregations demand everything in return—complete missional, financial and spiritual security.

What the doctrine of the Trinity reminds us is that, while we must imitate God, it is just as important in certain key moments to refuse to do so, to be willing to accept failure, stagnation, or imperfection, because this is what it means to be a creature. To be a creature, is also to be one who never gives perfectly unilaterally. We are needy, finite and incomplete beings trying to *become* who we were meant to be. Therefore, we must be realistic and honest rather than idealistic, in our expectations of one another. Only one love comes from a being with no needs. What we must recover then, is the conviction that to be a pastor, to be a Christian, and even to be a creature, is to live an indicative life. It is a life which says, "I can never give you what your heart desires, but I know who can."

---

34. Arendt, *Essays in Understanding*.

BIBLIOGRAPHY

Angelici, Ruben, trans. *Richard of Saint Victor, on the Trinity*. Eugene, OR: Cascade, 2011.

Aquinas, Thomas. *The Power of God*. Translated by Richard J Regan. Oxford: Oxford University Press, 2012.

Arendt, Hannah. *Essays in Understanding, 1930–1954: Formation, Exile, and Totalitarianism*. Edited by Jerome Kohn. New York: Schocken, 2005.

Augustine of Hippo. *The Works of Saint Augustine: A Translation for the 21st Century; The Trinity. Part 1, Volume 5*. Edited by Edmund Hill and John E. Rotelle. Brooklyn, NY: New City, 1991.

Burrell, David B. "The Christian Distinction Celebrated and Expanded." In *The Truthful and the Good: Essays in Honor of Robert Sokolowski*, edited by John J. Drummond, 191–206. Dordrecht: Kluwer Academic, 1996.

———. *Faith and Freedom: An Interfaith Perspective*. Malden, MA: Blackwell, 2004.

Charnock, Stephen. *The Complete Works of Stephen Charnock*. London: Nisbet, 1864.

Driscoll, Mark. *A Book You'll Actually Read on Church Leadership*. Wheaton, IL: Crossway, 2013.

———. "The Church and the Supremacy of Christ in a Postmodern World." In *The Supremacy of Christ in a Postmodern World*, edited by John Piper and Justin Taylor, 125–47. Wheaton, IL: Crossway, 2007.

———. "Trinity God Is." http://marshill.se/marshill/media/doctrine/trinity-god-is.

Driscoll, Mark, and Gerry Breshears. *Doctrine: What Christians Should Believe*. Wheaton, IL: Crossway, 2010.

Emery, Gilles. *The Trinitarian Theology of St Thomas Aquinas*. Translated by Francesca Aran Murphy. Oxford: Oxford University Press, 2010.

"From the Mag: 7 Big Questions." *Relevant*, August 28, 2007. https://relevantmagazine.com/faith/1344-from-the-mag-7-big-questions/.

Jones, Timothy Paul. "Prophets, Priests, and Kings Today? Theological and Practical Problems with the Use of the Munus Triplex as a Leadership Typology." *Perichoresis* 16 (2018) 63–85.

Kilby, Karen. "Perichoresis and Projection: Problems with Social Doctrines of the Trinity." *New Blackfriars* 81 (2000) 432–45.

Petry, Jonna. "My Story." https://joyfulexiles.files.wordpress.com/2012/03/jonna-mhc-story-29.pdf.

Sokolowski, Robert. *The God of Faith and Reason: Foundations of Christian Theology*. Washington, DC: Catholic University of America Press, 1995.

Tanner, Kathryn. *Christ the Key*. Cambridge: Cambridge University Press, 2010.

Volf, Miroslav. *Exclusion & Embrace: A Theological Exploration of Identity, Otherness, and Reconciliation*. Revised and updated. Nashville, TN: Abingdon, 2019.

Ware, Bruce A. "Tampering with the Trinity: Does the Son Submit to His Father?" *Journal of Biblical Manhood and Womanhood* 6 (2001) 4–12.

Webster, John. *The Culture of Theology*. Edited by Ivor J. Davidson and Alden C. McCray. Grand Rapids, MI: Baker Academic, 2019.

———. *God without Measure: Working Papers in Christian Theology*. Vol. 1, *God and the Works of God*. London: Bloomsbury T. & T. Clark, 2016.

Wright, Christopher J. H. *Hearing the Message of Daniel: Sustaining Faith in Today's World*. Grand Rapids, MI: Zondervan, 2017.

3

"You Must Not Do as They Do..."
Old Testament Israel's Distinctive Patterns of Leadership

Chris Wright

INTRODUCTION

IF WE WERE LOOKING for an Old Testament text parallel to the saying of Jesus in the title of this book, "Not so with you" (after he had described the typical authoritarian style of leadership in the pagan world), it would be the title of this chapter, which is taken from Lev 18.

> The Lord said to Moses, 2 "Speak to the Israelites and say to them: 'I am the Lord your God. 3 You must not do as they do in Egypt, where you used to live, and you must not do as they do in the land of Canaan, where I am bringing you. Do not follow their practices. 4 You must obey my laws and be careful to follow my decrees. I am the Lord your God. 5 Keep my decrees and laws, for the person who obeys them will live by them. I am the Lord. (Lev 18:1–5)

The immediate context speaks of a range of sexual practices that were to have no place in Israel, but the wider context, including especially Lev 19 and indeed the rest of Israel's charter for their constitutional and cultural life (especially Deuteronomy), presents Israel as a community that was self-consciously distinctive from surrounding nations. And this was not merely in the sense that they worshiped Yahweh rather than the gods of other nations; nor merely in the fact that they were committed to the worship of one God only, as distinct from their polytheistic neighbors. Rather,

> For Israel, exclusive commitment to Yahweh as sole deity was part of a covenantal structure of life that impacted every dimension of their social, economic, judicial, and political existence. And in doing so, it made Israel very distinctive indeed. This has been the conclusion of sociological studies of ancient Israel, which have shown that from a very early stage of its historical emergence, Israel had a deliberately articulated sense of national distinctiveness, which was expressed across the whole spectrum of ther social life—not just in their religion.[1]

THE DISTINCTIVENESS OF ISRAELITE SOCIETY

With its constitutional foundation in the covenant relationship with the sole God Yahweh, Israel was in a formal sense a theocracy—a nation ruled by God. Now "theocracy" has a very nasty aroma these days. It conjures up the image of a society ruthlessly regimented by a religious hierarchy purporting to embody the rule of the deity they claim to represent, a society in which personal or community freedoms are trampled and all power is concentrated in the hands of religious functionaries. Theocracy sounds like religiously sanctioned oppression.

Paradoxically, Israel's form of theocracy was the opposite: it relativized and dispersed power and guaranteed certain rights and freedoms to all Israelites in covenant relationship with Yahweh. So, for example, the fact that Yahweh, as covenant Lord, was simultaneously the supreme sovereign, supreme landlord, supreme lawgiver and judge, and supreme commander (all the normal ancient Near Eastern functions of kingship), meant that all human occupants of those roles had only relative power and authority, subject to Yahweh. And Yahweh demanded justice. Kings (if they chose to have them) were to be subject to God's law like all other citizens (Deut 17:14–20); Israelite families were like resident tenants on land ultimately belonging to Yahweh (Lev 25:23); judges exercised their responsibility under God's audit

---

1. Wright, *Old Testament Ethics*, 55. This book explores the social, economic, and political distinctiveness of Israel in considerable depth, as a factor in their theological and ethical significance.

(2 Chr 19:4–7); battles were to fought (when authorized by God) under the "commander of the army of the LORD" (Josh 5:14).

Human power "hubs" were thereby separated from one another, through common allegiance to the one divine Lord. This is reflected in the categories of civil and religious authority in Deut 16:18—18:22, where we find distinct roles and responsibilities for judges, kings, and priests—with prophets having the last word, as it were. Although this may not have been recognized in the formal constitutional sense of modern "separation of powers," it had a similar effect as a defense against tyrannical accumulation of executive, judicial, economic, and military power in single hands.[2]

As Ahab discovered, Israelite kings could not simply get what they wanted just because they were the king. It took Jezebel (from Phoenicia, where kings could do exactly that—notice her surprise at Israel's style of limited kingship, in 1 Kgs 21:7), to corrupt Israel's own judicial system in order to trample on the freedom and protection that Naboth and his family should have enjoyed under Yahweh's rule (1 Kgs 21). And that was something that Samuel had warned Israel about when they first hankered after a king—it would introduce distortions and abuses of power that would virtually enslave them, if they chose to reject the liberating kingship of Yahweh in favor of potentially oppressive human kings (1 Sam 8:1–20).

When God told Israel not to do as they do in Canaan, he meant it seriously—and especially in the realm of how power was exercised, economically and politically.

> For example, pre-Israelite Canaanite society was organized along "feudal" lines, with power residing at the elite top end of a highly stratified social pyramid in each of the small city-state Canaanite kingdoms. Israel by contrast was a "tribal" society. It had a kinship structure based on a three-fold division into tribes, clans and households. The third level consisted of a large number of "extended-family," land-owning households. These units, which were largely self-sufficient economically, performed most of the socially important functions in the villages and localities of Israel—judicial, economic, cultic, and military. Early Israelite society, then, as a fabric of such sturdy units enjoying considerable autonomy and social freedom, was socially decentralized and non-hierarchical. It was geared towards the

---

2. I remember being taught at school that the role of a constitutional monarch, such as Queen Elizabeth II, lies not in the power she exercises, but in the powers she separates. The legislature, executive, judiciary, and military all swear discrete allegiance to the crown, with the result that none has absolute power over the others—which leads to constitutional conflicts from time to time, of course, but is generally recognized as a strong defense of democratic freedoms and a healthy check on powerful ambitions.

social health and economic viability of the "lowest" units, not to the wealth, privilege or power of the "highest." ...

Turning to Israel's political life, we find that the patterns of political activity and power in the Old Testament followed the kinship patterns of Israelite society. They were diffused and decentralized. Power in decision making within the community, especially in judicial matters, resided in the network of elders. The elders were the mainstay of Israelite socio-political life at the broadest level throughout the whole Old Testament period. In the pre-monarchic period, this plural and corporate leadership was supplemented in time of military need by individual "charismatic" leaders. These "judges" were considered as raised up by God and were accepted by the people as mediating the rule of God. However, the stories of Gideon and Abimelech (Judg 8:22—9:57) indicate the difficulties facing any judge who was offered, or who sought, a wider or more permanent, dynastic, rule. Centralized power in Israel seems to have been strongly resisted until the external threat of the Philistines thrust it forcibly upon them. Such centralized "chieftaincy" seems to have been perceived as directly counter to the basic thrust of Israel towards locating power in the fabric of local households. Even after the monarchy was established, the system of local elders survived at village level and proved resistant to hierarchical and centralized government. Jehoshaphat's judicial reforms established royally appointed judges, but they applied only to the fortified cities (2 Chr 19:4–11). The administration of justice in town and village communities by their local elders presumably continued unaffected by these royal appointments. Although the Davidic, and especially the Solomonic state and its successors in the centuries that followed, centralized power in many ways, the narratives and the prophets indicate a steady resistance to such arrangements as being at odds with the more traditional understanding of Israel's covenantal social structure. So there was resistance in Israel to centralized power and a preference for diverse and participatory politics, which tolerated—indeed sought—the voice of criticism and opposition from the prophets, even if some of them paid a heavy price. Such decentralized power stands in marked contrast to contemporary ancient Near Eastern states which had highly stratified and pyramidal political and economic structures.[3]

---

3. Wright, *Old Testament Ethics*, 55–57.

Turning further to the area of power that is closer to the topic of this book—power exercised by religious leaders—we find something more radical still. For when God told the Israelites not to do as they do in Egypt, he meant that seriously too. In ancient Egypt, temples were major economic players in the state. They owned large tracts of land, employed large numbers of people, engaged in major agricultural and trading activity. Temples and their priests thus wielded considerable economic and political influence, even under powerful Pharaohs.

"It shall not be so among you" is virtually what Yahweh insisted on by stipulating that the priestly tribe, the tribe of Levi, even though it was the tribe of Moses and Aaron, was to be given no tribal lands whatsoever in the settlement of Canaan. They were allocated certain towns and surrounding pastureland, scattered throughout the other tribes (Num 35:1–5; Josh 21:1–42), but were explicitly excluded from the apportionment of tribal lands. Their "portion" was the LORD himself, and the care of the tabernacle and later the temple (Num 1:47–53; Josh 13:14; 18:7). This had some very significant implications.

It meant that the priests and Levites were to concentrate on their primary calling: to serve the tabernacle/temple, through its regular sacrifices, to teach the people the law of the Lord (Lev 10:10–11; Deut 33:10; Mal 2:4–7), and to be public health inspectors and sustain the cleanliness of the community (Lev 11–14). It meant that, far from wielding oppressive spiritual power over the rest of the people, they were in fact utterly dependent on the people for their own daily needs—which is why they were regularly included among the stock categories of the vulnerable and needy in Israel's community: widows, orphans, foreigners—and Levites.

And of course it meant that the priestly tribe could not wield political power in the nation from a position of economic wealth and accumulated resources (a lesson that the Christendom church somehow forgot). Theocracy in Israel was not to mean "hierocracy"—the unfettered rule of religious orders. It was only in the later monarchy that we find a corrupt priesthood in collusion with political power (temple and palace), perpetrating both religious apostasy and all kinds of social injustice and oppression, and opposing prophets like Jeremiah who protested (Jer 20:1–6). If that was true of the Levitical priesthood in Judah, how much more with the surrogate priesthood established by rebel King Jeroboam I, for the political convenience of his own breakaway northern kingdom (1 Kgs 12:25–33). No wonder, a century later, Amaziah the priest at Bethel in the reign of Jeroboam II evicted Amos, on the grounds that Bethel was "the king's sanctuary and temple of the kingdom" (Amos 7:13). Religious and political power in mutually protective collusion.

Stepping back at this point to our opening quotation from Lev 18:1–5, we must ask, Why was Israel instructed (and constructed) to be a nation of such contrast to surrounding nations? And the answer lies in the repeated affirmation: because "I am the LORD your God." Israel was to be the embodiment, in the political, economic and religious realms, of the character of Yahweh himself. They were to be a society that reflected their God, as the stark opening of Lev 19 made clear. "Be holy because I, the Lord your God, am holy." The social realities of Israel reflected profound theological realities about Yahweh—which must surely also be part of the message of this book. What kind of God (or god) is "seen" by society in the way those who are thought to represent him behave—especially those in positions of leadership and vocal authority?

> In other words, Israel was what it was as a society, because Yahweh was what he was as God. This is precisely the relationship envisaged in Deuteronomy 10:12ff. between the character of Yahweh and the social nature of Israel. There, to "walk in his ways", means to imitate Yahweh as the God who "shows no partiality, accepts no bribes, defends the cause of the fatherless . . ." The kind of society Yahweh desires and commands is based explicitly on the kind of God Yahweh is. This is supported extensively by the legal, prophetic and wisdom literature, and is reinforced by detailed sociological study.[4]

THE IDEALS OF ISRAELITE LEADERSHIP

Sadly we know (and ironically we know from Israel's own Scriptures in the former and latter prophets), that Old Testament Israel did not live up to the standards and ideals God held before them. But then what nation has ever lived up to the ideals of its own constitutional aspirations and charters? However, since our biblical authority resides in the revelatory words of Scripture, not in the empirical behavior of Israel (just as the ethical authority of 1 Corinthians resides in what Paul wrote, not in the actual behavior of the church in Corinth), we can give worthwhile attention to the qualities of leadership that are either explicitly commanded or modeled in these texts. Here are just three that surely also ought to characterize Christian leaders.

---

4. Wright, *Old Testament Ethics*, 61.

1. Modesty and Humility

The law of the king in Deut 17:14–20 is remarkably counter-cultural. First of all, it is interesting that God did not command Israel to adopt monarchy. For several centuries they resisted it. But if they chose to appoint a king, then God provides instructions on what that king should be and do. Basically, a king in Israel was to be unlike any king they might have known.

Ancient Near Eastern kings and emperors enjoyed spectacular extravagance of wealth and all the trappings of military power and greed (nothing much has changed in some countries of the modern world). Not so in Israel.

> The king, moreover, must not acquire great numbers of horses for himself or make the people return to Egypt to get more of them, for the Lord has told you, "You are not to go back that way again." He must not take many wives, or his heart will be led astray. He must not accumulate large amounts of silver and gold. (Deut 17:16–17)

God's law put a prohibition on military hardware (horses/chariots), harems, and excessive silver and gold. A king in Israel was not to accumulate the usual perks of the job: weapons, women, and wealth. Guns, girls, and gold. Or the classic trio, money, sex, and power. It was an ideal that scarcely survived David and got lost altogether during and after Solomon. It is still profoundly countercultural in today's world, and sadly stands in contrast to the egregious lifestyle of some church leaders.

And along with that ideal of material modesty went personal humility. The king must "not consider himself better than his fellow Israelites" (v. 20), but rather be as much subject to the law of the Lord as any of his own subjects were (vv. 18–19). The principle that nobody is "above the law" goes back a very long way.

God's standards for leadership, then, included the demand that those who are entrusted with power need to resist using it for personal enrichment or luxury, and not be tempted into grandiose self-exaltation above others.

2. Integrity and Accountability

"I know, my God, that you test the heart and are pleased with integrity" (1 Chr 29:17). So said King David towards the end of his life, after a lifetime in which he had proved the point positively and negatively in his own experience. Several of the psalms of David in the early part of the Psalter affirm his determination to rule with integrity and his battle against corruption and lies (e.g., Pss 5, 10, 17). However, while David's record in the matter of personal integrity could be said to be rather patchy and inconsistent, the example of the one who anointed him stands out, and indeed stood unchallenged by public endorsement—and that was Samuel.

Samuel was the last of the judges, though from his youth he also exercised the gifts of a prophet, and spent a lifetime in judicial, military, and political leadership. If the kings of Israel who followed him had been like him, the history of Israel might have been very different.

> At the close of his life, after Saul has been appointed as king and Samuel is about to step down as the leader of the people, Samuel takes a very significant step. He opens the books, makes himself accountable to the people. His words constitute an invitation for an audit of his tenure of office. He calls on the people as witnesses and God as judge. He is open for inspection. He claims that he has acted with integrity, but he submits that claim to public accountability. In fact, Samuel's accountability is a key factor in his integrity.
>
>> Samuel said to all Israel, "I have listened to everything you said to me and have set a king over you. Now you have a king as your leader. As for me, I am old and gray, and my sons are here with you. I have been your leader from my youth until this day. Here I stand. Testify against me in the presence of the Lord and his anointed. Whose ox have I taken? Whose donkey have I taken? Whom have I cheated? Whom have I oppressed? From whose hand have I accepted a bribe to make me shut my eyes? If I have done any of these things, I will make it right."
>>
>> "You have not cheated or oppressed us," they replied. "You have not taken anything from anyone's hand."
>>
>> Samuel said to them, "The Lord is witness against you, and also his anointed is witness this day, that you have not found anything in my hand."
>>
>> "He is witness," they said. (1 Sam 12:1–5)

This is a revealing account. Specifically, Samuel claims (1) that he had not profited from public office for personal gain and (2) that he had not betrayed public trust by corruption and bribery. The people accept and affirm his claim. He has discharged his public office with integrity and honesty.

Those are key standards for anybody in political life and leadership. They would still be held up, of course, as ideals in our own political realm. They are supposed to be protected by constitutional restrictions, emoluments clauses, avoidance of conflict of interest, and other forms of legal sanction. The principles go back a long way, and Samuel's simple words express them within the culture of Israel at that time. Those who are in positions of power must be transparently accountable and submit their integrity to public scrutiny.[5]

The paragraphs above refer, of course, to Samuel's record in public political office. But the principle surely applies, more stringently if anything, to those in spiritual and pastoral office. Sadly the opportunities for personal gain from religious leadership, and the temptations that money or other less tangible forms of bribery can offer to those wielding spiritual power, are perennially toxic. Indeed it is part of the tragic irony of the story of Samuel himself that he began his career by declaring God's condemnation of the sons of Eli for abusing their priestly office for personal greed, and ended his career with the agony of hearing that his own sons were likewise guilty of dishonesty and injustice (1 Sam 8:3).

3. Justice and Compassion

No demand ranks higher in God's standards for leadership in Israel than the requirement to "do justice." It is ubiquitous. Of course, this is not surprising since we have made the point that what God required of Israel as a society reflected the character of Yahweh as God, and Yahweh is above all the God of justice. Justice is what God loves (Pss 11:7; 33:5; 99:4; Isa 61:8). It is the very foundation of his throne (Ps 89:14).

God's justice is exercised in highly relational terms. It is not blind justice, merely "giving everyone their due." Rather, it means putting things right, by taking action against oppressors and wrongdoers, and rescuing or vindicating those who have been wronged. That is why God's righteousness and justice are strongly salvific and redemptive in action—as Israel knew from their own national epic of exodus liberation.

Accordingly, God's criterion for those who exercise power—especially those who do so in God's name among God's people—is the extent to which that power is exercised on behalf of the power-less. In Israel's society that especially included the family-less, the land-less, and the home-less, i.e., the classic listing of widows, orphans, foreigners or immigrants, slaves, Levites. That is why I included the word "compassion" along with justice in the heading. Justice was to be exercised especially out of compassion for

---

5. Wright, *Here Are Your Gods*, 89–90.

the vulnerable and needy—precisely as God had exercised his justice for Israel's sake when they were oppressed Hebrews in Egypt (e.g., Lev 19:33–34; 25:35–38; Deut 10:17–19; 15:12–15; 24:19–22).

The mother of King Lemuel (whoever he was) captured this dimension of leadership ethics perfectly when she advised her son:

> Speak up for those who cannot speak for themselves,
>   for the rights of all who are destitute.
> Speak up and judge fairly;
>   defend the rights of the poor and needy. (Prov 31:8–9)

I think Jesus would have agreed. And I can easily imagine Paul and James including such instructions among the duties of pastors and elders within the Christian church. It sits very well alongside the better-known demand of Micah,

> He has shown you, O mortal, what is good. And what does the Lord require of you?
> To act justly and to love mercy and to walk humbly with your God. (Mic 6:8)

THE MODEL LEADER

Moses had his faults, no doubt, but he is assuredly held up in the Old Testament as a model of leadership among God's people. And not just in the Old Testament. According to the book of Hebrews, only Jesus the Son surpassed Moses the servant in faithfulness within God's household (Heb 3:1–6).

What is interesting, in relation to the theme of this book, is that Moses's exercise of his leadership is connected in several places to the work or gifting of the Holy Spirit. His was unquestionably "spiritual" power. The clearest reference to this is Isa 63:10–14, where the Holy Spirit, or the Spirit of Yahweh, is mentioned three times, and linked to how God "sent his glorious arm of power to be at Moses's right hand." So we have leadership, the exercise of power, and the Holy Spirit, all bound together in the ministry of Moses.

The other place where the Spirit of God is linked to Moses is in the narrative of some of the most testing moments that he faced in his leadership, in Num 11–14. This is a context in which, given the urgent and threatening problems he faced, we might have expected to find Moses exercising power in the form of decisive, authoritative, and self-assured actions, through which his superb leadership qualities would be demonstrated. In fact, we find something very different indeed. What we find is power without pride, power without jealousy, and power without ambition.[6]

1. Power without Pride

> Now Moses was a very humble man, more humble than anyone else on the face of the earth. (Num 12:3)

> This is a remarkable testimonial. The word here translated "humble" is "anaw," and indeed it can mean meek and humble (e.g., Prov 3:34 and 16:19, where it is contrasted with the proud). But most often it means, not so much a subjective virtue or an inward personal characteristic, as an objective state inflicted by others. The word describes people who are lowly because of some affliction, people who suffer by being put down and demeaned by others (which was true enough of Moses a lot of the time, even as a leader).

> The vast bulk of the occurrences of this and related words denote the position of people who have been humbled or afflicted in one way or another. It suggests people who are weak in some respect. They lack resources or power.[7]

> Is this not very ironic? Those who are lowly, by definition, "lack resources or power." Yet Moses was a man of incredible power. Even secular historians would agree that Moses has to be included among the greatest of all human leaders and nation-builders. ... Moses was a leader, and a very great one. Yet Moses was a servant, and a very lowly one. A leader, and a servant. A servant-leader, or a leading-servant. Is it possible to be both? According to our text the answer is yes, because the Bible affirms both of these paradoxical truths about him. The secret of Moses' power lay in the Spirit of God, and the secret of his humility lay in his lack of self-sufficiency.[8]

The classic example is the story of Num 11. Faced with mutinous demand for meat to supplement the manna, Moses collapses in panic before

---

6. I explore these points in greater depth in Wright, *Knowing the Holy Spirit* (originally published in 2007 by Monarch; now included in Wright, *Knowing God through the Old Testament*.
7. Goldingay, *Old Testament Theology*, 311.
8. Wright, *Knowing God through the Old Testament*, 438–39.

God. He cannot imagine how much mutton, beef, or fish would be required (Num 11:21–22). So Moses does not come up with an immediate plan of action. God, however, promises that meat will be delivered—poultry on the wing. But meanwhile God proposes also to share "some of the power of the Spirit that is on" Moses with seventy other leaders (Num 11:16–17, 24–25). And from that we learn two things: that Moses had no self-sufficiency but was dependent on the Spirit of God himself; and that he had no problem with God sharing the gifts and power of the Spirit around with others. The more the better, it seemed. He was humble enough neither to imagine he could cope on his own nor to resent God providing spiritual gifts for others to share the load. Some Christian leaders never learn either lesson.

2. Power without Jealousy

The story of Num 11 proceeds from one crisis to another. Two of the elders are not present when the Spirit is distributed, but nevertheless the Spirit rests on them "in the camp," and they start "prophesying." This outbreak of unscripted charismatic activity beyond Moses's immediate presence and control scares his Number Two, Joshua, who calls out "Moses, my lord, stop them!" (v. 28). And then we have Moses's classic response:

> Are you jealous for my sake? I wish that all the LORD's people were prophets and that the LORD would put his Spirit on them! (v. 29).

> I can't help thinking that there was a twinkle in Moses' eye as he put Joshua in his place. "Is it me you're really concerned about, or yourself? What is happening here is no problem for me; why is it a problem for you?" Moses had no personal jealousy, for his status, office or privilege—or even for a monopoly of God's Spirit and his gifts. If God wanted others to enjoy (if that's the right word) the experience of his Spirit and all the manifestations that went with it, that's fine by Moses. They'll find out soon enough that it isn't all standing about prophesying, by any means. There is a lot of work to be done, not to mention all the hungry people out there. For the moment, whatever power God's Spirit would give Moses was power without jealousy. He would gladly share it. In fact, if God wanted to share the Spirit more widely still, he would welcome that too.[9]

---

9. Wright, *Knowing God through the Old Testament*, 443–44.

We know from elsewhere that Moses had a uniquely intimate personal relationship with God (Num 12:7–8). So he was utterly secure in his own status before God and had no need to boost his authority by jealously claiming a monopoly on the gifts and power of God's Spirit. Sadly, again, we have to say that many Christian leaders jealously protect their alleged spiritual authority, in a way that hinders the spiritual growth and ministry of others in their community, thus damaging both themselves and those they lead.

3. Power without Ambition

Numbers 14 recounts an even more threatening crisis. After the majority of the spies bring back a massively discouraging report on the land, the whole community threatens to stone Moses and Aaron and go back to Egypt. God appears in great wrath and proposes to Moses the same thing that he had been on the cusp of doing at Mount Sinai in response to the idolatry of the Golden Calf (Exod 32).

> The LORD said to Moses, "How long will these people treat me with contempt? How long will they refuse to believe in me, in spite of all the miraculous signs I have performed among them? I will strike them down with a plague and destroy them, but I will make you into a nation greater and stronger than they." (Num. 14:10–12).

> It was an incredible temptation, if one can look at it like that. What was God proposing? He was offering to transfer to Moses all the promise that he had made to Abraham (that he would be a great nation), and its implications. God still had his ultimate purpose in mind. But he would carry it out by a different route. Forget the tribes of Israel. From now on, it will be the children of Moses. He will be known as the God of Moses. Moses will be the patriarch of a new nation, his own descendants. Just God and Moses and his seed forever. And wouldn't they get on so well together, if only these people were finally out of the way? Such thoughts could easily have fed Moses' ambitions—if he'd had any. He could step away from the burdens of leadership of this rancorous mob, and step into the limelight of history.[10]

But, in an extraordinary repetition of his intercession at Mount Sinai, Moses not only pleads with God to spare the people (you can read his memory of the event in Deut 9:23–29), he bluntly rejects God's offer to start

---

10. Wright, *Knowing God through the Old Testament*, 447.

all over again with Moses. He was a leader totally devoid of personal ambition for his own glory or future legacy.

> Moses had been called by God to serve God by serving these people. And he was not going to be deflected away from that calling—not even by God himself! He had no personal ambitions to be the father of a great nation in his own right. His job was to be the servant of God and the servant of these people—no matter what. But what people they were! Moses probably had the most critical, rebellious, awkward, ungrateful, unreasonable congregation of grumpy old men that any leader or pastor could ever have. Think of some of the things he has had to cope with in these narratives in the book of Numbers alone:
>
> - Administrative overload
> - Catering problems
> - Charismatic outbursts
> - Family feuds and disapproval of his own marriage
> - Refusal to follow the vision God had given through him
> - Attacks from outside the community
> - Sexual immorality within the community
>
> And God suggests, "Let's get rid of all of that and all of them, and you can be the head of a new community altogether." Tragically, apart from actually killing people, that seems to be what some leaders do—whether leaders of churches or mission organizations. In fact that's how some of them became leaders in the first place—by jumping out of a church or organization they didn't like, or one that caused them too many problems, and just starting up a new one, preferably named after themselves (with "international" or "incorporated" tacked on to add importance). Any such temptation, any such ambition, is precisely what Moses flatly refuses here. The power of his leadership, and certainly the power of his intercession at this precise moment, was that it was power without selfish ambition.[11]

CONCLUSION

Moses, then, provides the preeminent model in the Old Testament for what the exercise of leadership and power should look like among God's people.

11. Wright, *Knowing God through the Old Testament*, 448–49.

And it is countercultural and paradoxical—in a way that surely challenges so much that passes for spiritually powerful leadership in today's church.

> The paradox of the power of Moses, then, is this. The greatest evidence of the presence of the Holy Spirit in his life was precisely the absence of those things that are commonly linked with great and powerful people: pride in one's own self-sufficiency; jealous defence of one's own prerogatives; driving ambition for one's own legacy. This is the power of the Holy Spirit in a human life. This is power with humility.
>
> The church needs leaders. And leaders need power, if they are ever to get anything done (or, more properly, if God is ever to get anything done through them). But the kind of power they need is not the kind of power by which the world generally assesses leadership—"Not by might nor by power, but by my Spirit," says the LORD. (Zech 4:6)[12]

BIBLIOGRAPHY

Goldingay, John. *Old Testament Theology*. Vol. 1, *Israel's Gospel*. Downers Grove, IL: IVP Academic, 2015.

Wright, Christopher J. H. *Here Are Your Gods, Faithful Discipleship in Idolatrous Times*. London: InterVarsity, 2020.

———. *Knowing God through the Old Testament: Three Volumes in One*. Downers Grove, IL: IVP Academic, 2019.

———. *Knowing the Holy Spirit through the Old Testament*. Oxford: Monarch, 2006.

———. *Old Testament Ethics for the People of God*. Leicester, UK: InterVarsity, 2004.

---

12. Wright, *Knowing God through the Old Testament*, 450.

4

Sin and Why We Need to Take It More Seriously

Nick Mackison

I. INTRODUCTION—EVANGELICAL NAÏVETÉ

ABUSERS HAVE PERPETRATED THEIR dark deeds in the church since its beginning. Yet, while church-based abuse is nothing new, social media platforms have propelled it into the public square with fresh urgency. Hardly a week passes without whistleblowers directing troubling allegations at oncetrusted pastors and thought leaders, no matter their denominational stripe. Covert abusers—from sexual predators, to fraudsters, to bullies—have been uncovered in every corner of evangelicalism whether Baptist, Presbyterian, Anglican, or Independent. That is to say, abusers are not someone else's problem; they are our problem. Now, one might ask why this happens at all? How can abusers operate at such scale and with such impunity? Surely the church, of all places, would provide a "safe space" from bad actors? Questions like these reveal the evangelical mindset surrounding abuse. For many, the exposure of predators among their ranks has produced profound cognitive dissonance whereby, in finally being faced with real evil, they question whether their faith can account for it. But what this crisis reveals is a fickle grasp of the Bible's teaching on evil, despite Scripture's repeated testimony to what the Puritans described as "the exceeding sinfulness of sin." While revulsion in the face of evil is good and necessary, astonishment is not. And one reason why many of us are astonished is our naïveté.¹ In other words, whatever we may verbally profess about the nature and extent of evil, we just don't believe our own doctrine of sin. As Jeff Crippen comments

> [A] factor working in the abuser's favor is the fact that many Christians, though in theory they believe in 'the exceeding sinfulness of sin,' . . . in practice believe that everyone is basically good, or at least that we all struggle with sin in basically the same way and feel the same kind of guilt about it."²

Evangelical naïveté leaves the church vulnerable to exploitation, where leaders are ill-equipped to respond to evil within the church with the necessary wisdom and firmness. If the church is to ward off abuse and protect the vulnerable, it must be prepared to reckon with the implications of a biblical doctrine of sin.

a. The Sinfulness of Sin

A biblical doctrine of sin should disabuse us of naïveté. The doctrine of total or radical depravity, common to most evangelical expressions,³ is derived from serious engagement with texts like Gen 6:5 which asserts "every inclination of the thoughts of the human heart [is] only evil all the time."⁴ While "total depravity" can be misunderstood to imply the depth of human corruption (that someone is as wicked as he or she could possibly be), it instead denotes its breadth, where each individual is "wholly defiled in all the parts and faculties of soul and body."⁵ Furthermore, as Bavinck notes, our common ancestry implies that "humanity is not an aggregate of individuals but an organic unity."⁶ Thus the sin and corruption of Adam is the sin and corruption of the whole human organism (Rom 5:12). Total depravity

---

1. "Especially people who grew up in safe families and safe churches and safe schools can be incredibly naïve as to the realities of the dark deeds of hypocrisy." Crippen and Davis, *Unholy Charade'*, Ch 6.

2. Crippen and Davis, *Unholy Charade'*, 22.

3. Calvinist, Lutheran and Arminian theologians all hold to this position with some minor variations.

4. While it may be objected that this text was describing the crescendo of human evil prior to the flood and so cannot be considered normative, John Frame is right to observe that 'God's judgment of man's moral condition is virtually the same after the flood: "the intention of man's heart is evil from his youth" (Gen 8:2). Frame, *Systematic Theology*, 861.

5. Westminster Confession of Faith, 6.2.

6. Bavinck, *Sin and Salvation*, 102.

therefore describes the extent of sin's reach over both individuals and communities; it is universal in its sweep. Furthermore, though sin has a variety of manifestations, its common denominator is rebellion against God.[7] The various prohibitions of God's law may identify a vast array of sinful behaviors and attitudes, but the cumulative effect is to boil down sin's essence to that of "lawlessness" (1 John 3:4). Any sin against the law is a sin against the Law-giver, which explains why breaking even a solitary commandment is tantamount to a breach of the entire legal code (Jas 2:10). As James writes, the inclination to show partiality to the rich (Jas 2:9) flows from the same defiled well that overflows in adultery and murder (Jas 2:11). In one sense, therefore, there are no "big" or "little" sins insofar as they are all expressions of a single principle. Nevertheless, the consequences of certain sins outweigh those of others and Jesus notes that some infractions of the law are "weightier" than others (Matt 23:23). Consequently, any Christian capable of making peace with seemingly "innocuous" or "respectable" sins is also capable of indulging in habits that are even more shocking and destructive.

The Bible's teaching on the extent of sin confronts us with the problem as the common affliction of every human being, including those within the church. If James could warn God's people of their continuing liability to sins of adultery and murder, we have no reason to suppose that abuse is merely a problem for those outside the church. In practice, this means that not every "believer" we encounter will be a "nice guy"; abusers are not just "out there," they can also be "in here." However, we must take care that vigilance in this matter does not degenerate into self-righteousness. Coming to terms with church-based abuse can lead one to suppose he is a moral hero merely for recognising something to which others appear willfully blind. But, a sober understanding of sin means we are all implicated and precludes the Pharisaism that says, "I thank you God that I am not like this abuser" (Luke 18:11). If sin is the common problem of every person, then we are all potential participants in abuse, whether as victims, bystanders, or perpetrators.

b. Sin as Misused Power to Abuse

In challenging naïveté, however, it is not enough to speak about sin in general, we also need to face the specific issue of sin's potential to corrupt the power dynamics playing out in churches. The exploitation of power is not a new phenomenon. Contemporary categorizations of abuse and pathologies of abusers may well reflect new terminology, but they do not reflect a new reality. Scripture candidly documents exploitative behavior in the covenant

---

7. Lev 11:44–45; 19:2; 20:7; 1 Pet 1:6.

community, alerting the people of God to sin's ancient provenance and continued presence. Even a cursory reading of the biblical record reveals multiple examples of exploitative, malevolent conduct *within the confines of* God's people: rape, financial fraud, battery, and even murder. What is happening now has happened before. In providing a responsible account of misused power, it is necessary that we situate it within the larger frame of biblical teaching.

The idea of *misused* power carries with it a recognition that "power" per se is not sinful. A common thread on the doctrine of sin, from the early church Fathers, through the Middle Ages to the Reformation, involves framing sin in terms of its deleterious impact. Sin has no ontological existence of its own but, instead, involves a parasitic feeding on that which is good; it is "privation." Power itself is no abstract entity but is a human descriptor of God's simple essence as all capable.[8] Before Adam fell, God called him to reflect divine rule by exercising "dominion" in Eden (Gen 1:26). Power imbalances are not intrinsically evil but, ideally, constitute God's plan for the healthy functioning of civil societies.[9] The misuse of power involves therefore a privation of the good; a warping of the perfect ordering of relationships involved in pre-fall power dynamics.[10] That is to say, the abuse of power involves a perversion of the necessary imbalance that exists between two parties in such a way that the stronger does harm to the weaker party. For instance, there exists a necessary power imbalance between a doctor and a patient. The sick patient who arrives at the doctor's surgery in need of help does so in a state of vulnerability. The "power" exercised by the doctor involves diagnostic abilities to isolate the patient's illness and prescribe suitable treatment. This imbalance necessitates trust on the part of the patient and responsibility on the part of the doctor. The widespread recognition of this imbalance, and its potential for abuse, is reflected in the routine proscription of romantic relationships between doctors and patients by regulatory bodies.

A working definition of abuse must recognize the dynamic of trust and betrayal. We might therefore describe abuse this way: "Exploiting power and trust to the damage and injury of another." It may be "physical (including sexual) and non-physical (verbal and emotional). It can be active (physically or verbally) or passive (not speaking, not acting). Abuse, therefore, is

---

8. Various adjectives denoting power are ascribed to God in Scripture. For example, God's eschatological victory over sin and death is repeatedly celebrated in Revelation with the assertion that God is "Almighty" (see 1:8; 4:8; 11:17; 15:3; 16:7, 14; 19:6, 15; 21:22).

9. Cf. Prov 8:15, 16; Rom 13:1, 2, 4.

10. See Gen 3:16 where sin corrupts the power imbalance between the man and the woman.

not limited to physical assault."[11] The damage caused by betrayal of trust can scarcely be overstated, and especially so when caused by Christian leaders who claim to model Christ's example.

II. WHEN ABUSE IS "SPIRITUAL"—SHEPHERDS DESTROY THE FLOCK

It needs to be restated that power imbalances are not wrong in themselves; any form of leadership involves this imbalance. The answer to abuse of power is right use, not no use. However, when power imbalances and trust are exploited within the community of God's people, the resultant damage has its own, distinctively darkened hue:

> 1 The word of the LORD came to me: 2 "Son of man, prophesy against the shepherds of Israel; prophesy and say to them: 'This is what the Sovereign LORD says: Woe to you shepherds of Israel who only take care of yourselves! Should not shepherds take care of the flock? 3 You eat the curds, clothe yourselves with the wool and slaughter the choice animals, but you do not take care of the flock. 4 You have not strengthened the weak or healed the sick or bound up the injured. You have not brought back the strays or searched for the lost. You have ruled them harshly and brutally. 5 So they were scattered because there was no shepherd, and when they were scattered they became food for all the wild animals. (Ezek 34:1–5)

The Lord's indictment of these "savage shepherds," who exercised leadership in Israel,[12] concerns conduct antithetical to the purpose of their office. The function of leaders within God's covenant people was to "shepherd" the nation in faithfulness to the Lord. It involved a duty of care (v. 2–3) towards those members of society who, like sheep, would be prone to stray from their covenantal obligations (v. 4) and into the dangers of the covenant curses (Deut 28:15–68). This is why kings had to be avid students of God's law (Deut 17:18, 19), not considering themselves above others in this obligation (Deut 17:20). Instead of feeding the flock, however, these shepherds fed *upon* the flock (v. 3) and scattered the sheep (v. 5). The precedent is established here—leaders amongst God's people may in fact be

---

11. Crippen and Davis, *Unholy Charade*, chap. 2.

12. "Kings and leaders often were called "shepherds" in the ancient Near East (see Isa 44:28; Jer 2:8; 10:21; 23:1–6; 25:34–38; Mic 5:4–5; Zech 11:4–17). These 'shepherds' were more than military-political leaders. They bore a primary responsibility for the moral and spiritual direction of the nation." Cooper, *Ezekiel*, 298.

feeding themselves upon God's sheep instead of feeding God's sheep. Accordingly, not every Christian leader we encounter will be a "good guy," however charming or gifted he may seem. There will be leaders who hide their abuse behind theological orthodoxy, leadership prowess, great giftedness, or winsome demeanor.

At this point, one may object that the Old Testament setting of these episodes merely highlights the need for Christ's coming as the true Shepherd, bringing intimacy with God for all his people (e.g., Jer 31:34) and the gift of the indwelling Spirit (e.g., Ezek 36:25–27). Surely these New Covenant benefits would preclude the presence of systemic abuse today? Sadly not. The epistle of Jude deploys Ezek 34:1–5 in an expose of abusers who had infiltrated the church.[13] "These people are blemishes at your love feasts, eating with you without the slightest qualm—shepherds who feed only themselves. They are clouds without rain, blown along by the wind; autumn trees, without fruit and uprooted—twice dead" (Jude 1:12). Jude directly applies Ezekiel's description of "shepherds who feed only themselves" to the presence of destructive leaders within the New Testament church—and Jude is not alone in doing so. Paul also warned the Ephesian elders of shepherds just like those in Ezek 34:1–5; "savage wolves [who] will come in among you and will not spare the flock" (Acts 20:29). The danger of abusive spiritual leaders is common to Old and New Testaments.

a. The Subtle Nature of Spiritual Abuse

The nature and consequences of "spiritual abuse"[14] cannot be limited to its more overt manifestations such as physical battery, financial fraud, and sexual predation. Though these are terrible evils in their own right, Ezek 34:1–5 frames abuse as including any conduct that damages the victim's relationship with God. That is to say, spiritual abuse is behavior that scatters the sheep from the covenant community and from their Lord. The effects of such conduct may not be immediately obvious to either the perpetrator or the victim, and so this spiritual abuse has a subtle power all of its own:

> Spiritual abuse is the mistreatment of a person who is in need of help, support or greater spiritual empowerment, with the result

---

13. Jude warns the church that these people had "secretly slipped in among you" (v. 4).

14. Note the point made elsewhere in this volume: "If everything church leaders do wrong is called spiritual abuse, the issue is trivialized." Blue, *Healing Spiritual Abuse*, chap. 1.

of weakening, undermining or decreasing that person's spiritual empowerment.[15]

Abuse victims frequently testify that the harm experienced led to disillusionment with, and even abandonment of, the Christian faith itself. The casualties who remain within the church often encounter psychological difficulties in relating to God, whether in private prayer or Scripture study. In *Escaping the Maze of Spiritual Abuse*, psychologist Lisa Oakley observes that often abuse victims "are very fearful of the Bible or simply see it as a tool of control . . . the impact of this experience often leaves people unable or scared to read the Bible again."[16] This is why ministerial malpractice is so serious. If pastoral sin generally carries a greater weight of judgment (Jas 3:1), what of its more nefarious manifestations? If there is potential for any Christian to destroy the faith of a "weaker" brother or sister by misusing legitimate freedoms (1 Cor 8:11), how much greater the potential for harm when a pastor abuses his position?

Sadly, many churches have failed to provide sufficient protection for victims of abuse. In many cases where pastors have been caught in illicit sexual relationships with congregants, there is a contemporary trend towards what appears to be an all-too-quick restoration for the sinning leader. Such practice illustrates a callous disregard for the victims of pastoral abuse. The imbalance of power means that, no matter how much "consent" is thought to be given, such behavior is, by definition, abuse of leadership and the quick restoration of the leader looks like support for the abuser. An all-too-familiar pattern emerges of public announcements from a fallen evangelical celebrity that he is going through the process of "healing" and "counselling," but rarely with anything that approaches real accountability. The desperate haste to return to ministry at minimum suggests that the seriousness of the sin and its consequences has not been faced adequately. It also invites the question of whose needs and reputation are being served?

Quick restoration is another outworking of naïveté about sin and its consequences. Facile justifications offered by those involved in the restoration process—for example, invoking David's restoration to kingship, following adultery and murder, as providing warrant for ministerial return—betray a skin-deep understanding of evil. As noted earlier, while all sin incurs God's displeasure, some sins are worse than others (e.g., Ezek 8:6, 13, 15) and merit greater condemnation (1 John 5:16), especially those committed against the vulnerable (Mark 9:42). The potential consequences determine what sins are "worse" than others and helps explain why those

---

15. Johnson and VanVonderen, *Subtle Power*, chap. 1.
16. Oakley and Humphreys, *Escaping the Maze*, chap. 3.

holding positions of influence will be judged more severely (Jas 3:1). To insist therefore that certain sins have a disqualifying impact on church leaders, is neither legalistic nor graceless; it is responsible. Indeed, while biblical teaching on sin should raise questions about the practice of quick restoration, a question remains as to whether adulterous pastors can be restored at all. In *The Stain that Stays*, John Armstrong argues that pastoral adultery "is an even greater sin than adultery in general."[17] He reasons that such sin "compromises [a pastor's] past ordination . . . before the church body, makes their vows to be faithful to their ministry meaningless, and scandalizes their entire congregation, especially those new and weak in their faith."[18] While an immoral pastor may be restored to regular church membership, Armstrong makes a strong case for his never being restored to office. While it is beyond the scope of this paper to provide an extended analysis of Armstrong's position, the uncommon seriousness with which he treats pastoral sin is commendable.

b. Pervasive Spiritual Abuse

The problem of spiritual abuse is not restricted to isolated individuals; it may be intrinsic to entire churches or organizations. In Ezekiel, abusive leaders in Israel had "scattered" (34:5) the sheep. The whole community suffered and the scale of the problem led to the shepherds *en masse* being denounced. The lack of exceptions suggests that abuse had become a systemic problem. This issue continued from Ezekiel's day to the advent of Christ, where the abusive religious establishment left the people as "sheep without a shepherd" (Matt 9:36; Mark 6:34). Jesus described the scribes, who comprised the theological teaching-body of Judea, as akin to the devouring shepherds of Ezek 34. In like manner, these scribes would "devour widows' houses" (Luke 20:47). Jesus' lack of restraint is notable as he condemned the institution that was supposed to promote and teach biblical truth, but instead harmed people. With apparent lack of concern for the reputation of the religious establishment, Jesus issued blanket condemnations of the scribes and Pharisees by painting them all as spiritual abusers. He added none of the modern-day qualifiers like "Some of these men . . ." or "There are some bad apples in the establishment." Rather, the presence of abuse, together with practices and structures that sustained it, earned Jesus's harshest condemnation (e.g., Matt 23:15).

---

17. Armstrong, *Stain That Stays*, 65.
18. Armstrong, *Stain That Stays*, 67.

Ezekiel confronts the common notion of the abuser as the individual operating in secret, unseen. Rather, the problem is a much greater one, where patterns of abuse occur covertly at a systemic level, sometimes tolerated and even sanctioned by the religious setup. It is idealistic, therefore, for us now to expect the same religious institutions, that have sometimes enabled and tolerated abuse, to deal justly with abuse victims. It is not unusual for victims of abuse to find church procedure protecting perpetrators and further harming victims. We might legitimately ask again, in such situations whose reputation is being protected? Encouragements by church officers to victims like "Just be patient while the denomination investigates," are often accompanied by every effort to bury scandal in the background. At the same time, we must affirm the necessity of rigorous procedures for dealing with such issues. Perhaps we might say that procedures that prevent transparency and public honesty are part of the problem. Abuse flourishes in the dark.

The candor of Scripture here should serve as a model for how we respond to spiritual abuse. Often, a misplaced fear that scandal will irreparably damage the reputation of the church fuels efforts to conceal the details of pastoral abuse. This attempt to "cover up," however, is another instance of a defective understanding of sin. The scriptural prescription for "covering" sin involves nothing less than the "covering" provided by atoning sacrifice. The Hebrew word for "atone" means literally "to cover" (i.e., *kipper*),[19] and its cognates in the Greek New Testament reflect the semantics of this. God in Christ has provided the definitive "covering" (i.e., *hilaskesthai*) for his people's sins (Heb 2:17). Attempts at covering up abuse by means of silencing victims and obstructing the exercise of pastoral discipline betray the misunderstanding that sin is manageable, as if something less than the blood of the incarnate Son is sufficient to "cover" our offences. If we understand the extent of sin (and therefore the extent of the atonement), then we have nothing to fear from truth—no matter how terrible. The truth always exposes sin by casting light upon it.[20] Only when sin is exposed can it be covered, that is "expiated," through the blood of Christ. The readiness to cover up ministerial sin betrays both a low view of sin and a lack of confidence in the gospel itself. It arrogantly presumes that we are better at dealing with sin and its consequences than is God.

---

19. This word occurs variously throughout Lev 4:20—23:28 to describe the sacrificial practices, i.e., the blood of a sacrifice "covers" sin.

20. Cf. John 1:5; 1 John 1:5–7.

c. Spiritual Abuse Involves Exploitation

With a narcissistic insistence on "having the best of everything,"[21] the shepherds in Ezekiel would use "the choice animals" of the flock for their own purposes. The same is true today. As Blue notes, it is "the most committed believers [who] are often the most vulnerable to abusive religion."[22] Those with the greatest desire to serve the Lord and his church are most at risk of having their goodwill manipulated by an abusive spiritual leader.

At this point it is worth noting that the pathology of the spiritual abuser lies on a spectrum, from the deliberate abuser who sadistically feeds on the pain he inflicts, to the unwitting abuser who is quite unconscious of any harm caused. Like a toddler at the wheels of a bus, the good intentions of the unwitting abuser cultivates a fantasy that insulates his view of the accumulating wreckage in the rearview mirror. According to Blue, this latter phenomenon is the more usual manifestation of church-based abuse:

> Spiritual abuse may differ from some other forms of abuse in that it is rarely perpetrated with intent to maim . . . spiritual abusers are curiously naive about the effects of their exploitation.[23]

This point cannot be emphasized enough—spiritual abusers will, more often than not, defend their behavior with an appeal to good intentions. But a common feature in the diverse examples of abusive spiritual leadership is a belief that people are somehow expendable in the service of some "greater good." It makes no difference whether this "good" is construed as the advancement of a noble ideal on the one hand or the satiating of avarice on the other; people will be sacrificed with remarkably little compassion or empathy. Chuck DeGroat notes from the criteria for narcissistic personality disorder,[24] the common element in abusive leaders involve "impairments of empathy or intimacy. The narcissist is always out of touch with himself and others."[25] This insight speaks directly to the mentality of the abuser and the traits inherent to any leadership abuse.[26]

---

21. The Mayo Clinic, "Narcissistic Personality Disorder," para. 18.
22. Blue, *Healing Spiritual Abuse*, chap. 1.
23. Blue, *Healing Spiritual Abuse*, chap. 1.
24. See American Psychiatric Association. *Diagnostic and Statistical Manual*.
25. DeGroat, *Narcissism*, chap. 2.
26. Eds: We are being extremely careful here to avoid throwing around diagnoses of full-blown narcissistic personality disorder, not least because it is a contested diagnosis in the UK. However, it seems relatively uncontroversial to identify narcissistic traits in spiritually abusive leaders.

We must be alert, therefore, to abuse perpetrated in God's name. "Vision statements" for reaching the lost, proffered by apparently "kingdom-minded" pastors, may be noble in intent and helpful in motivating genuine concern for the health of the church. But they may also express baptized empire building, thus justifying the relentless exploitation of the "choice animals" who must sacrifice their time, talents, careers, finances and families for the "sake of the church." Sadly, burnout or ostracism for failure to perform is a common factor in the decline of erstwhile disciples, many of whom spiral into a state of spiritual crisis. But for the narcissistic pastor, the human cost of this "kingdom" expansion is inevitable "collateral damage." The pastor's growing congregation thus degenerates into what DeGroat describes as "grandiose narcissistic systems."[27]

On top of all this, there is the ever-present pitfall of the Pharisee, who places burdens on the vulnerable (Matt 23:4) while neglecting "the weightier matters of the law: justice and mercy and faithfulness (Matt 23:23)." Scripture can so easily be wielded as a weapon to control people's behaviors, while all the time neglecting their actual good. The many forms of legalism and the examples of leaders applying behavioral rules to their congregations, is one further expression of a deficient view of sin. The issue of total depravity cannot be dealt with by enforcing behavioral codes.[28]

III. CONCLUSIONS

A robust understanding of the Bible's teaching on sin should leave us unsurprised by the reality of abusive leadership within the church and able to face it honestly. How then should we respond?

a. Take Courage from the Example of Jesus

Having noted Jesus' repeated broadsides against the spiritual abusers of his day, victims can take comfort from the fact that abuse is a matter of utmost importance to God. Blue is not overstating the case when he says: "Jesus was so focused on the problem of spiritual abuse that it was the only social evil

---

27. DeGroat, *Narcissism*, chap. 6.

28. One of the more subtle forms of abusive leadership today is one that makes people expendable in the name of biblical fidelity. An example of this would be the promotion of the so-called marriage-permanence view. Rightly recognizing the importance of marriage, this position goes beyond Scripture and would deny even abused spouses the just (and biblical) recourse of divorce. Testimonies abound of abused spouses being commanded to stay in situations that are not only damaging but positively dangerous.

against which he ever developed a platform."[29] When sheep are scattered by abusive leaders, Jesus' heart is moved for those "harassed and helpless" ones (Matt 9:36). Love for his oppressed people motivated Jesus' explosive invectives against the scribes and Pharisees and, though our anger is rarely without sin, Christ's example validates the anger felt by spiritual abuse victims. If anger towards abuse and abusers is legitimate, it is vital that victims are given the safe space in which to express this in appropriate ways. Exhortations to "forgive and forget" are often issued too early and often reflect discomfort with victims' pain and unwillingness to face sin honestly.

b. Learn from Jesus's Exercise of Power

In coming "not to be served, but to serve" (Mark 10:45) Jesus demonstrated servant-leadership as the only "leadership style" commended by Scripture. Any model that reduces the people to servitude in the interests of structural power is a perversion of the biblical witness. The leader-as-servant motif also establishes clear boundaries for the pastor who must frame his vocation in terms of submitting his own interests to the service of his Father (Phil 2:3). In turn, this protects the church from pastoral overreach. A leadership model that moves beyond the biblical parameters of preaching and church discipline for certain sins (e.g., 1 Cor 6:9) has stepped outside of the God-ordained boundaries for pastoral authority. An illustrative incident, involving the apostle Paul, records that despite his "strongly" urging Apollos to visit the Corinthian congregation, Apollos remained unwilling (1 Cor 16:12). For Paul, to insist on Apollos's assent would constitute apostolic overreach. Would that many "visionary" church leaders could learn from his example.

c. Reject Idealism

Notwithstanding the seriousness of abuse, its presence and prevalence does not necessarily cast aspersions upon a church's legitimacy.[30] That there is no such thing as the ideal church is a truism that bears repeating. If savage wolves could infiltrate and dominate *bona fide* apostolic churches of the first century, it would be naïve to suppose any difference today. This outlook

---

29. Blue, *Healing Spiritual Abuse*, chap. 1.

30. Similarly—and very uncomfortably—abusive leaders are not necessarily unconverted and change, though extraordinarily difficult and usually very long term, can happen. DeGroat makes the point well that the narcissist is not entirely doomed never to change, though it is a long, long road to recovery, reconciliation, and healing.

should free us from the slavery of idealism. There never was a "golden age" in church history devoid of abusive leaders. If we have suffered spiritual abuse or have become disillusioned by reports of abuse within the church, we must guard against "calling it a day" with the faith. "Giving up" is a lament to the passing of a church age that never existed and, ultimately, comprises a further capitulation to the presence of evil.

Instructive here is the story involving the "poor widow" of Luke 21:2 who deposited a gift into the temple treasury.[31] It is significant that Luke placed the episode immediately after Jesus condemned the scribes for devouring widows' houses in 20:47. This widow was no doubt aware she belonged to a demographic which provided fodder for rapacious leaders. Indeed, Luke's placement of the story at minimum raises the question of whether her poverty was caused by financial exploitation at the hands of the scribes. Strikingly, however, the scribes' conduct had not allowed the widow to become cynical. She gave sacrificially to the temple because she could distinguish between the temple itself and the stewards of the temple. Accordingly, we must guard against exaggerating the importance of leaders in the church to the extent that we forget the church itself is God's new temple, his dwelling place. Paul himself distinguished between the function of leaders and the reality of the church when he wrote, "For we are co-workers in God's service; you are God's field, God's building" (1 Cor 3:9). That the farmers and builders are abusive does not entail that the farm or building is illegitimate. This realism, shaped by a rigorous biblical understanding of sin, is a truth that will set us free from the naïve idealism that leads so often to heartbreak, disillusion, and despair. Rather than becoming slaves of idealism, we will have the boldness to look evil straight in the eye and say, "though you slay me, I will continue to hope in the Lord."[32]

BIBLIOGRAPHY

American Psychiatric Association. *Diagnostic and Statistical Manual of Mental Disorders: DSM-5*. 5th ed. Washington, DC: American Psychiatric Association, 2013.
Armstrong, John H. *The Stain That Stays: The Church's Response to the Sexual Misconduct of Its Leaders*. Fearn, Scotland: Christian Focus, 2000.
Bavinck, Herman. *Reformed Dogmatics: Sin and Salvation in Christ*. Translated by John Vriend. Grand Rapids, MI: Baker Academic, 2006.
Blue, Ken. *Healing Spiritual Abuse: How to Break Free from Bad Church Experiences*. Downers Grove, IL: InterVarsity, 1993.

---

31. I owe the following insight to my pastor Rev. Norman Mackay latterly of Govan Free Church, Glasgow.

32. Adapted from Job 13:15.

Cooper, LaMar Eugene. *New American Commentary.* Vol. 17, *Ezekiel.* Edited by Ray E. Clendenen. Nashville, TN: B & H, 2014.

Crippen, Jeff, and Rebecca Davis. *Unholy Charade: Unmasking the Domestic Abuser in the Church.* 1st ed. Tillamook, OR: Justice Keepers, 2015.

DeGroat, Chuck. *When Narcissism Comes to Church: Healing Your Community from Emotional and Spiritual Abuse.* Downers Grove, IL: InterVarsity, 2020.

Frame, John M. *Systematic Theology: An Introduction to Christian Belief.* Phillipsburg, NJ: P & R, 2013.

Johnson, David W., and Jeffrey VanVonderen. *The Subtle Power of Spiritual Abuse: Recognizing & Escaping Spiritual Manipulation and False Spiritual Authority within the Church.* Grand Rapids, MI: Bethany, 2010.

The Mayo Clinic. "Narcissistic Personality Disorder." https://www.mayoclinic.org/diseases-conditions/narcissistic-personality-disorder/symptoms-causes/syc-20366662.

Oakley, Lisa, and Justin Humphreys. *Escaping the Maze of Spiritual Abuse: How to Create Healthy Christian Cultures.* London: SPCK, 2020.

5

The Power of the Imago Dei and the Imago Dei in Power

Mark Meynell

WE KNOW THE EPISODE well.[1] A lawyer itches with questions for Jesus. He wants "to justify himself," Luke tells, so it is only natural to ask the obvious question, "What must I do?" (Luke 10:25, 29). Jesus steers him towards the obvious answer: love God; love your neighbor. But perhaps that was too open-ended for him. For all his affability and apparent curiosity, he needs lawyerly clarity in defining "neighbor."

Jesus' legal case study, more conventionally categorized as a parable, is nothing if not profoundly provocative. This is undoubtedly why the lawyer is left unwilling even to utter the despised word "Samaritan," as if his very ethnicity somehow renders him unworthy of neighborly assistance. Or to be more accurate to Jesus' narrative, as if the Samaritan's ethnicity renders him unworthy of being a *model* of neighborly love.

The lawyer's second question is crucial for the topic at hand. For, if it is truly common to all humanity, then we must surely conclude that anybody created in God's image must therefore be my neighbor. It follows naturally, then, that my neighborhood must constitute the whole of humanity, every single person who shares in the *imago Dei*. This seems to be Jesus' implicit point in the case study: *all* people, regardless of race, skin color, culture, sexuality, class, education, wealth, status, politics, *all* are neighbors. The

---

1. Based on a paper originally given at the Oak Hill College School of Theology on 14th July 2020, published in Primer 11—A Little Lower than the Angels (published by FIEC and Oak Hill, 2021).

Samaritan shows breathtaking but practical love for a fellow human being reduced to his most vulnerable.

Put like this, however, neighborhood love seems unfeasible and unattainable. How is it even remotely practicable? The Good Samaritan surely prompts a despair similar to that of those who overheard Jesus' interaction with the rich ruler. The only hope lies in Jesus' counterstatement: "What is impossible for man is possible for God" (Luke 18:26–27) Nevertheless, forgiven people are never exempted from the demands of gospel love. Jesus' challenge of "Go and do likewise" remains (Luke 10:37). Therein lie the great dramas of ethics, of course, and the myriad debates are a constant, especially as a result of the need to navigate the gap between idealism and realism. Yet, without one crucial ingredient, all such debates are vain and futile.

That ingredient is power.

The potential to wield power and authority is God-given, a crucial function derived from being created in God's image. We must never reduce the image to this or any other function. But loving well often requires real power. Especially for those who lack it or who are the most vulnerable. As the Harvard firebrand and philosopher Cornel West put it, "Never forget that justice is what love looks like in public."

But we have a problem—or rather, five. Power is tricky to scrutinize at the best of times; and especially in the current climate. But I don't hear it discussed very much in evangelical circles at all. And we must; and this is *not* just because everybody else seems to be.

1. FIVE IMPEDIMENTS . . . OR WHY MANY EVANGELICALS JUST DON'T (WANT TO?) GET IT

(i) The Blindspot of the Enlightenment?

We can almost say this is *the* Enlightenment blindspot. Unfortunately, Evangelicalism is far more shaped by the Enlightenment project than we care to admit. So much of enlightened thinking, and therefore the Modernist era it spawned, evolved from the revolution of granting preeminence to reason and thought, and thus to ideas and ideologies. These consequently lay at the heart of its assaults on religion and Christianity in particular. No wonder, then, that Christians' responses to gospel assaults for perhaps the last three centuries focused on philosophical defenses. We cannot afford to stop that altogether. Truth still matters.

Yet we now live in an environment whose hostility is characterized, not so much by philosophy as sociology. Since Nietzsche and especially the twentieth century's unique horrors, all must now concede that truth claims are *never* neutral or objective. They are inescapably tied to the power wielded by their advocates. Failure to recognize that fact was an enlightenment blindspot. But then, the totalitarianism of Hitler and Stalin made it impossible to ignore. The acid of skepticism that fueled the Enlightenment's pursuit of truth and objectivity proved ineluctable. It proceeded to corrode the knowability of truth itself. So today, we are all primed to assess not only the content of a person's truth claims but the apparent agendas behind them. So if someone in the West fifty years ago, say, started investigating Christianity, a primary question would likely have been, "Is what these people believe true?" Today, in the increasingly unlikely situation of someone unilaterally doing the same, he or she is more likely to ask, "Am I safe with this crowd?" Yet, because we have tended to be oblivious to underlying culture shifts, our attempts to reach the world for Christ today get swatted away. Still so shaped by enlightenment frameworks, we don't even see these assaults coming. We might patiently be articulating what seem (to us, at any rate) supremely convincing arguments, while our interlocutors closed their ears the moment they discerned our power privileges. Whether we realized it or not, the church and her gospel, having once been dismissed as a mere irrelevance, are now recast as categorically dangerous and worthy of "deplatforming."

Troubling though this obviously is, there is something strange about our predicament. Our blindspots actually concealed what the Bible has said all along. This is ironic, since we are the very people supposed to take the Scriptures seriously. We will return to this in a moment.

The next impediment to discussing power is perhaps more recognizable, however. The reluctance derives from a natural suspicion of cultural bandwagons, an innate resistance to political correctness or wokeness or whatever other disparaging label seems appropriate.

(ii) The Reductionism of Critical Theory?

While awareness of the tenets and concerns of so-called *critical theory* may be limited, we can undoubtedly recognize its pervasive effects in the West. In some circles, mere mention of its somewhat-anodyne label to Christian leaders will be sufficient to increase temperatures and raise hackles. For example, Shenvi and Sawyer's 2019 piece for *The Gospel Coalition*[2] is largely helpful and informative, but some will presume to restrict their engagement to gleaning the headline terminology and warding their people off with dog-whistle labels like "cultural Marxism." As the article makes clear, the

2. Shenvi and Sawyer, "Incompatibility of Critical Theory."

various schools of thought operating under the critical theory banner did not spontaneously emerge from the ether, nor do they lack any intellectual or experiential bases. There is undoubtedly truth in their analyses, without which it could never gain the traction it has, not least in those with long memories of oppression and abuse.

Taking its cue from Nietzsche, it faces the harsh reality that nature is red in tooth and claw. The defining factor in human survival and coming out on top is simple. It is a matter not merely of accepting but embracing the necessity of the will to power. Where this has been impossible historically, so the narrative goes, it is now time, for the sake of justice, to bring transformation, to complete the revolution. This is about empowering the voiceless and vulnerable, showing them kindness, and providing restitution for victims of injustice.

But there are problems. Not, I hasten to add, because that oppression—*of non-white races, of women, of sexual minorities, of classes or political opponents, etc.*—is a figment. For ironically, the flaw lies not in going too far, but in never going far enough.

At its worst, the approach identifies and blames power abuse as the cause of *every* social ill; its concomitant solution is to cast victims as therefore the only valid inheritors of power. Disputing that is then complex, with opponents routinely silenced by means of a humiliating exposure of vested interests fearing the loss of privilege.

But what then? What happens when former victims take charge? Will they differ from any other cohort in power? The monarchs and aristocrats were evidently not up to it, so we looked to the bourgeoisie; they failed, so it needed to be given to the workers; but the workers in power simply created a new aristocracy. And now we give it to oppressed minorities? Then what? Is it too much to expect that these formerly oppressed will resist the temptation to become oppressors?

Critical theory seems to have little to say about this, apart from self-destructive contests about victimhood trump cards. But the Bible does! Take liberation theology, at its height in Latin America in the sixties and seventies. They claimed inspiration from both Moses and Marx—and they saw evidence of God's liberating grace in both ancient Egypt and twentieth century revolutions. They rightly exposed the rank hypocrisy of the failure of those with orthodox beliefs to give more than lip service to helping society's vulnerable and weak. Hence their urgent cries for improved praxis. But their flaw? To put it crudely, they assumed that divine providence started with the Exodus, in effect, whereas the biblical narrative, of course, opens with creation and the fall. That offers a political diagnosis that goes *far* deeper than critical theory ever has. For it underscores the reality of human sin and evil. Even within our neighbors made in God's image. Even within ourselves. As Solzhenitsyn famously realized during his Gulag incarceration.

> In the intoxication of youthful successes I had felt myself to be infallible, and I was therefore cruel. In the surfeit of power I was a murderer, and an oppressor. In my most evil moments I was convinced I was doing good, and I was well supplied with systematic arguments. And it was only when I lay there on the rotting prison straw that I sensed within myself the first stirrings of good. Gradually it was disclosed to me that the line separating good and evil passes not through states, nor between classes, nor between political orders either—but right through every human heart—through all human hearts . . . even in the best of all hearts, there remains . . . an uprooted small corner of evil.[3]

Despite never having experienced anything like the extremes he describes, I for one cannot deny the reality of his observations in my own heart.

So if there are such flaws in the whole approach, should we not avoid talk of victimhood altogether? It certainly has currency today, with features in the news on an almost daily basis, but surely this is a faddish distraction?

(iii) The Currency of Victimhood?

Because sin is true, our preaching may not duck the fact we are all perpetrators. As my former colleague, Rico Tice, always says when training leaders for *Christianity Explored* courses, the gospel demands that we cross cultural pain barriers. This is always difficult. But the danger is we miss something crucial in our cultural resistance and that is the objective reality of victimhood.

We must preach victimhood *as well*, regardless of its cultural currency. People *do* suffer at the hands of others, through no fault of their own, especially at the hands of the powerful. It is as simple as that. Every single one of us is both a perpetrator of personal sin and a victim of others' sin. There is such a thing as innocent suffering. To deny victimhood is to deny that fact, which is, after all, the central point of the Bible's oldest book, the book of Job. To deny it is to make a reductionism of our own. Furthermore, the denial of victimhood renders people vulnerable to the strongest advocates of critical theory, especially if their suffering was caused by preachers of the so-called "simple gospel."

---

3. Solzhenitsyn, *Gulag Archipelago*, 312.

(iv) The Insecurity of Privilege?

This is perhaps another subconscious reason for avoiding the power discussion. There is currently much talk of "white privilege" and "white supremacy" and it is not the place to engage that debate here. But one thing is clear: those with privilege (of any sort) are always the last to recognize it as privilege.

We may not articulate it in such terms, but if we enjoy privilege, the real possibility of fearing its loss must be faced as a motivation. After all, even if you must share a privilege, it is no longer a privilege, is it? So akin to President Trump's suggestion that coronavirus infections can be reduced simply by reducing the number of tests, we prefer ignorance and denial to facing the truth, especially if there is a risk of costly change.

(v) The Aversion of a Generation?

Some shy away from authority altogether, not out of temperament but precedents. The failings of forebears who wielded authority badly and even abusively is paralyzing. The media love to expose hypocrisy (apart from its own, of course), and what is juicier than ecclesiastical examples? There have been some horrendous stories in recent months in both the UK and USA, and so we recoil. After all, we just want "to love people." We take Lord Acton's adage seriously—power corrupts so let's avoid power. But societies which lack leaders and authority are anarchies that degenerate into survival of the strongest.

Authority and power are not the problem. Consider electricity. A substation will have mandatory warning signs to deter trespassers: Danger of death! But does that make electricity morally bad? Of course not. It is morally neutral. The issue is its application. So it is with God-given authority. For example, one writer asked a fascinating hypothetical question.[4] If it had been possible to form a modern-style symphony orchestra in the perfection that was the garden of Eden—a paradise without a hint of sin or selfishness—would it require a conductor? The answer is obvious: of course it would. The best conductor functions to enable every player to contribute and play to the best of their abilities. The best conductor will forge something that far exceeds the sum of the parts so that together all flourish, more than they would if playing alone.

No, as we have always known, it is not power per se that is the biggest problem but the human heart. Yet perversely, evangelicals have too often failed to pay attention to how sin twists our own wielding of whatever power

---

4. Austin, *Up with Authority*.

we do have. It is hard to grasp the urgency of this question, though. So to buttress what is at stake here, we must step back to a broader context for which there is now a near universal consensus: the abolition of slavery. That surely constitutes the greatest conceivable abuse of a neighbor, barring only murder.

2. THE ABOLITIONIST'S CAUSE: AM I NOT A BROTHER?

On 12th May 1789, William Wilberforce rises to his feet in the House of Commons. First elected in 1780 at only twenty-one, he had dedicated the previous two years to investigating slavery, urged on by close friend and now prime minister, William Pitt. The challenge was formidable. The Commons was largely skeptical—not least because the Privy Council had commissioned a report into West African slaves' conditions by a Liverpool delegate, Robert Norris. Among several claims, one deceit stood out as especially grotesque: slaves were somehow *better off* for their capture.

Wilberforce roundly condemned the Norris Report, accusing it of drawing "a film over the eyes, so thick that total blindness could do no more."[5] Armed with statistical details and eyewitness accounts, he carefully debunked each claim with new evidence and moral force. He spoke for four hours. Here are just a couple of excerpts.

> When first I heard, Sir, of these iniquities, I considered them as exaggerations, and could not believe it possible, that men had determined to live by exerting themselves for the torture and misery of their fellow-creatures. I have taken great pains to make myself master of the subject, and can declare, that such scenes of barbarity are enough to rouse the indignation and horror of the most callous of mankind.[6]

After itemizing some appalling statistics from the Middle Passage—the westward, Atlantic voyage which caused vast numbers of Africans to die—he concludes with evidence that slave mortality was almost entirely the consequence of their horrendous treatment rather than any culpable behavior.

> Here the Divine Doctrine is contradicted by the reverse action—That sympathy is the great source of humanity. . . . As soon as ever I had arrived thus far in my investigation of the slave trade,

---

5. Wilberforce, "Let Us Make a Reparation," para. 24.
6. Wilberforce, "William Wilberforce Speech."

I confess to you sir, so enormous so dreadful, so irremediable did its wickedness appear that my own mind was completely made up for the abolition. A trade founded in iniquity, and carried on as this was, must be abolished, let the policy be what it might,—let the consequences be what they would, I from this time determined that I would never rest till I had effected its abolition.[7]

Wilberforce's marathon marked a sea change and it was soon regarded as one of the greatest speeches Parliament ever witnessed. Yet because of the weight of financial, not to mention prejudiced, self-interest, the public square duel *for* the powerless *against* the privileged was now only picking up steam. It took eighteen years and multiple legislative attempts before the transatlantic trade was outlawed. Then, the abolition of slavery itself within British territories would require parliamentary slog for *another* twenty-seven years.

Notice Wilberforce's argument. Such treatment of human beings contradicted "Divine Doctrine." As fellow creatures, their createdness alone should be sufficient to elicit our "sympathy [which] is the great source of humanity." Of course, Wilberforce was by no means the only agitator for change. He was simply one of the most visible.

But what of the voices of those directly afflicted? Thankfully, there are *many* testimonies of those who escaped or were freed, on both sides of the Atlantic. Most famously, the letters of composer and actor Ignatius Sancho (published soon after his death in 1780) and Olaudah Equiano (also known as Gustavus Vassa, whose autobiography came out in 1789) have rarely gone out of print. Then a generation or so later came the account of Mary Prince, published in 1831, in which she described her multiple sales and journeys from Bermuda to Britain via Antigua.

But one of the most powerful and compelling voices of all was that of Frederick Douglass. He left a remarkable legacy of speeches, letters, and books. Here is but one example from an open letter he published in his local press. It is both heartbreaking and infuriating that it was necessary.

> A letter to the American slaves from those who have fled from American Slavery (The North Star—Sept 5 1850)
> Afflicted and Beloved Brothers:
> The meeting which sends you this letter, is a meeting of runaway slaves. We thought it well, that they, who had once suffered, as you still suffer, that they, who had once drunk of that bitterest of all bitter cups, which you are still compelled to drink

---

7. Wilberforce, "William Wilberforce Speech."

of, should come together for the purpose of making a communication to you.

> . . . Join no political party, which refuses to commit itself fully, openly, and heartfully, in its newspapers, meetings, and nominations, to the doctrine, that slavery is the grossest of all absurdities, as well as the guiltiest of all abominations, and *that there can no more be a law for the enslavement of man, made in the image of God, than for the enslavement of God himself.* . . . Better die than insult yourself and insult every person of African blood, and insult your Maker, by contributing to elevate to civil office he who refuses to eat with you, to sit by your side in the House of Worship, or to let his children sit in the school by the side of your children.[8]

Again notice the nub of the argument. If we each bear the Imago Dei, there is a givenness to human value, dignity, and equality, and therefore rights. Without such a conviction, it is ultimately impossible to defend the dignity, let alone sanctity, of each person's individual life. This is the desperate conundrum for the modernist and postmodernist world. It can offer no alternative to Richard Dawkins's bleak acquiescence to dancing to "the music of our DNA."[9]

Slavery is, of course, a morally extreme, if *still* present, reality. The suggestion that it might even remotely resonate with modern evangelicals in leadership will sound absurd. Yet, sadly, there are *some* parallels, especially since there is a spectrum of the ways in which power and authority are wielded. Which is where things get unsettling . . .

3. HANDLING HUMAN POWER: IN WHOSE INTERESTS IS IT WIELDED?

If the capacity for power over others and, relatedly, the authority that is derived from that, are indeed functional features of being created in God's image—part of the givenness of our nature—then there was evidently a divine purpose behind this gift. Elsewhere, we are called to love our neighbors as ourselves. So the question is not *whether* we use our power (as derived from personality and charisma, or privileges, or roles and job descriptions), but *how* we use power. This is because not wielding our power is itself a choice made possible by that power and privilege. I should add that this is a

---

8. Douglass, *Frederick Douglass*, 261.
9. Dawkins, *River Out of Eden*, 133.

question for every believer, not just those with church titles or responsibilities, because it gets to the heart of how anybody treats anyone else.

Before I meet or engage with any other person, the starting point must be that each possesses the same unshakable dignity and honor as we do. At the same time, since that *Imago* has been distorted and broken, such that every single one is tempted to sin and *is* sinful, we must assume each person has a capacity for evil. The paradox is that neither negates the other. Both are true. As Luther said, we are "*simul iustus et peccator*" (at once a justified one and sinner), to which we might well add that we are "*simul creatus ad imaginem dei et peccator.*"

The implications for the life of a Christian community are tremendous, but we will restrict ourselves to two.

(I) HUMAN POWER AND TRUTH

As a culture, we are now more attuned to the whiff of dark agendas than ever. We no longer take statements at face value; and I'm not just referring to Prime Ministerial press conferences. The prevailing assumption is that *everybody* is hiding something. Arch-cynics will retort, "So what? Conceal away. Speak not to convince but to move; not to reason, but to cajole, manipulate, control!"

Yet for the follower of Christ, this is unconscionable. We know we should let our yes be "yes," our no, "no" (Matt 5:37). We know that our convictions about the truth of Christ ought automatically to inspire a commitment to truthfulness like Christ. After all, what is a lie? It is a rejection of "true" truth, of reality, certainly. But it is much more. It is an attempt to mould another person's perception of reality to my own ends, which is in effect an attempt to gain power over another.

The German Catholic philosopher Josef Pieper unpacked this brilliantly in his 1974 essay *Abuse of Power*. As one whose life spanned twentieth-century Germany—he was born in 1907 and died 1997—he had observed this phenomenon. For it was Josef Goebbels who had declared, "We do not talk to say something, but to obtain a certain effect."[10] Do you see it? It achieves power through the mere *illusion* of truthfulness. Yet, if I am encountering a neighbor, a fellow image-bearer, how is it even possible to justify such treatment?

> Whoever speaks to another person—not simply, we presume, in spontaneous conversation, but using well-considered words,

---

10. Quoted in Meynell, *Wilderness of Mirrors*, 46.

and whoever in so doing is explicitly not committed to the truth—whoever, in other words, is in this guided by something other than the truth—such a person, from that moment on, no longer considers the other as partner, as equal. In fact, he no longer respects the other as a human person. From that moment on, to be precise, all conversation ceases; all dialogue and all communication comes to an end. But what's then taking place?[11]

Not considering the other as equal—but someone only useful, at best. He continues:

Rather, he has become for me an object to be manipulated, possibly to be dominated, to be handled and controlled. Thus the situation is just about the opposite of what it appears to be. It appears, especially to the one so flattered, as if a special respect would be paid, while in fact this is precisely *not* the case. His dignity is ignored. I concentrate on his weaknesses and on those areas that may appeal to him—in order to manipulate him, to use him for *my* purposes . . . an *instrument of power*.[12]

Finally:

This lesson in a nutshell says: the abuse of political power is fundamentally connected with the sophistic abuse of the word, indeed, finds in it the fertile soil in which to hide and grow and get ready, so much so that the latent potential of the totalitarian poison can be ascertained, as it were, by observing the symptom of the public abuse of language.[13]

Sadly, what is true in politics is true in every other human sphere. Including the church. Nobody ever claimed the church was immune from worldliness. In fact, it is arguable that every single one of Paul's letters was provoked by some kind of worldliness that hadn't yet been identified or rooted out. So consider these situations from ministry life.

How committed in practice are we to both truths about Christ and truthfulness like Christ? Or are we too quick to justify lying, or "half lies," or accept a little "economy with the truth"? Perhaps to massage our own reputations or to protect the supposedly good name of our ministry? Or even to convince potential members that "our lot" is a better bet than "that lot"?

The problem can be far more subtle than that, however. Consider the tendency towards instinctive, or even deliberate, reductionism. Imagine

---

11. Pieper, *Abuse of Language*, 21.
12. Pieper, *Abuse of Language*, 22.
13. Pieper, *Abuse of Language*, 32.

a heated debate is taking place in the wider church (when isn't there?). It could be about anything really, but when it is especially contentious or complex, most pastors are likely to be deeply, and reasonably, concerned about church members heading down what seem to be blind alleys. Furthermore, on top of all the regular demands on a pastor, the temptation to use a quick-fix to save time and effort is great. We all know that a speedy, damning, and alarmist label will successfully deter perhaps nine out of ten members.

- "Oh, you're resorting to that classic, *liberal* argument now, are you?" After all, who wants to end up in that camp?
- "Oh she's gone all *social-gospel* with this race stuff. It's a slippery slope, you know?" After all, nobody wants to end up slipping right out of the body and even becoming an enemy of the cross?
- "Yes, Fred has started saying X. And sadly, that surely reveals he's no longer committed to scriptural authority." That is a guaranteed clincher in some circles, and deployed with alarming ease.

It is all very easy when you know how. But if truth be told, it is disingenuous and deceptive. It uses language not for the sake of truth but for its effect. It may start with exhaustion and being over-stretched. We are too tired to battle on yet another front. Yet this does not alter what is happening.

The gains are usually only short term. Spin and propaganda invariably get exposed in time. But here is a privilege we rarely acknowledge. One of the most significant features of a Christian leader's power is hidden. It is a phenomenon that occurs far more in churches than almost any other human organizations: we are trusted. This does not include what happens outside, since polls and surveys consistently reveal declining trust in clergy in Western culture. But inside? We will be readily believed, and so we are able to exploit that whether we acknowledge the fact or not. I vividly remember the first time it struck me with real force. The real shock, however, is that I was so slow on the uptake. Being on the preaching team at All Souls, Langham Place for nine years was a great if daunting privilege. Several years in, I walked up as usual into the unique pulpit (a gift to the church after the 1975 refurbishment it is very much of its time, resembling a large prop on a Kubrick science fiction film) and was suddenly stunned. Within a few seconds, almost a thousand people will sit in expectant silence for thirty or forty minutes, listening to my every word, taking notes and wrestling with ideas, ready and willing to put what I say into practice. What other contexts in modern life regularly allow for such rapt attention? Not many. This is astonishing power. So a time-saving reductionism thrown in will have quite the effect.

What are we implying about those we manipulate? Have they not become objects, rather than neighbors? We no longer consider them fellow *Imago Dei creatures*. In our subconscious calculations they have ceased to be persons; they have become instruments. Just as our words have ceased to communicate truth; they have become tools. This seems extreme, but only just. For ultimately, they become enslaved. After all, did not Aristotle explicitly describe slaves as "live tools"?[14]

The second implication will bring the connection to slavery into sharper focus.

(II) HUMAN POWER AND FREEDOM

How do we relate to one another in community life? One writer who has had a profound effect on me in this area is Dietrich Bonhoeffer. He did not engage with critical theory per se, but his insights have vital applications to the power dynamics within our communities and churches. His *Life Together* is so dense and rich that I can normally digest only a few pages at a time, but that Confessing Church learning community learned a great deal in Finkenwalde despite only existing between 1935–37.

After a challenging section on the personal discipline of withholding sinful thoughts and guarding the tongue in community life, Bonhoeffer grounds his argument on the givenness of our creation.

> God did not make others as I would have made them. God did not give them to me so that I could dominate and control them, but so that I might find the Creator by means of them. Now other people, in the freedom with which they were created, become an occasion for me to rejoice, whereas before they were only a nuisance and trouble for me. God does not want me to mould others into the image that seems good to me, that is, into my own image. Instead, *in their freedom from me* God made other people in God's own image. I can never know in advance how God's image should appear in others. That image always takes on a completely new and unique form whose origin is found solely in God's free and sovereign act of creation. To me that form may seem strange, even ungodly. But God creates every person in the image of God's Son, the Crucified, and this image, likewise, certainly looked strange and ungodly to me before I grasped it.[15]

---

14. Aristotle, *Pol.* 1253b23–1254a17 (p. 63).
15. Bonhoeffer, *Life Together*, 71–72, my emphasis.

This idea then gets picked up a few pages later.

> First of all, it is the *freedom of* the other . . . that is a burden to Christians. The freedom of the other goes against Christians' high opinions of themselves, and yet they must recognize it. Christians could rid themselves of this burden if they didn't release the other person but did violence to him, stamping him with their own image. But when Christians allow God to create God's own image in others, they allow others their own freedom. Thereby Christians themselves bear the burden of the freedom enjoyed by these other creatures of God. All that we mean by human nature, individuality, and talent is part of the other person's freedom—as are the other's weaknesses and peculiarities that so sorely try our patience, and everything that produces the plethora of clashes, differences, and arguments between me and the other. Here, bearing the burden of the other means tolerating the reality of the other's creation by God—affirming it, and in bearing with it, breaking through to delight in it.[16]

As we consider how we need to heed this insight, it is important to identify the various ways by which a Christian leader's authority, for good and ill, is manifested:

- *Influence and Vision*: is it overt or is its effect on council or elders' meetings more subtle? Does it facilitate and inspire a sense of ownership and mutual growth? Whose vision is it, in fact? Is it God leading his people through the agency of the leaders he has placed there; or is it more a matter of what one or two leaders have decided "on God's behalf"?

- *Preaching and Training*: is the pulpit a place of equipping and stretching, refreshing and inspiring? Does it both inform and transform disciples? Or is this a sphere of domination and thought control, especially when it comes to the demarcation of a narrow tribal identity? In other words, does it insist on a uniquely authoritative grasp on gospel truth while silencing dissent or doubt?

- *People and Teams*: some of the most egregious power abuses occur within leadership or staff teams. For an insecure leader, the freedom of the other is precisely where a threat lies, especially in situations of having to work closely together. How will they be aligned and work together? Is it partnership, albeit with differing roles (in which some necessary distinctions in authority are marked out), or is it a matter of curtailing others' freedom for the sake of the leader's freedom?

---

16. Bonhoeffer, *Life Together*, 78–79.

But I want to consider the area of discipleship, since it relates to all three of these. In some of the worst failings of recent years, it is in the aims, patterns and methods of discipling others, especially when there are significant age gaps, that the ground has proved fertile for abuse. This is necessarily a cursory glance, so the hope is that this stimulates further discussion.

It is no surprise, after the cases that reached the national press as well as those that have not, for some to seek a prohibition of one-to-one discipleship ministry altogether. It is only the naive or complacent who would not concede its inherent dangers, even when advocating for it on account of biblical precedent and personal benefit.

Furthermore, one aspect that makes this so complex is the fluidity with which human beings relate to one another. A single relationship can largely contain healthy dynamics despite containing some negative and even toxic elements. So even the best of them will feature less than ideal elements. Conversely, even the worst and most abusive are likely to feature at least some positives, albeit tarnished by coercive agendas or twisted generosity. We should expect nothing less of those who bear God's image, yet are fallen. We are neither the holy creatures God made us to be, nor are we infernal devils with the *imago* eradicated.

This fluidity must force us to discern a spectrum here. The Twitter soundbites of our aggressive shaming culture fail to allow room for that. Everything is binary (except, ironically enough, for the biological realities that generally *are* binary). It's never a matter of "that was a racist statement" or "this is a homophobic thing to do." Uttering an X statement exposes someone as an X-ist. End of story. That is their identity forevermore. The motivation behind identifying such social dynamics, of course, was certainly positive; its outcomes, unfortunately less so.

What was one of the supreme goals of enlightenment thinking? Both American and French Revolutions were waged in order to bring it to the people.

- Across the English channel, it was *"Liberté! Égalité! Fraternité!"*
- Across the Atlantic, the Declaration of Independence stated in 1776 that all human beings have three inalienable rights granted by the Creator—"life, liberty and the pursuit of happiness." When crafted a few years later, the new constitution made it clear that liberty lay at the very heart of this new nation. The Preamble identifies one of several purposes of the Union being to "secure the blessings of Liberty."

That is hardly a bad thing. There are far worse goals that people have fought for. And I for one would far prefer to be free than enslaved. Who wouldn't?

Yet it was precisely at this point that another significant flaw in this enlightenment thought lay. Nobody could ever fully agree on what that liberty was *for*. How should it be expressed? What was to happen when one person pursuing happiness resulted in another enduring misery? The right to pursue happiness is clearly one root of the modern individualism that cares little or nothing for the community. In contrast, the Scriptures never make this mistake. Humanity's redemption was never to result in a shapeless or subjective liberty. It was a freedom *from* slavery, certainly. But a careful reading of the book of Exodus reveals a potent paradox. The people were freed *from* Egypt, but *for* the worship of Yahweh.

As was said in subsequent centuries, it is precisely in the service of Yahweh that we find perfect freedom, a context in which we truly flourish; where we can fully express what it was we were created to be. It is akin to a musician submitting to the ideal orchestral conductor, one who enables playing at their very best, making the sum infinitely greater even than great individual parts. That is ultimately what being in God's image leads to.

Notice how a person thus never loses their identity or individuality in the community (which is where communism leads). Nor does their inherent selfishness override the needs of that community (which is where libertarianism leads). This offers unity without oppressive uniformity; diversity without corrosive atomization. As if that was not paradoxical enough, here is the greatest of them all, in the light of all we have considered. God's community offers genuine freedom to serve without selfishness; slavery without the slightest hint of humiliation or dehumanization.

How is that possible? Well it comes back again to the issue of *how* we use our power. God himself is to be our model for that. Here is Richard Middleton at the conclusion of his major work on the *Imago Dei*.

> Genesis 1 artfully shatters both ancient and contemporary rhetorical expectations and, instead, depicts God as a generous creator, sharing power with a variety of creatures (especially humanity), inviting them (and trusting them—at some risk) to participate in the creative (and historical) process. In Brueggemann's summary, the picture of God in Genesis 1 and of humanity as *imago Dei* foregrounds "the creative use of power which invites, evokes and permits. There is nothing here of coercive or tyrannical power, either for God or for humankind." Drawing both on the text's rhetoric of God's "gracious self-giving" as the model for human action and its protest against ancient Near

Eastern views of human servitude, Brueggemann concludes: "The text is revolutionary."[17]

So here is our spectrum.

Given that I possess power and authority, to what use should I put it; my own purposes or for the flourishing of another? The closer we get to the former, the more it enslaves the other. It gravitates towards a relationship of control and coercion. That other person has ceased to be my neighbor; he or she has become an instrument or tool to possess and use.

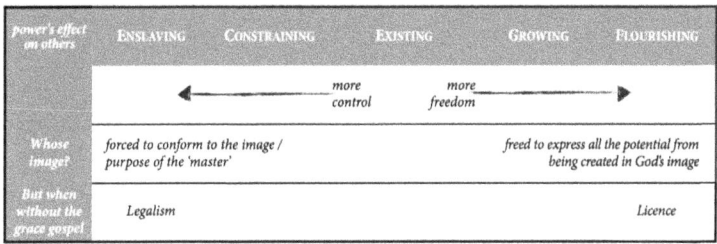

Another additional dynamic needs to be factored in here. For if we omit the gospel of grace from our praxis (which is perfectly possible even in those whose preaching is full of it), there are devastating consequences for people along this spectrum.

All in ministry long for people to grow in maturity and Christlikeness. We want to see the fruit of the Spirit. Like any preacher, I find that my preparation process invariably stimulates ideas about how a text should be applied. Our motives for doing so will naturally be mixed. We might simply want to appear impressive or authoritative; or we are desperate for some visible validation for the effectiveness of our efforts. But even without these traps and with the best of intentions for others' growth, a graceless ministry will inevitably lead to two pastoral errors.

- We become legalistic, detailing every sub-clause in the application of a truth, offering visible and verifiable checklists, a path that will offer a sense either of achievement or abject failure. This is a ministry that gets results. Achievement is the operative word, of course. Yet this is a form of enslavement. We will never find legalism in the Bible, so a legalistic message must by definition be a form of deception, and therefore of subtle manipulation. It is a leader's means of usurping God's authority over people's discipleship. As well as hubristic, it is enslaving.

17. Middleton, *Liberating Image*, 267.

- Conversely, perhaps out of a fear of legalism, we become advocates of license. We offer freedom, but only freedom of a sort. It is effectively enlightenment liberty, which we might even go so far as to describe as sin. It is creaturely freedom without creator worship; it is the Red Sea without the tabernacle; it is Exodus without Genesis.

Paul dealt with both so brilliantly in Galatians. Then as he explained to Titus, it is ultimately grace *alone* that teaches us to say "No" to worldliness and "Yes" to Christ. (Titus 2:11–15) Grace is always transformative.

Yet, here's the rub. As a Christian leader, my longing is for people to grow in holiness, while my temptation is to avoid the hard, slow graft of ministry and take short cuts. That will mean I begin to justify any means in that work. Even if it means abusing my power by which I curtail my neighbor's freedom. In other words, I limit their freedom to have agency and responsibility for their own lives.

I think this is one of the worst things about the John Smyth horrors which started coming to light in the UK media in recent years. He deliberately targeted young and impressionable boys and then inflicted grotesque punishments on them in the name of Christian discipline and sanctification. This happened not just in the UK but also in Zimbabwe. They were manipulated and controlled. How was such activity not identified and ended? The answer in part is because of the guile and deception of abusers: they tend to be masters of concealment and threats.

Yet it must also be said that he was able to hide within distortions that grew within the culture of Iwerne camps. I should say that I personally gained much from Iwerne camps and was a leader for seven years (despite never having gone as a teenager). I am thankful to God for all I gained there, not least in the deep Christian friendships that I still value to this day. I should also say that in recent years, significant rather than token changes were made to the network's culture. Smyth was before my time and I only learned his name when it reached the front pages, and having learned more about him, there is little doubt that Smyth was an extreme outlier; his appalling activities were truly monstrous, especially because they clearly influenced others to act in similar ways.

Nevertheless, at its worst, there *was* a culture of what C. S. Lewis famously articulated as the "Inner Ring."[18] In part because of the deliberate mission of reaching students from the "top schools" and around the more magnetic personalities in the leaders' room, there *was* a sense of being elite and set apart. Most importantly, there were some unspoken, unhealthy, and even controlling discipleship methods, which is what made Smyth's

---

18. Lewis, *Weight of Glory*, 141–57.

extremes less discernible. Too often, a fatal boundary was crossed by a number, though they were by no means in the majority. In discipling someone, usually one far younger and more impressionable, a mentor would act not simply as a fellow pilgrim, offering wisdom as one a little further along in the Christian road. He effectively took on responsibility for that person's progress and holiness. He presumed to exercise a role, normally exclusive to the Holy Spirit, his job to bring about transformation.

For example, he might well discern arrogance in the young believer. That is certainly common enough! But *then*, the mentor assumes the role of sanctifier. This is not to exclude the place for a gentle challenge or even rebuke. Their effectiveness or expediency will often depend on factors such as the quality of trust between the pair, the mentor's ownership of his or her own sin, the younger believer's teachability and honesty. However, there is a fine line between a divinely appointed challenge and bringing someone "down a peg or two." Some of the tried and tested means included playing squash or tennis with the sole aim of resounding victory; or employing a harsh word or sarcastic put-down in a team meeting; or giving a deliberate cold shoulder for a period "until he learned his lesson." There will no doubt be various pastoral justifications for such treatment. Yet in the light of Bonhoeffer's insights, the "freedom of the other" has been trampled in actions that have already degenerated into control. Such manipulations are hardly healthy for *either* party.

Henri Nouwen was remarkably astute about how ministry goes wrong. He is adamant, however, that the kind of ministry he describes here, one which we can no doubt recognize regardless of our denominational or cultural contexts, is emphatically not gospel ministry.

> When I ask myself the main reason for so many people having left the church during the past decades in France, Germany, Holland, and also in Canada and America, the word "power" easily comes to mind. . . . The temptation to consider power an apt instrument for the proclamation of the Gospel is the greatest of all. We keep hearing from others, as well as saying to ourselves, that having power—provided it is used in the service of God and your fellow human beings—is a good thing. With this rationalization, crusades took place; inquisitions were organized; Indians were enslaved; positions of great influence were desired; episcopal palaces, splendid cathedrals, and opulent seminaries were built; and much moral manipulation of conscience was engaged in.[19]

---

19. Nouwen, *In the Name of Jesus*, 58.

This is but one legacy of the gradual Constantinian revolution begun with the Edict of Milan in AD 313. No doubt Christians had faced this temptation before that point, but now the might of the State could be allied with the church's already significant influence for whatever ends (especially after the Edict of Thessalonica made Christianity Rome's official religion in AD 380).

Nouwen's insight, however, is fascinating. As Chuck deGroat's fine if chilling analysis of narcissism elaborates,[20] such temptations suggest a deeper problem.

> One thing is clear to me: the temptations of power are greatest when intimacy is a threat. Much Christian leadership is exercised by people who do not know how to develop healthy, intimate relationships and have opted for power and control instead. Many Christian empire-builders have been people unable to give and receive love.[21]

If correct, and deGroat clearly indicates that he is, then the antidote to such behavior will necessitate a long and painful road of self-discovery and confession at the very least. It is a problem as far from the realms of the quick fix as it is possible to be. What we can say for certain is that these problems force us to recognize afresh the profound transformation that our Lord Jesus Christ's revolution demands of us. He walked the path of powerlessness despite, or even because of, his power. He is the King of Kings and Lord of Lords, yet adopted the degradation and invisibility of the slave. Weakness has never looked so potent.

> Powerlessness and humility in the spiritual life do not refer to people who have no spine and who let everyone else make decisions for them. They refer to people who are so deeply in love with Jesus that they are ready to follow him wherever he guides them, always trusting that, with him, they will find life and find it abundantly.[22]

4. ACID TESTS: SOME DIAGNOSTIC QUESTIONS

I will close with a barrage of diagnostic questions to help us discern where we might unwittingly be crossing lines or lazily exploiting our privileges.

---

20. DeGroat, *Narcissism*.
21. Nouwen, *In the Name of Jesus*, 60.
22. Nouwen, *In the Name of Jesus*, 63.

- Who are the weak and strong/powerful outside our church neighborhoods? Do these demographic groups feature in our church? If so, are the power dynamics the same within and without? In other words, perhaps the neighborhood includes affluent yuppie types, alongside those with more menial social roles, such as shopkeepers, council workers, cleaners, those often from immigrant or deprived backgrounds. If this social range is represented church, do they function in the same kinds of roles? Are the yuppies the only ones in leadership as elders or PCC? Is there any sense that the people regarded by the world as inferior are especially treasured and valued, not just because they clean the toilets faithfully and well but because everybody has something to learn about Christ through and from them? We're part of a body. Every part matters (especially those parts that the world treats as embarrassing or somehow shameful). All are neighbors.

- How do questioners and doubters fare? Is there a limit to how they're handled or tolerated? Or do they know they are truly welcome, even if they perhaps need to pick better moments for their questions? Does the preaching help them or does it assume everything in the Christian life is "sorted" and straightforward? Can the leaders be questioned? Publicly? Or is that crossing a line? Then how is humor used? Is it a sarcasm used to keep people in their place or differentiate insiders from outsiders? Is it used to divide and conquer or to bring lightness and joy?

- When it comes to the disciplines of the Christian life and those who lead the charge on church discipline, is there an acceptance of "the freedom of the other" or is it more honored in the breach, whereby behaviors are patrolled without leeway for conscience, differences of opinion or struggles? Is it determined by just one person or a small group? Are these questions ever publicly discussed, by which I do not mean public discussion of an individual case (unless there are safeguarding concerns, naturally); rather, an airing of the general issues and how these might be tackled.

- How are church ministry strategies decided? Obviously no fellowship can do everything. We all have to focus and prioritize. However, how are the criteria decided? Is there any point at which these criteria are merely worldly? Are we just valuing those that the world values and so seek to do ministry with them?

For surely, if we have learned nothing else from all this, one thing is clear. There can be no limits or boundaries to my neighborhood. Certainly not the boundaries of race and color, wealth and status, education and privilege. All are made in the image of God. Which surely means, there is *no such thing* as a strategic person. How can there be? At least not in a way that we can discern. God undoubtedly has his plans and purposes, but who are we to know precisely what they are until long after the moment.

So whenever I encounter an individual person, I must acknowledge and embrace the fact that, *without exception,* each one is my neighbor.

BIBLIOGRAPHY

Aristotle. *Politics*. Translated by Thomas A. Sinclair. Rev. ed. London: Penguin, 1992. Kindle ed.
Austin, Victor. *Up with Authority: Why We Need Authority to Flourish as Human Beings*. London: T. & T. Clark, 2010.
Bonhoeffer, Dietrich. *Life Together*. Translated by John W. Doberstein. London: SCM, 2005.
Dawkins, Richard. *River Out of Eden: A Darwinian View of Life*. London: Phoenix, 1996.
DeGroat, Chuck. *When Narcissism Comes to Church: Healing Your Community from Emotional and Spiritual Abuse*. Downers Grove, IL: InterVarsity, 2020.
Douglass, Frederick. *Frederick Douglass: Selected Speeches and Writings*. Edited by Philip Sheldon Foner. Adapted by Yuval Taylor. Library of Black America. Chicago: Lawrence Hill, 1999.
Lewis, C. S. *The Weight of Glory*. Grand Rapids, MI: Eerdmans, 1949.
Meynell, Mark. *A Wilderness of Mirrors: Trusting Again in a Cynical World*. Grand Rapids, MI: Zondervan, 2015.
Middleton, J. Richard. *The Liberating Image: The Imago Dei in Genesis 1*. Grand Rapids, MI: Brazos, 2005. http://www.loc.gov/catdir/toc/ecip054/2004028522.html.
Nouwen, Henri J. M. *In the Name of Jesus*. London: Darton, Longman & Todd, 1989.
Pieper, Josef. *Abuse of Language, Abuse of Power*. Translated by Lothar Krauth. San Francisco: Ignatius, 2007.
Shenvi, Neil, and Pat Sawyer. "The Incompatibility of Critical Theory and Christianity." *The Gospel Coalition*, May 15, 2019. https://www.thegospelcoalition.org/article/incompatibility-critical-theory-christianity/.
Solzhenitsyn, Aleksandr Isaevich. *The Gulag Archipelago, 1918–56: An Experiment in Literary Investigation*. London: Harvill, 2003.
Wilberforce, William. "Let Us Make a Reparation to Africa." http://www.emersonkent.com/speeches/abolition.htm.
———. "William Wilberforce Speech against the Slave Trade." https://www.biographyonline.net/politicians/quotes/wilberforce-speech.html.

6

Symbolic Capital and the Dynamics of Leadership
The Gospel and the Idolatry of Status

Grant Macaskill

THIS ESSAY WILL RECONSIDER what Paul means when he speaks of his "own righteousness"—literally, the "righteousness of myself"—in Phil 3:4–16. Complex issues of status are at work in this expression and they continue to constitute dangerous forces in the lives of Christians, even of those who proclaim "salvation by grace." We will consider particularly how this impacts practices of leadership.

Paul's reasons for "confidence in the flesh" (3:4) have usually been understood to be his "legalistic" convictions. I argue he is presenting a more embracive account of social identity and the logic of personal worth and value and that this is what Paul understands the gospel to challenge. This logic of worth continues to permeate the life of the church and to compromise the conduct of its leaders, requiring Paul to confront it.

In order to probe this logic, and to show how Paul contrasts it with the gospel, I will make use of a modern philosophical and sociological category that I think labels its qualities effectively, that of symbolic capital.[1] Once I

---

1. I am not the first to apply this category to Paul's representation of confidence in the flesh and there is nothing particularly innovative in the core observations I make concerning it (although I trace more thoroughly than others have the use of "capital" and "ownership" language in Phil 3). John Barclay makes extensive use of the concept

have read the elements of Phil 3:1–16 in relation to this category, I will consider how the dynamics it labels might particularly compromise leadership practices, if not carefully identified and challenged.

We commonly read Phil 3:4–16 as reflecting Paul's abandonment of his older commitment to a "works righteousness." This is equivalent to a "legalism" in which a person believes that salvation can be earned through the performance of an obedience that will secure God's approval. This definition of righteousness often employs the central image of the "balance sheet": if the person performs enough good to be in credit with God, they can expect salvation, and their moral performance is directed accordingly. The gospel of grace, by contrast, represents sin as constituting a level of universal debt on this ledger that can never be balanced by our efforts and can only be addressed by the sharing of Christ's credit of righteousness with us. This is appropriated by faith and not works. Since evangelical definitions of the gospel as a message of grace exclude such beliefs, evangelicals commonly see "works righteousness" or "legalism" as someone else's problem, a belief that other traditions or religions might propound but that we reject. Philippians 3:4–6 is taken as a specimen example of works righteousness, with the following verses describing Paul's repentance from this way of thinking.

By contrast to this, I will argue that what Paul has in view here is as much about how we are seen by other people as it is about how we might be seen by God. It is about the currency that we perceive ourselves to have and expect to be recognized by others, what some theorists describe as "symbolic capital." This is fundamentally opposed to Paul's identification of the "righteousness that is of God." I hope that readers will see the essential qualities of "symbolic capital" and the transferability of the concept from Paul's ancient context to our contemporary one. The essay will also consider the particular perils that this "of-ourselves-righteousness" represents for those involved in leadership within the church at any level, as the native (but often un-self-aware) desire to accrue symbolic capital subverts our ministries. I am convinced that many instances of power and abuse that we have seen within evangelical ministries in recent years reflect such dynamics.

1. SYMBOLIC CAPITAL

The language of "symbolic capital" was developed by philosophers and social theorists, particularly those interested in power relationships and identity,[2]

---

in his important study (Barclay, *Paul and the Gift*) which I discuss further, below. He explicitly uses the terminology on p. 469 of that work.

2. The language of "symbolic capital" is particularly credited to Pierre Bourdieu,

and has been important in some recent studies of the New Testament. The term labels the kind of reputational stock or social currency—status—that an individual or group might be perceived to have, such that association with this individual or group carries with it some kind of benefit. The language of "honor" (and its opposite, "shame") has sometimes been used as a label for this, particularly by biblical scholars interested in cultural anthropology, but concerns have been raised about the way the term has been used by Western anthropologists, so I simply use here the concept of symbolic capital.[3]

The factors that generate such perceptions of capital will be discussed below, but as a starting point for understanding this concept, we might think of the groups that form within schools, the perceptions attached to them and the inter- and inner-group dynamics that characterize them. There is probably a "cool group." The word "cool," used in this way, may well be a word of a particular era (and I may show my age by using it . . .) but it usefully represents the concept we need to understand. It is not necessarily easy to define precisely, but members of this group are perceived to own it, and thus to possess a certain status within the wider community. Outsiders to the group may, on occasion, be associated with it and derive a certain coolness from that association, often of a more temporary kind. Within the group, there will probably be hierarchies of coolness, often linked to the performance of particular roles or identities, but perhaps also to other factors of status that individual members may enjoy (like beauty or clothing). There will probably be other groups in the school, including a nerdy group, and they may not have much respect for what makes the cool group "cool"; they may have their own hierarchy based on different valued characteristics. The groups may exist with a certain competition. Because they are embedded in a bigger community (the school), the value of association with one group or another might come into play for an individual. It's a standard trope of high school drama: someone from the nerd group becomes useful to someone in the cool group, they like the sudden coolness they obtain

---

who developed it in Bourdieu, *Distinction*. Bourdieu has explored the various kinds of capital and their role in sociology and culture. See, for example, his lectures on the topic, published as Bourdieu, *Forms of Capital*. There is a related concept of "social capital" and the two expressions are sometimes used rather interchangeably, but "symbolic capital" is the more useful and inclusive category for my purposes here.

3. For the background to the category of honor in anthropology, and criticisms of its use, see the accessible study Engelke, *Think Like an Anthropologist*, 94–110. For New Testament scholarship, the most widely influential work is that of Malina, *New Testament World*. The book has been released in multiple updated editions and remains influential on the field. While the book has rightly been subjected to criticism for its handling of honor and shame, it remains an important contribution.

by that association, but their involvement with the nerd group is thereby compromised, creating tensions and estrangements.

One of the reasons I use this particular illustration is that the groups in question are not formally bounded, with technical categories of membership; the factors at work operate also in formalized contexts, but can permeate all kinds of groupings, because they are really social dynamics that often operate at a sub-intentional level. A second reason that I use this illustration is because it highlights that these dynamics are universal, even if they manifest themselves in characteristic ways in particular societies or communities. One of the problems that afflicted some of the early scholarship on honor and shame was that it sometimes represented the dynamics as if they were features of certain *kinds* of society, collectivist ones that were particularly oriented to the identity of the community and membership of it.[4] While distinctions can be made between kinds of societies (with a greater degree of collectivism in some contexts such as my own background in Gaelic-speaking village communities; collectivism is not just an "Eastern"[5] quality), the dynamics of symbolic capital affect all cultures in some way. My discussion of high school groups may have reminded some of the movie *Clueless*; it is worth noting that this movie is actually an updating of Jane Austen's novel, *Emma*. The settings of book and film are geographically and temporally different, as are many of the cultural particulars, but the dynamics are parallel, easily translated across time and place.

This initial illustration of the concept is a useful starting point. It highlights the pervasiveness of the phenomena associated with symbolic capital—they are found in any group, including religious ones—and the fact that the social "stock" is often accrued on the basis of a combination of factors, some intrinsic and some performed. Wealth, strength, beauty and property are all factors, but so is the role that individuals might play. Their identity always involves a blend of natural and *performed* characteristics.

To really get to grips with its implications for Christian identity and leadership, however, we need to think a little about how symbolic capital functions for groups that have more defined boundaries that set them apart from the wider populace. Not everyone in the group will be particularly preoccupied with these boundaries (this will turn out to be important for some of the dynamics I discuss below), but many will. The points of demarcation may or may not include formalized categories of membership but they will

---

4. This tendency is entangled with the complex phenomena labeled by Edward Said as "orientalism," with its underlying tendency to other those outside of the Western cultural elite and present them, in some sense, as more primitive or unenlightened. See Said, *Orientalism*.

5. By this, again, I invoke Said's category of Orientalism.

certainly involve markers or characteristics differentiating those inside from those outside, with these markers being *generally* accepted by the group in question. Now the performative characteristics take on particular importance, as the individual member is expected to enact, embody, or affirm the distinctive qualities or values associated with the group. The person who clearly and competently acts or thinks like a member of the group will be affirmed or highly valued; the person who does not enact this identity with such proficiency, saying or doing things that are not *quite* right, will be less highly valued. Depending on the extent to which they fail to embody the ideal, they may increasingly be treated with suspicion. The group may also see its own status as being threatened by that latter person's behavior. This in turn may be a factor in negative valuation reaching the point where a person is removed and excluded from membership. The status of the insider, meanwhile, is further enhanced not merely by embodying the distinguishing characteristics of the group, but also promoting and defending them. The articulate proponent of the group's values may be celebrated as a champion.

As a brief but important aside, and by way of a disclaimer of sorts, this notion of "boundary maintenance" has been made to do a lot of work in some recent biblical scholarship, particularly around the values of some Jewish groups in Antiquity (primarily, the Pharisees) and the relationship of Jesus and the early church to these. While affirming the concept of boundary maintenance in general, and its relevance to the social dynamics of leadership in Christian groups, I consider many of these approaches to early Judaism to be grossly misrepresentative of the groups in question, often to the point of constituting a rather anti-Semitic discourse. They depict Jesus and Paul as heroic champions of an evangelical resistance to an embodiment of Judaism that has lost its sense of global vocation and of the true purpose of the law. I do not consider this to be a legitimate representation of the groups that comprised Judaism in Antiquity, but I am also deeply concerned that such accounts miss what is really going on in these interactions and thus fail to see that how they may be replicated in the contemporary church (or academy, for that matter).

This anthropological discussion of symbolic capital also highlights two further points. First, the economic quality of the language is not simply metaphorical: this kind of currency has real-world economic significance. We don't necessarily see that because we are familiar with an economic discourse that is based on monetary transaction for currency and goods; we tend to confine the language of "economy" to this. Both historical and contemporary anthropological study, though, has highlighted that services, goods and even names can be exchanged for associative value and that this is an important part of economy more comprehensively understood. The giving of gifts, for example, can be a way of obtaining status through association with the recipient, or of conferring a favor on that person that can be returned at some point in the future. This has been an important theme in some recent New Testament scholarship that has highlighted the mistake of assuming the imagery of salvation as gift in the New Testament *in itself* conveys the idea of something given to those who do not deserve it. Classically, gifts were given to those who might be worthy of them, who might be worth giving a gift to because they can do something splendid in return, or whose honor might be associated with the giver.

John Barclay, who has developed this line of study most extensively in New Testament research, has highlighted that this can cause us to overlook how Paul's emphasis on salvation as gift actually radicalizes the idea of the undeserving recipient; it doesn't presume it.[6] Socially, in Antiquity, one would expect a powerful God to give his gift of salvation to those who are worth that kind of investment, who can reciprocate with outstanding service, and this might begin to lead us to see what is going on with Paul's description of his old self and status in Phil 3. In economies that operate on a largely nonmonetary basis, this kind of gift giving is conspicuously part of day-to-day business. But even in economies that are principally monetary, symbolic capital is significant: rosters of eminent clients or endorsements from celebrated individuals directly benefit the perceived values of companies, and individuals often progress because they are supported emblematically by influential people.

Second, the study of symbolic capital has highlighted that the value associated with the individual or group is precisely what they are considered to be worth and consider themselves to be worth. That is, tacit evaluative decisions become functionally constitutive of a genuine stratification, in which one person is considered more valuable than another. I note this, not to affirm it, but to expose it. We have a commendable discourse today that we are all of equal value and honor, and that everything else is just circumstance, but the study of symbolic capital shows that whatever we might say, people *actually* perceive worth to vary between people according to their symbolic stock. If we are honest with ourselves, we don't often *act* as though people are equal: we treat some as more valuable than others, in ways that can be quite context-specific. Pastorally, this will be crucial to what I will discuss below.

Once we have understood what symbolic capital is, we can begin to think about the factors that contribute to our perceived stock, which really

---

6. For an accessible version of his work, see Barclay, *Paul and the Power*. The author's seminal work on the topic is Barclay, *Paul and the Gift*.

emerges from our involvement with multiple groups in the complex activity of living within society. These factors may vary across cultures and between subgroups, but several things tend to emerge consistently, entwined with the elements discussed above: wealth, beauty, family name, lineage, heritage, perceived intelligence, and the perceived performance of an ideal identity (where the "ideal" conforms to the expectations of the particular grouping).[7] All of these qualities are public, in some sense, though the scope of the public to which we perform might change and the last two elements might be especially specific to the values of particular groups. Crucially, of course, if we are involved with multiple groups at once—and most people will be—these dynamics will be very complicated; sometimes they will create tensions within the individual, but sometimes these can be resolved by the effective compartmentalization of our group involvement.

If we think for a moment about "evangelicalism," we can begin to appreciate how some of these dynamics might operate. The word has been used to label a range of sub-cultures, its application always intended to mark them out from other Christian subcultures. The distinctive features of these subcultures are actually quite varied, even if members of the group believe that all evangelicals will look just like themselves. That the group seeks to define itself in contrast to related groups is important; it is a key element in the cherishing of certain performed identities and identity markers (the "boundary markers" that I discussed above). Doctrine is often considered definitive, though when you look closely it is actually one of the places where there is most variation within evangelicalism and the least distinctiveness from other traditions. In reality, what defines evangelicalism is a kind of accepted identity, a composite of agreed ethical standpoints on specific issues and doctrinal emphases (note: "emphases" rather than "doctrines" as such).[8] Evangelicals expect other evangelicals to look, act, and speak in particular ways. Those who perform this identity well will enjoy high levels of symbolic capital within the group, while those who perform it badly or less consistently will have less. Some may be treated with suspicion: they may not qualify as "real evangelicals" for all that they self-identify as such.

Remember two things. First, "identity" is about *who* we are and *who* we see ourselves as being, whether at a conscious or subconscious level.

---

7. For an accessible but sophisticated consideration of the intersectional elements of identity and evaluation, informed by the context of the Global South but sensitive to the role of the modern West in shaping discourse on identity, see Appiah, *Lies That Bind*.

8. The classic study of evangelicalism as a social phenomenon defined by modern values and dynamics, rather than a distinct doctrinal tradition, is Bebbington, *Evangelicalism*. Bebbington's claims have been both affirmed and challenged. See the collection of essays in Haykin and Stewart, *Emergence of Evangelicalism*.

Performing an identity is always a "who" thing. Second, the phenomena of symbolic capital are manifest in all cultures, even if the prized characteristics are culturally specific. We are all affected by them, even if we would like that not to be the case. And this means that the dynamics outlined in the last paragraph will *naturally and universally* come with a pressure to perform, unless they are identified for what they are and reconstructed. In any context where there is an audience, even an audience of one, we will feel a pressure to perform identity well and may even engage in those performances competitively. We may not do so consciously, but we do it nonetheless; we feel affirmation or anxiety variously according to our perception of our own performance.

So basic is this to our psychology—it lies deeper than we are able to recognize—that it likely also colors how we think about our relationship with God. We may *talk* about salvation in terms of grace, but we naturally *think* and *act* in terms of performed identity and its associated capital. Ironically, an evangelical who prizes the language of grace might judge and be judged according to how they use that language in the performance of a particular identity. In the next section, I will reflect on how Paul presents the gospel precisely as something that exposes this tendency and does so because the perilous instinct to judge according to symbolic capital remains a powerful driver of our identity.

2. READING PAUL'S LANGUAGE OF RIGHTEOUSNESS AS SYMBOLIC CAPITAL

In Phil 3:1–16, in describing how he used to think about himself and God before his encounter with Jesus, Paul uses the language of symbolic capital. The account is often read as contrasting his formerly "legalistic" way of thinking with his new convictions about grace, but this does not really do justice to his language nor to the reason he deploys it as he does. Once we appreciate how the concept of symbolic capital casts light on what Paul is doing here, we can begin to see that what he describes is not someone else's problem, a legalistic account of salvation from which real Christians have been liberated, but is about a universal human instinct that remains a threat to the individual Christian and to the health of their community.

Little of what Paul talks about in relation to his old way of thinking and being is actually about legal obedience. Little, if any, of it can really be categorized as "legalism." He certainly talks about being "as to the law, a Pharisee," and "as to righteousness under the Law, blameless," but before he gets to these he has listed several other things which cannot be credited to his own agency or understood principally in terms of legal obedience: his status as circumcised (something in which he had no agency), his ethnicity, his tribal association. Effectively, when discussing his reasons to feel confident, Paul begins by saying, "I'm from the right race, I come from a good family, with one of the most respected family names." I am the right kind of person. This is the kind of the thing that is associated with symbolic capital and we need to allow it to contextualize the other elements in Paul's account.

The suspicion that the key dynamic in Paul's discussion of "self-righteousness" is one of symbolic capital is reinforced by the language that Paul uses to introduce these elements and then to contrast them with the righteousness of God that he now enjoys by faith. It is easy to pass over the use of the verb "to have" in 3:4.

> I, too, have [*echōn*] confidence in the flesh . . . I [have] more. (Phil 3:4)

Paul effectively says of himself here, I am an "owner" of a body with status. Interestingly, the verb he uses for the subject's impression of confidence is *dokeō*. That verb is here translated as "suppose" but can mean "to seem." It is related to the label of a heresy called Docetism that rejected the goodness of the body and considered Jesus's incarnation to be a mere semblance of flesh; a glamour. At the risk of reading into Paul's words, it may be helpful to see him here as labeling his sense of personal capital precisely as a glamour, as something not real. Glamour, as we know, can be a truly powerful dynamic, but it is built on lies and photoshop.

The language of commodification resurfaces in verse 7:

> Phil. 3:7 Yet whatever gains [*kerdē*] I had, these I have come to regard as loss [*zēmia*] because of Christ. 8 More than that, I regard everything as loss because of the surpassing value [*hyperechon*] of knowing Christ Jesus my Lord. For his sake I have suffered the loss of all things, and I regard them as rubbish, in order that I may gain [*kerdēsō*] Christ.

If we use slightly different words—simply to break our familiarity with a text we may have read often—the economic quality of the language becomes more striking: "whatever capital I had, I now consider to be a deficit because of Christ." As he drives that home, the language he uses continues to be that of ownership; I regard everything as deficit because of the "hyper-having" of the knowledge of Christ Jesus. The word that he uses is a cognate to the one he used earlier of being an owner of confidence, with the well-known prefix "hyper" intensifying it. So, really, Paul is contrasting two kinds of capital: the worse-than-worthless capital he used to consider valuable and the knowledge of Jesus that he now sees to be truly worth something.

The capital language extends further in verse 8: those things he used to think of as valuable capital—the stuff of status—he considers deficit and actually shameful[9] in order that he may "gain Christ." The verb for "gain" here is cognate to the word he used for "gains" at the beginning of verse 7: Paul considered those things "gains" (*kerdē*), *but now he seeks to "gain" (kerdēso)* Christ and be found "in him." This is the language of union of Christ. And here, at this climactic contrast of the two kinds of capital, Paul's language shifts to emphasize the true ownership that is at work: to gain Christ is not to turn him into another commodity, but to be incorporated into him. The language is ironic: Christ is the object that Paul seeks to apprehend, to own, but in that apprehension he discovers that Christ is the owner who has apprehended him. That same inversion occurs in verse 12: "I press on to take hold of that for which Christ Jesus took hold of me."

The contrast in verse 9, then, is between a righteousness that is "mine" or that is "of me" (i.e., one that *inheres* in my person) with one that is "of God, though faith" (one that *inheres* in God's person and is shared with me). So, righteousness (false and real) is represented in capital terms, and the key to obtaining true righteousness is to be laid hold of, to be owned, to be "found in him."

Now, none of this means that a notion of stringent obedience to the law is not part of the picture of "self-inhering righteousness"; it simply means that is embedded within a bigger complex of symbolic capital. Living a "commendable" or "praiseworthy" life is part of this, but that is not necessarily because one thinks that this will contractually oblige God to save us; rather, it is part of a bigger and all-embracing sense of who we are, our sense of personal capital, which is at once embodied before other people and before God. At the risk of belaboring the point, let me note this. One of our problems is that we tend to consider the notions of righteousness and sin in terms of a balance sheet, or a bank balance, but that is to think of a person's capital balance in purely monetary terms; we even talk about our property as things our money is tied up in. When we reduce the notion of "capital" to the bank balance, we then also tend to reduce the credit and deficit to one issue: obedience or keeping the law. But in Paul's time, money was just one strand of the economy and there were other forms of capital: gift exchange,

---

9. The term that is often translated as "rubbish," *skubala*, is used in ancient literature both of garbage in streets and of faeces (the latter usage encountered in technical medical writing, such as the works of Aretaeus and Galen). So, while "rubbish" captures one translational possibility, it may not convey the force of Paul's language about how he now regards what he once considered treasure.

service provision, reputational associations, perceived qualities. Within religious groups, the performance of religious identity was part of that. So, it's not simply that Paul thought he had done enough to be rewarded by God; it is that he thought he was the right kind of person with the right kind of capital and could therefore expect God's favor and the favor of God's people. If that is the real problem, a basically wrong sense of self and significance, then the antidote is not merely to be pointed to someone who does what you can't do—and then to try to do something similar in gratitude—it is to be pointed to the person who is who and what you are not, and to live within his identity.

In fact, Paul's references to the law and Pharisaism may not have the significance that we think even in relation to this notion of self-righteousness. Most scholars of ancient Judaism and of the New Testament think that the Pharisees have been misrepresented as "card-carrying legalists" and that what characterized them was not a belief that meticulous obedience would save, but that obedience should have a *particular* shape, based on *particular* interpretations of Scripture.[10] Or, to put this differently, what characterized them was a *particular* way of thinking about how God's word should be read, interpreted and applied. So, when Paul says, "as to the Law, a Pharisee," his words are not primarily intended to say that he kept the law really well, but that he kept the law in a very particular way (which is why he still adds another clause to say that he was blameless under the law). For a certain subgroup within Judaism, his performance of this specific identity would have secured him further capital.

As an aside, distinctive identities such as those of the Pharisees can become more important in cultures where a spectrum of religious embodiments exist and where some might want these to be differentiated. The Pharisees were a movement characterized by particular views on how the Bible should be read, and there is no question that adherence to their values would result in members being *visibly* different from gentiles, at a time when many were considered to be assimilating to Greek or Roman cultural practices. Contextually, this is not dissimilar to the present time, when there is a spectrum of Christian identities embodied within a complex society with diverse values; the ease with which some of these can seemingly be distinguished from the identities around them can be attractive for those nervous about matters of identity. I use the word "seemingly" here, because the reality is that some of these apparent distinctives may actually embody the underlying values of the surrounding society, just in ways that are cleanly labeled as "Christian" or "evangelical."

10. See the recent collection of essays in Sievers and Levine, *Pharisees*.

Once we recognize all of this, we can begin to see that the problem, for Paul, does not lie in the beliefs of Pharisaism, but in the presumptive evaluation of his status as a Pharisee, linked to his performance of Pharisaic identity. This is actually quite similar to the performance of evangelical identity (which is, likewise, not necessarily a bad thing in itself) and the status that we might consider it to earn for us with others who share in that identity. And this takes us to the nub of the issue: the problem is precisely our tendency to put stock on the performance of that identity as a means to capital, rather than recognizing the characteristics of that identity to be derivative or contingent manifestations of the presence of Christ.

To be sure, this whole discussion is occasioned by the need to challenge a group advocating a particular kind of law adherence within the church, the "mutilators of the flesh" that Paul describes in 3:1–2, who are generally understood to be advocating the circumcision of gentile believers. But when read in relation to what follows, we can see that the problem with this group is not their confusion over the place of the law, but their confusion over how identity and performative markers function within this. The unfortunate irony is that many evangelicals will condemn this group's advocacy of circumcision as a "works righteousness" and "legalism," while themselves fixating with the performative markers of the true evangelical.

In the preface to *Living in Union with Christ*, I wrote the following as a kind of confession that maps Paul's language onto this:

> I was idolatrous in the worst of ways because I thought I was being faithful—in between my moments of undeniable sin. I was an evangelical of evangelicals, of the tribe of Knox; as to zeal, a defender of all evangelical truth claims and attender of all services; as to doctrine, faultless (in my own mind, at least). Yet over time, I have come to see that the most basic problem I had was the way that I thought about my self: I had not really come to terms with the implications of the gospel for who I identified myself to be, although this was a big part of my Reformed theological heritage. This affected all of my piety, all of my relationships, and all of my service.[11]

3. SYMBOLIC CAPITAL AND LEADERSHIP

The quotation with which I ended the last section is a useful transition to thinking more specifically about how the issue of symbolic capital might

---

11. Macaskill, *Living in Union*, x.

bear particularly on the dynamics of evangelical leadership. Once I have outlined these, I will close the essay by returning to Philippians and considering some of the practices Paul advocates that deflate our actually hollow stores of capital and reorient us towards the righteousness of God in Christ.

Philippians seems to be written to a church struggling with internal divisions and politicking. Some of these are connected to explicit identity markers and the performance of a particular boundary maintaining identity (see, particularly, his comments on the circumcision group in 3:1–2, discussed earlier), but others seem more about the dynamics of personal capital and the factions that form around it. Paul's plea to Euodia and Syntyche to be of "the same mind" in the Lord (4:2) focuses a concern that has run through the letter, that competitive thinking should be abandoned, driven as it typically is by some kind of self-interest. In particular, there are a number of interesting connections with Phil 2, and its famous description of Christ's self-giving servanthood. These suggest that there is a close integration of the two chapters, which are central to the work as a whole.

In particular, Paul seems concerned with how we think: notice how often the language of mind and of thinking or cognition occurs. He calls his readers to participate in the mind of Christ (2:5) and to be of the same, singular mind (2:2); the form of words is very similar to what he addresses to Euodia and Syntyche. This is a summons to set aside competition in their thinking, in alignment with Christ's own attitude. It is interesting that his example is presented using the imagery of capital disbursement. The key verb used in Phil 2:7, in relation to Christ's taking the form[12] of a servant, is *kenoō*, which has an essential association with the act of making something empty; it is used, for example, of emptying a storeroom or a chest.[13] It is sometimes translated as "made himself nothing" (as in NIV) but can also be rendered as "emptied himself" (NRSV). The full significance of the imagery requires to be considered within the broader contours of the epistle, but it is interesting to note that at its core is a verb that contrasts with that of the one seeking to acquire or to hoard their capital. Christ does not consider his equality with God something to be stored, but something to be disbursed.

Paul, then, considers the gospel of this Christ to hold to account the natural, "fleshly" instinct to accrue symbolic capital for self. The centrality

---

12. The use of "form" (*morphē*) and the paralleled occurrence of "likeness" (*homoiōma*) probably itself reflects issues of symbolic capital: Christ takes on the appearance, the visible symbolic characteristics, of one who is devoid of symbolic capital.

13. This is the typical usage in Classical Greek writing, as described in the major lexicons. In the Greek translation of the Bible, it occurs in Jer 14:2 and 15:9, associated with the ruin of Judah and the emptying of Jerusalem by the Babylonian conquest.

of this theme to the letter suggests that he sees it as one of the principal factors in disunity and perhaps abuse.

How, then, might this bear on the dynamics of leadership, whether formal or informal? Most obviously, the status of leadership itself can constitute an attractive kind of symbolic capital. It is attractive not because it brings us money, but because it brings us importance, and because that sense of importance is "self"-affirming. Some people may be especially vulnerable to this allure, and any nervousness or insecurity about identity will obviously contribute to this. There may be particular risks for young people, but the issues are hardly confined to the young.

In principle, the common recasting of leadership as a role of service, informed by Phil 2:5–11, should function as a kind of antidote to this. But it is important to recognize the ease with which the idea of "servant-leadership" can become just rhetoric or linguistic posturing, where leaders claim to be servants but act like dukes. I suspect that a tendency to represent the narrative of atonement in Phil 2:5–11 as a heroic act, rather than as a manifestation of true self-abasement and abandonment of capital, enables this.

It is important to note, too, that leadership (and its associated capital) might be formal, associated with a title, but it extends beyond that to the perception that a particular individual is, in some sense or another, a leader among their peers. This may be a matter of being considered a particularly insightful or instructive voice in a Bible study, for example, something that can often be linked to the confidence and effectiveness with which we communicate our interpretations.

If leadership is associated with symbolic capital, then it also becomes shaped by the need to perform the identity that will enhance that capital, which will often be about the performance of the distinctive values of a group, including its boundary-marking values. For groups explicitly defined by their commitment to the authority of Scripture, there is a particular risk associated with the role of the interpreter or teacher: perceived expertise in Scripture, or excellence in its interpretation and application, can be a basis for capital. Scripture can then be handled as if it were a commodity, rather than a speaking agent. I have written elsewhere about this danger, which is often linked to a distorted identification of Scripture and how it functions (particularly linked to the image of the manual or handbook), which reinforces the dynamics of status associated with the scriptural expert.[14]

More subtly, the pressure to perform and embody the identity of the group, particularly in relation to its boundaries, mean that this "expertise" in

---

14. Macaskill, *New Testament and Intellectual Humility*, especially chap. 8, "Intellectual Humility and the Reading of Scripture."

Scripture is subjected to a set of prior expectations. What marks one group off from another may be a particular interpretation of Scripture or how its teaching is to be applied in the contemporary world; the retaining and enhancing of capital within that group requires the expert teacher to reinforce that interpretation and not jeopardize it. When interacting with those outside the group in the presence of an audience that includes group members, the expert might feel a pressure to play to their own galleries (perhaps without even recognizing this). Rather than engaging in genuinely open discussion about what Scripture might say, the interpreter will subscribe to and defend the group's reading; this may well be a good reading, but it may also be vulnerable to criticism, and the point is that the tacit pressure to sustain the group's values (and thus maintain one's capital) makes such criticism something that is *personally* threatening. The interpreter needs to defend, and be *seen* to defend, the reading accepted by the group, if their identity is to be maintained and not jeopardized.

This obviously creates a barrier to meaningful exchange across group boundaries, which is often shaped less by a redemptive or constructive instinct to truly communicate and more by a desire to build in-group capital. But it can also contribute to some dangerously manipulative in-group dynamics. Leaders can feel threatened by those in the group who may question the standard interpretation that supports their capital and can feel the need to shut down any dialogue on the matter. Importantly, the dynamic of this might include some strategy to limit the capital that is associated with those who take a contrary view, marginalizing them in some way or another; they may not be excluded from the group, but their own status might be called into question. This has been a strikingly recurrent feature of the various testimonies that have come from churches and ministries that have come to be seen as toxic.

This problem is also entangled with a use of Scripture itself as capital; that is, the invoked authority of Scripture can be used as a means to purchase power over competitors within the group. The one who claims their position as "biblical" (a word that only really started to be used extensively in the last decade of the nineteenth century and became visibly more popular from 1980 on),[15] appropriates a powerful currency to assert themselves over others, to the point of excluding their opponents. The problem, of course, is that often what is labeled as "biblical" is either a particular creative synthesis of elements lifted from Scripture, or a decontextualized reading of one or

---

15. The statistics can be loosely traced through online tools that analyze digitized resources (which now include most older publication), such as Google Books. https://books.google.com/ngrams/graph?year_start=1800&year_end=2019&corpus=26&smoothing=7&case_insensitive=on&content=biblical.

several verses. The word "biblical" can often be deployed to bypass the more serious work of regulated scriptural interpretation and theological or ethical discourse. This is widely recognized. My concern here is to note how this problem can be enmeshed with the dynamics of symbolic capital, at once enabling these and compromised by them.

Equivalent points could be made about the usage of other adjectives, some of which have only recently come to be used in this way, that are intended to indicate an essential difference (and a correlated boundary) between one group and another. The adjectival use of words like "gospel" exemplifies this and, along with words like "sound," can serve to mark the perception of graded subgroups, even within a bigger identity-group like evangelicalism. Once we recognize the extent to which these are phenomena of identity, linked to the dynamics of symbolic capital (and with a certain nervousness about both), we can begin to appreciate how it might compromise a genuine concern to ask what the Scriptures might say on this matter or that, particularly if the results of such an inquiry are not reducible to a straightforward position.

Of course, while single issues may dominate the identity of a specific group at a specific time (the debates in some quarters about the role of women in ministry is an example of this), identity is a complex thing and the dynamics just outlined will usually involve the combination of multiple values and characteristics at once. Those whose embodied complex of views and activities (which may also be linked to their personality) reinforce the identity of the group will be celebrated and those who threaten it will be marginalized, if not thoroughly excluded. For those not yet in leadership, the pursuit of that particular capital can involve learning to perform this particular identity, a pressure that may operate at a sub-conscious level.

It is also, of course, vital to note that the pursuit of capital often has a competitive quality, because stocks are measured relative to each other. While this can manifest itself in the process of attaining symbolic capital, as one's reputation grows, it can also manifest itself in the conflict between figures who have acquired significant capital already. In Philippians, the tensions between Euodia and Syntyche may well reflect this kind of division; the divisions between factions apparent in 1 Cor 1–4 seem also to reflect such a dynamic.

As with Paul's background in the Pharisee movement, many of the key issues may involve genuine convictions around matters of scriptural interpretation, and the positions adopted may be good ones. It is crucial to recognize, though, that it is possible to hold the right view in the wrong way. To put this differently: it is possible to advocate a virtue viciously. Once the matter is driven, without our necessarily recognizing it, by the need to maintain capital within the group, even the most laudable of moral positions becomes a matter of loss with God.

CONCLUDING COMMENTS: LEADERSHIP AND THE ECONOMY OF THE GIFT

Much more could be said on Paul's strategies for challenging the dynamics of symbolic capital in the Epistle to the Philippians. It is notable, for example, that once the problem is exposed for what it is, a space opens for a more constructive approach to personal reputation. Paul presents himself as a model, worthy of imitation by his readers, even as he participates in the self-giving of Christ (3:17). This is an important topic, worthy of discussion in itself, but it is enough here to recognize that this kind of self-presentation is legitimated precisely by its reorientation of the concept of personal capital towards Christ. In fact, such a claim to be worthy of imitation would be difficult for most evangelical leaders because it does not conform to the similitude of humility, the façade of self-deprecation they are expected to perform by which capital is maintained.

It is also notable, I think, that Paul presents thanksgiving and joy as key practices for the follower of Christ, by which anxiety is addressed. To give thanks is to acknowledge a gift, to acknowledge that the economy of God is precisely one of gift—of undeserved gift, moreover—and not one of personal capital. The anxiety involved in the pursuit of symbolic capital, meanwhile, can be challenged by the intentional practice of thanksgiving, by which we acknowledge that our place in God's economy is not accomplished or acquired, but is received.

These points are important and deserve further reflection. The core point on which they rest, however, is the substance of what I have considered here. Paul's gospel is not presented narrowly as a matter of deliverance from deserved punishment, but as liberation from an entire "economy," one in which we are enslaved by the dynamics of symbolic capital and its acquisition. Our enslavement is a complex participation, constituted differently by having and not-having such capital, but the way out is to embrace a different kind of economy, one of gift, in which the stores of all our capital, with each other and with God, lie in the one to whom we are united, in whose identity we participate. The devastating point is this: if we reduce the gospel to deliverance from punishment, and lose sight of its economic implications, then we can continue to operate our churches as capital economies, with leaders unwittingly vicious in their pursuit of social stock. They can see themselves as shepherds, tending their flocks, when in truth they are wolves, greedy to consume. This may sound overly dramatic, until we read the testimonies of those who have escaped cultures of abuse, perpetrated and perpetuated by church leaders. The word "culture" there is an important one: cultures and economies are intertwined and an unreconstructed ecclesial economy of symbolic capital will always generate a culture that is abusive.

BIBLIOGRAPHY

Appiah, Anthony. *The Lies That Bind: Rethinking Identity, Creed, Country, Color, Class, Culture*. Liveright paperback edition. New York: Liveright, 2019.
Barclay, John M. G. *Paul and the Gift*. Grand Rapids, MI: Eerdmans, 2015.
———. *Paul and the Power of Grace*. Grand Rapids, MI: Eerdmans, 2020.
Bebbington, David. *Evangelicalism in Modern Britain: A History from the 1730s to the 1980s*. London: Routledge, 1988.
Bourdieu, Pierre. *Distinction: A Social Critique of the Judgement of Taste*. Translated by R. Nice. London: Routledge, 2010.
———. *Forms of Capital: General Sociology*. Vol. 3, *Lectures at the Collège De France 1983–84*. Translated by Peter Collier. London: Wiley, 2021.
Engelke, Matthew. *Think Like an Anthropologist*. London: Pelican, 2017.
Haykin, Michael A. J., and Kenneth J. Stewart, eds. *The Emergence of Evangelicalism: Exploring Historical Continuities*. Downers Grove, IL: InterVarsity, 2008.
Macaskill, Grant. *Living in Union with Christ: Paul's Gospel and Christian Moral Identity*. Grand Rapids, MI: Baker Academic, 2019.
———. *The New Testament and Intellectual Humility*. Oxford: Oxford University Press, 2018.
Malina, Bruce J. *The New Testament World: Insights from Cultural Anthropology*. Louisville, KY: John Knox, 1981.
Said, Edward W. *Orientalism*. 1st ed. New York: Pantheon, 1978.
Sievers, Joseph, and Amy-Jill Levine. *The Pharisees*. Grand Rapids, MI: Eerdmans, 2021.

7

Use, Not Abuse
An Augustinian Approach to Loving People

Graham Shearer

WE LIVE IN TIMES in which we have become acutely aware of the dynamics of power: its patterns, problems, uses and abuse.[1] We recognize that power is not merely inherent in those who occupy great offices of state or who possess the means of physical coercion, but can take many forms, including what Michel Foucault calls "pastoral power."[2] Those who serve people's spiritual needs, therefore, necessarily have significant power and influence in their lives, whether this is admitted or welcomed or otherwise. We are sensitive, therefore, to what pastors teach about how people should be treated. How then, would we react if a pastor published a book that raised the question "whether humans ought to enjoy one another or use one another" and then answered that Christians *should*, in fact, use people. Yet such is the argument of Augustine of Hippo (AD 354–430) in his work *On Christian Teaching*. To those familiar with Kant's dictum that "So act that you treat humanity . . . always . . . as an end, never merely as a means"[3] Augustine's words seem grotesque.

---

1. This is an expanded version of an essay originally published by Ad Fontes, the journal of The Davenant Institute. I'm grateful for their permission to include it here.
2. See Foucault, "Subject and Power," 777–95.
3. Kant, *Metaphysics of Morals*, 429, italics omitted.

Isn't using people the very definition of abuse of power? Have we found in Augustine the root of so much of the pastoral abuse we now see? How can Augustine urge us, urge pastors, to use people rather than enjoy them?

I'd like to explore Augustine's argument and suggest that, far from being a license or a vehicle for abuse, it is actually an effective prophylactic for the kinds of pastoral abuse and mistreatment that presently occupy our podcasts and social media feeds.

THINGS AND SIGNS

Augustine is writing to teach teachers and he begins by making a famous distinction between signs and things. Signs are things but not every thing is a sign, for the nature of a sign is to point beyond itself to something else. Likewise, Augustine says, "some things are to be enjoyed, some which are to be used, and some whose function is both to enjoy and use."[4] Augustine explains the distinction: "To enjoy something is to hold fast to it in love for its own sake. To use something is to apply whatever it may be to the purpose of obtaining what you love."[5]

The distinctions between sign and thing and use and enjoyment are in parallel. It is the things which are to be enjoyed, those loved for their own sake, that signs signify and other things are used to get to. Augustine uses the metaphor of a journey. Imagine travelers going to their homeland, he says, who are so taken up with the journey that they never arrive at the destination where they can truly be happy. This is the danger for those who enjoy what is meant to be used.

USING PEOPLE, ENJOYING GOD

What, then, are the things to be enjoyed? Augustine has a clear answer: "The things which are to be enjoyed, then, are the Father and the Son and the Holy Spirit, and the Trinity that consists of them, which is a kind of single, supreme thing, shared by all who enjoy it."[6] It is only the Triune God, who is unchangeable wisdom and truth and goodness, who is ultimately to be enjoyed. Everything else points to the supreme goodness of the Trinity and merely reflects it. Augustine then goes on to summarize how the Triune God has enabled those who are broken and wounded by the love of lesser

---

4. Augustine of Hippo, *Doctr. chr.* 1.3.3 (p. 9).
5. Augustine of Hippo, *Doctr. chr.* 1.4.4 (p. 9).
6. Augustine of Hippo, *Doctr. chr.* 1.5.5 (p. 10).

things, created things, to be healed and restored and returned to that happy homeland: enjoyment of the Trinity.

This, then, is the backdrop for Augustine's question which is best read in the context of the whole paragraph:

> Among all these things, then, it is only the eternal and unchangeable things which I mentioned that are to be enjoyed; other things are to be used, so that we may attain the full enjoyment of those things.... It is therefore an important question, whether humans ought to enjoy one another or to use one another or both. We have been commanded to love one another but the question is whether one person should be loved by another on his own account or for some other reason. If it is on his own account, we enjoy him; if for some other reason, we use him. In my opinion, he should be loved for another reason. For if something is to be loved on its own account, it is made to constitute a happy life, even if it is not as yet the reality but the hope of it which consoles us at this time. But "cursed is he who puts his hope in man" [Jer. 17:5].[7]

Augustine's logic is that if we love another person for their own sake, if they become our journey's terminus, as it were, then we have made that person "constitute a happy life." That person bears the weight of all our hopes and expectations of our soul's happiness.

Laid out like this, we can see why Augustine insists that people should not be loved for their own sake, as an end in themselves. For, since human beings, though bearing the divine image, are finite, and now flawed, they are not a safe object of our strongest desires. Within the created order, human desire is like a howitzer in a bowling alley: an instrument of immense power in want of an appropriate target. No matter how precisely aimed, infinite human desire unleashed on a finite human object will only lead to disaster for both the lover and the loved.

Augustine provides an example of this in his autobiographical *Confessions*. In Book 4, Augustine records his limitless grief at the death of a friend. Grief made him, he tells us, "become to myself a place of unhappiness in which I could not bear to be; but I could not escape from myself."[8] Reflecting on his desolation, Augustine tells us that "the reason why that grief had penetrated me so easily and deeply was that I had poured out my soul on to the sand by loving a person sure to die as if he would never die."[9]

---

7. Augustine of Hippo, *Doctr. chr.* 1.22,21 (pp. 16–17).
8. Augustine of Hippo, *Conf.* 4.7 (p. 60).
9. Augustine of Hippo, *Conf.* 4.8 (p. 60).

Augustine is not, of course, condemning grief at the death of a friend, we will return to this point later, yet he diagnoses in the catastrophic nature of *his* grief a sign that he had loved his friend as if he were infinite.

Of course, it is not just in death that people reveal their finitude. No amount of human attention, care, or praise is sufficient to sustain another human soul. And none of us gives to others all the care or attention we are capable of, given our sinful and broken condition. What Augustine says of finite creatures in general is no less true of human beings: "something temporal is loved more before it is possessed, but will lose its appeal when attained, for it does not satisfy the soul." It may not emerge as grief but in some other form: loveless withdrawal, overbearing anger, smothering control, or the inability to believe that the object of our love has ever done anything wrong. All these and more can be a sign that we have begun to make someone an end in themselves.

Faced with the discrepancy between our need and what is supplied by the finite object of our desire, we have two options. Denial, where we seek to convince ourselves and others that the object of our love *really* does meet our need; numbing ourselves to the pain of the shortfall so like the leper we can leave our hand in the fire. Or, we blame the one on whom we have leaned for not being able to bear our weight and direct upon them all our bitterness for the hunger of our soul. In neither case do we actually love the other person as they really are. Either we idealize them, ceasing to perceive them as finite beings, or we demonize them, blinded to their created goodness.

LOVING FOR GOD'S SAKE

Augustine, then, proposes an alternative. Having explained that we should not love even ourselves on our own account, he writes: "So if you ought to love yourself not on your own account but on account of the one who is the most proper object of your love, another person should not be angry if you love him too on account of God."[10] We are to love others, not for each other's sake, but so that we might reach our "permanent goal," the "supreme reward" of knowing God. This is what it means when Augustine says we are to "use" people. He does not mean people are to be regarded as tools to be picked up and discarded according to our wishes. He is not contrasting "use" with "love" as if we can only do one but not the other. Rather, Augustine is seeking to show *how* we are to love people. Whether we love our neighbor "on his own account," that is as the final object of all our desire or

---

10. Augustine of Hippo, *Doctr. chr.* 1.22.21 (p. 17).

whether we love him "on God's account," as a precious traveling companion who helps us on the journey to our eternal home him with.[11]

A moment's reflection discloses how liberating this is. Seeking enjoyment in the Triune God, I am freed no longer to require from others that their goodness, their care, their compassion should somehow quench the thirst of my inner being. I am released simply to appreciate the way they reflect in some finite way the unquenchable goodness of the infinite God. If I appreciate your sense of humor or kindness, I do not have to be crushed if I find in you an occasional irritability because what I enjoyed in you has led me not to you, but your source: the Triune creator. Each peal of laughter, each word of kindness or spark of insight I find in another person is a reminder to me of my destination, my true place of rest, the unchanging, infinite goodness of the Triune God. Reflecting on Jesus' command to love God with heart, soul, and mind, Augustine writes,

> any object worthy of love that enters the mind should be swept towards the same destination as that to which the whole flood of our love is directed. So a person who loves his neighbor properly should, in concert with him, aim to love God with all his heart, all his soul, and all his mind. In this way, loving him as he would himself, he relates his love of himself and his neighbor entirely to the love of God, which allows not the slightest trickle to flow away from it and thereby diminish it.[12]

It is only by loving our neighbor, friends, spouses, and children for the sake of another, God himself, that we can love them truly and fully. Loving our neighbor in God risks no disappointment, no bitter taste of disillusionment for,

> When you enjoy a human being in God, you are enjoying God rather than that human being. For you enjoy the one by whom

---

11. In an influential article, Oliver O'Donovan argues that Augustine's use of the term "use" was "quite simply a mistake, with which Augustine cannot live." Certainly it is a provocative use of vocabulary and seems to cut against the grain of Augustine's strong emphasis on neighbor love in the rest of his writing. However, Sarah Stewart-Kroeker has argued in a recent article that O'Donovan's argument is mistaken, that "use" and "enjoyment" are not synonymous with "means" and "end" and that Augustine's terminology allows for others to be both "used" and "enjoyed" when the terms are understood correctly. Readers who wish to pursue the question further are directed to her article. See O'Donovan, "'Usus' and 'Fruitio'"; Stewart-Kroeker, "Resisting Idolatry and Instrumentalisation."

12. Augustine of Hippo, *Doctr. chr.* 1.22.21 (p. 17).

you are made happy, and you will one day rejoice that you have attained the one in whom you now set your hope of attaining him.[13]

Everything good in our neighbor sweeps us towards the source of all goodness: the unchanging goodness of God. Everything flawed and finite in them provokes compassion, just as our sin provoked compassion in God.

Of course, loving God, and others, in this way, is not instinctive, indeed it is counterintuitive. This, according to Augustine, is not because love for God is unnatural to man nor that God is somehow inadequate as an object of our love. Rather it is that in our fallen condition, the gaze of our hearts naturally tilts downwards towards created and material things, like a mirror too heavy for its stand. To lift ourselves up, away from, or perhaps better beyond, created things now requires a spiritual discipline that is foreign to most of us. Trying to lead his congregation towards perceiving God as the fitting object of their desire, as he preaches on Ps 27:4, Augustine says,

> Let your heart stretch beyond all familiar things, let its gaze go beyond all the things you are accustomed to think about which are derived from the flesh, all the thoughts drawn out from the fleshly senses and any kind of fantasies. Drive the whole lot out of your mind; whatever presents itself to your thoughts, turn it down. Recognize the weakness of your heart, and whatever occurs to you, say of it, "That is not the real thing, for if it had been, I could not even have imagined it." In this way you will be desiring something good.[14]

Augustine first insists that his hearers prescind any creaturely finitude in their conception of this "something good," a task that necessarily requires them to go beyond the limits of their imagination. What, though, is left once the resources of the human mind are exhausted? Augustine continues,

> What sort of good? The Good of all good, from which all good derives, the Good to which nothing can be added to explain what goodness is. For a person is described as good, and a field as good, and a house as good, and an animal as good, and a tree as good, and a body as good, and a soul as good; and every time you said "good," you added something. But there is a simple good, sheer Goodness-Itself, in virtue of which all things are good, the Good itself from which good things derive their goodness. This is the delight of the Lord, this is what we shall contemplate.[15]

---

13. Augustine of Hippo, *Doctr. chr.* 1.33.37 (p. 25).
14. Augustine of Hippo, *Exp. Ps.* 279.
15. Augustine of Hippo, *Exp. Ps.* 279.

Augustine is seeking to communicate what infinite, perfect goodness must be. He points out that nothing called "good" in creation has goodness added to it. There are good animals but not all animals are good—to be animal and to be good are different, separable, things. But Augustine says, this is not the only way to be good. Another way to be good is to be goodness itself, to be the good from which all other goodness derives. God is that goodness, "sheer Goodness-Itself," goodness that is pure, infinite, and unadulterated and, by necessity therefore, contains every shade and aspect of created goodness. Having drawn this contrast between created and uncreated, finite and infinite goodness, Augustine asks his congregations to compare the two and ask themselves which is likely to produce greater joy.

> Now, brothers and sisters, if the things which are called good delight us, if we are delighted with things not intrinsically good (for no changeable things are intrinsically good), what will the contemplation of the unchangeable good be like, the good which is eternal and abides the same for ever? Indeed, those things which are called good would in no way delight us unless they were good, and they could not possibly be good unless they derived from him who is intrinsically good.[16]

Uncreated goodness, as the source of all created goodness, must be infinitely superior to all others. If created goodness, whether in a person or a place or an artefact, can command our love, how much more must the infinitely full expanse of divine goodness? As I say, this way of thinking is not instinctive to us, and it is a path that has become overgrown with the thickets and brambles of post-Kantian philosophy and Western material prosperity. Nevertheless, it remains the only path that allows the human heart to avoid the pitfalls of perceiving people as tools or threats, to either deifying or demonizing them.

SOME OBJECTIONS

At this stage, we might have two objections. First, isn't this just "don't make an idol out of people," the kind of advice that you can find in countless evangelical publications about relationships? Of course, that is at the heart of what Augustine is saying. But where his analysis goes further is identifying *how* we can make someone an idol: by failing to continue traveling, by failing to make the last connection of relating our love for them to their creator and instead stopping, as if their finite goodness could be an adequate object

---

16. Augustine of Hippo, *Exp. Ps.* 279–80.

for our infinite desire. As Rowan Williams puts it, Augustine is warning "against an attitude towards any finite person or object that terminates their meaning in their capacity to satisfy my desire, that treats them as the end of desire, conceiving my meaning in terms of them and theirs in terms of me."[17] Without this element, the injunction not to make people an idol can appear to make our love for people and our love for God a zero-sum game, that we can only ensure that we love God by *not* loving people. But Augustine's analysis uproots that error. The problem with our love for people is *not* that it is excessive but that it ceases too soon, instead of rolling on and through towards its eternal source and satisfaction.

This helps answer the other potential objection we might have: doesn't Augustine sound like a cold fish? Doesn't this talk of "using" people, no matter how qualified, make Augustine sound like one of those people that inspired Douglas Coupland to write, "Looking a convert in the eyes was like trying to make eye contact with a horse. They'd be alive and breathing, but they wouldn't be a hundred percent there anymore. They'd left the day-to-day world and joined the realm of eternal time."[18] Do Augustine's reflections on his grief over his friend's death suggest he is guilty of this? That, I think, is to misread him. For Augustine writes,

> Yet the idea of enjoying someone or something is very close to that of using someone or something together with love. For when the object of love is present, it inevitably brings with it pleasure as well.[19]

"Using" people in this Augustinian sense does not preclude deriving pleasure from them, appreciating them, and therefore, feeling loss and sadness if we are parted from them. Friendship was a central theme of Augustine's life, so much so that he could write, "what consolation have we in this human society . . . except the unfeigned faith and mutual affections of genuine, loyal friends?"[20] In the same passage Augustine speaks of the "burning sorrow that ravages our hearts" when we hear of misfortune befalling our loved ones. No, Augustine's approach is not one of cold indifference, he does not rebuke us for the joy, the elation, the sadness and sorrow that human society involves; rather he urges us to let our love for our neighbor ascend to its highest intensity, and therefore abound to its highest object: the Triune God who is love itself.

17. Williams, "Language," 140.
18. Coupland, *Hey Nostradamus! A Novel*, 27.
19. Augustine of Hippo, *Doctr. chr.* 1.33.37 (pp. 25–26).
20. Augustine of Hippo, *Civ.* 19.8 (p. 862).

Only by placing ourselves and our neighbor in this frame can we truly love them, for only in this frame do we see ourselves and them as we truly are. We no longer require another human, finite as they are, to satisfy the limitless longings that swell like the sea beneath our conscious thought. Nor need we set ourselves the task of meeting their infinite needs with our finite capacities. Instead, we are able to be to them what we really are, a finite, fallen echo of that infinite triune goodness that dwells in eternity, a mere snatch of melody of a heavenly symphony. Likewise, they can be to us what they truly are, a finite gift from an infinite giver, a sign of something beyond themselves, whose every facet, like a diamond, speaks of the love, kindness, and generosity of the one who gives them to us.

USE, LOVE, AND ABUSE

It should now be clear how what Augustine is saying is the very opposite of the kind of "bodies piling up behind the bus" pastoral approach of some church leaders. If we are to use people it is as signposts to the infinite, unconditioned goodness of the Triune God. Using people to get something *more* limited than a human being, such as power, popularity, money, or success, would strike Augustine as utterly perverse, traveling in the wrong direction, like someone booking a hotel in order to visit a bus stop. Relative to the rest of creation, Kant's dictum is right—no created object is worthy to be an end for which other people are the means. Only the uncreated Triune God, Father, Son, and Spirit, can qualify as an end for which human beings can serve as means. Everything else is decaying and failing—things that lose their appeal when attained. The paradox is that only when people are used in the right way, used to obtain and enjoy that triune goodness, are people loved as they really are: created echoes of that goodness uniquely made in the image of God.

Therefore, when we see pastoral abuse, we see guides who do not know the destination; pastors who do not know the eternal joy that is in the Triune God, the only thing that is "loved more passionately when obtained than when desired." No amount of money or success, power or praise, can ever be the final source of enjoyment for the soul "whose true and certain abode is eternity."[21] And so, those pastors who use people to get to them are traveling in the opposite direction to the one Augustine recommends. The bright lights on the horizon they point to are not the fires of home but merely the signaling on the railway line: useful for the journey, deadly as a destination.

21. Augustine of Hippo, *Doctr. chr.* 1.38.42 (p. 28).

Instead, Augustine would have us use each other to move towards the infinite love, goodness and glory of the Father, Son, and Spirit and enjoy all things in him. When we realize that is our true destination, then we can truly begin to use our power, pastoral, or otherwise, and everything else we possess, in a way shaped by that divine love, "which allows not the slightest trickle to flow away from it and thereby diminish it."[22]

BIBLIOGRAPHY

Augustine of Hippo. *The City of God*. Translated by Henry Bettenson. London: Penguin, 2003.

———. *Confessions*. Translated by Henry Chadwick. Oxford: Oxford University Press, 1998.

———. *Expositions of the Psalms*. Edited by John E. Rotelle. Translated by Maria Boulding. Hyde Park, NY: New City, 2000.

———. *On Christian Teaching*. Translated by R. P. H. Green. Oxford: Oxford University Press, 2008.

Coupland, Douglas. *Hey Nostradamus!: A Novel*. New York: Bloomsbury, 2010.

Foucault, Michel. "The Subject and Power." *Critical Inquiry* 8 (1982) 777–95.

Kant, Immanuel. *Groundwork of the Metaphysics of Morals*. Edited by Jens Timmerman. Translated by Mary J. Gregor. Cambridge: Cambridge University Press, 2014.

O'Donovan, Oliver. "'Usus' and 'Fruitio' in Augustine, 'de Doctrina Christiana I'." *The Journal of Theological Studies* 33 (1982) 361–97.

Stewart-Kroeker, Sarah. "Resisting Idolatry and Instrumentalisation in Loving the Neighbour: The Significance of the Pilgrimage Motif for Augustine's Usus–Fruitio Distinction." *Studies in Christian Ethics* 27 (2014) 202–21.

Williams, Rowan. "Language, Reality and Desire in Augustine's 'de Doctrina'." *Literature and Theology* 3 (1989) 138–50.

---

22. Augustine of Hippo, *Doctr. chr.* 1.22.21 (p. 17).

PART 2

Practical and Pastoral Reflections

AN INTERLUDE

How did we come to define "success" as the avoidance of the very conditions Jesus associates with happiness and flourishing in the Beatitudes? What if we end up with the "anti-Beatitudes"?

Miserable are:

- Those who are full of themselves, because they're disqualified from the kingdom of heaven
- Those who are complacent and at ease with things as they are, because they forfeit true comfort
- Those who are self-assertive, self-confident, and demand and get their rights, because that's all they'll get and they'll lose everything that really matters
- Those who are content with conforming to behavioral standards that confer social status, because they will be empty inside
- Those who demand justice of others and are highly critical of them, because they will find that others treat them the same way
- Those whose hearts are full of selfish and self-centered desires for pleasure and gain, because the true God is ever hidden from them
- Those who create division and dissension and are proud of their tribal belonging, because there is no place for them in the kingdom of heaven
- Those who are celebrated, praised and famous, because that's all they'll get . . .

(Mark Stirling: from a meditation on the Greek text of Matt 5:2–12)

One thing is clear to me: the temptation of power is greatest when intimacy is a threat. Much Christian leadership is exercised by people who do not know how to develop healthy, intimate relationships and have opted for power and control instead. Many Christian empire-builders have been people unable to give and receive love.

Henri Nouwen, *In the Name of Jesus*.

8

When a Church Becomes a Cult
Twenty-Five Years On

Steve Wookey

AROUND TWENTY-FIVE YEARS AGO I wrote a book entitled *When a Church Becomes a Cult*. It was an attempt to define why it is that all too often churches which start as mainstream churches, with seemingly well-grounded ministries, get hijacked by over-authoritarian leaders, and end up becoming quasi-cults, in the process causing an immense amount of damage.

I have to admit that the book was not particularly well written, and I have felt slightly ashamed of it ever since—except that from time to time I get phone calls from people who are wrestling with exactly the issues I was referring to, and I realize that the situation today is, if anything, worse than at that time. In fact if I were to write a similar book today there would be, tragically, a hugely increased number of examples.

I have spent the last twenty-five years in a small market town where these things can seem far away—we are neither city center, nor cutting edge. But even in the North Cotswolds, I have seen again and again the damage done to the faith of sincere Christian people by leaders who distort the gospel, who lead their flock astray, but above all who betray their Lord and Savior.

Often it has been some sexual misdemeanor. The minister of a neighboring parish had to stand down after being caught in a compromising situation with the partner of a famous rock star. Another local evangelical minister left for a high-profile post, only for it to become clear that he was leaving behind a trail of ungodly behavior and damaged people—within two years he had to leave the ministry altogether. Another local minister stood up in the pulpit one Sunday to announce that he and his wife were splitting up. The minister of the largest church in the area—one of the largest in the country—had to resign over an extramarital affair.

Every time it happens there is always a long list of casualties—wives, husbands, children devastated, congregation members disillusioned, enemies of the gospel secretly, or sometimes not so secretly, rejoicing.

Though these examples are all of abuse of power expressed in sexual sin, spiritual abuse is by no means restricted to sexual behaviors. A particularly exclusive Christian group near where I was working recently built a large, new meeting hall. A number of former members of this group came to our congregation with disturbing stories of the behavior of the elders, and the pressure applied to members and even former members.

In addition, I, like many others, have been shocked by the recent revelations concerning certain evangelical leaders, particularly two whom I knew and respected. I knew nothing of what had been going on, and even now find it hard to believe. I also knew some of the victims reasonably well, or so I thought, and had never suspected anything was wrong.

Consequently, I find myself feeling at times very angry about it all, especially when we see the anguish it has caused, and the sincere believers whose lives have been turned upside down. It never occurred to me writing the book twenty-five years ago that I would find examples of what I was trying to describe so close to home. Why did I not spot it?

I have heard it said that the root of all heresy is a defective view of sin. Where we underestimate sin we are liable to go wrong. And perhaps that is the first lesson I have had to learn, that at the heart of all that has happened is original sin, the truth that in our hearts all of us are fallen. Even those we admire the most have a fault line running through them. As soon as we start to place them on a pedestal, we are setting ourselves up for inevitable disappointment.

I have often reflected on why so many of the great characters of the Bible were so deeply flawed. Even David, the "man after God's own heart" (1 Sam 13:14), committed adultery, then murder to cover up his adultery. Solomon, the so-called wisest man in the world (1 Sam 3:12), turned away from God in his later years, and committed appalling apostasy (1 Kgs 11:4-6). We should never be surprised at the depth of sin both in our own hearts, and in the hearts of those we most admire.

Too often today we divide the world into goodies and baddies, but, as Solzhenitsyn wrote, "the line separating good and evil passes not through states, nor between classes, nor between political parties either, but right through every human heart, and through all human hearts."[1] The political world is riven with tribalism, where one's judgement of others is determined not so much by their character as by their allegiances. Never was this more clearly seen in the UK than over Brexit, over which you could make or lose friends very quickly. I was deeply depressed by many of the comments made by certain Facebook friends who claimed to be Christian yet were utterly scathing in their denunciations of those they disagreed with.

The Christian world itself is also often split into different camps, sometimes over trifling issues, at other times over major issues. But the temptation is to see those we agree with as being the goodies, and those we disagree with as the baddies. Hence we will excuse or overlook the faults, in ourselves or in others, provided we/they are on the right side. Equally we will be quick to recognize and point to the faults in others who do not belong to our particular tribe. But in reality of course, we all are sinners in need of God's grace, even the most respected of Christian leaders.

A recently retired bishop was asked what had been his greatest surprise when he took on the role. He said simply but shockingly: "The immorality of the clergy."

But I believe there are other factors which have caused leaders to fall and people to be led away, and I want to focus on two.

THE PROBLEM OF THEOLOGICAL IGNORANCE

There is an increasing ignorance of the Bible, even in Bible-believing churches. For large numbers of churches, the sermon has become less important than "ministry" with the result that congregations are less and less well-taught, and increasingly dependent on special words, or revelations. As a result, they are less able to spot misleading teaching when it comes around.

The best antidote to any false teaching is true teaching. I often quote the introduction to Walter Martin's book, *The Kingdom of the Cults*, probably the fullest and best book ever written on cults. He wrote:

> The American Banking Association . . . each year sends hundreds of bank tellers to Washington in order to teach them to detect counterfeit money . . . It is most interesting that during the entire two weeks of the training program, no teller touches counterfeit money. Only the original passes through his hands. The reason for this is that the ABA is convinced that if a man is thoroughly familiar with the original, he will

---

1. Solzhenitsyn, *Gulag Archipelago*, 312.

not be deceived by the counterfeit bill, no matter how much like the original it appears.[2]

In other words, to avoid falling into error we must become familiar with the truth. That is equally true for the Christian, and to do that we need the Bible. So many of the problems that face the church today stem from the fact that we do not know the Bible well enough, and when we do, we refuse to accept its teaching. And that perhaps is particularly true of those who seek to lead.

I do wonder whether the introduction of part-time training for many of our clergy (at least in the Anglican Church) has meant that more and more people are ordained with a very limited understanding of basic Bible truths. As an example of this I was very struck by some comments passed by a member of our diocesan staff at a clergy conference a few years back. His job was to interview potential ordination candidates, prior to their being recommended for training. Over a period of two years, he had interviewed around twenty-five candidates, male and female, and from all traditions. He was impressed by their enthusiasm and their commitment. But he was less impressed by three common problems that he had observed. I would be surprised if these were restricted to Anglicans.

First, he became aware that most of them had at best a very basic Bible understanding. They did not really know what the Bible was about, did not appreciate the thread that runs all the way through, and were thus unable to teach it with any confidence. Very few even thought of themselves as Bible teachers. Despite the fact that the ordination rites stress the role of teaching the faith as being the first responsibility of the minister, somehow no one had ever explained that to them.

The first three questions asked at the ordination of a deacon are these:

> Q. Do you accept the Holy Scriptures as revealing all things necessary for eternal salvation through faith in Jesus Christ?
> A. I do so accept them.
> Q. *Will you be diligent in prayer, in reading Holy Scripture, and in all studies that will deepen your faith and fit you to bear witness to the truth of the gospel?*
> A. By the help of God, I will.
> Q. *Do you believe the doctrine of the Christian faith as the Church of England has received it, and in your ministry will you expound and teach it?*
> A. I believe it and will so do.

---

2. Martin, *Kingdom of the Cults*, 16.

In other words, the primary role of the minister is to be a teacher and defender of the truth. It is no surprise that a church which neglects its primary purpose to teach and instruct will inevitably be more liable to be led astray.

Secondly, he discovered that not one of them had a regular daily devotional time, whether it was a time of Bible reading and prayer, or the daily office. Every Christian knows that our personal relationship with Christ is of preeminent importance. But very few of us, evidently, even those putting themselves forward for full-time Christian ministry, seem prepared to give the time to developing that relationship.

But thirdly, and most remarkably, he asked each one of them to give a brief overview of the Christian gospel. Not one of them, from whatever tradition they may have hailed, even mentioned the cross. How is it possible to speak of the gospel without the cross? For two thousand years it has been the very symbol of the Christian faith, for the simple reason that without the cross there would be no gospel. It is why Paul determined when visiting the Corinthians that he would "know nothing while [he] was with [them] except Jesus Christ and him crucified" (1 Cor 2:2).

Somehow or other we are breeding a generation of believers who do not grasp even the most basic truths of the Bible, have never really understood the gospel itself, and are thus heavily dependent on their own church leadership. They are thus at a much greater risk of falling for error.

THE PROBLEM OF CELEBRITY LEADERS

The second issue, which naturally follows, is an ever-increasing dependence upon individuals, focusing on magnetic personalities and great gifting rather than Christian character, such that certain leaders effectively become untouchable. We have placed them on such a pedestal that they can effectively do what they like. Christian leadership conferences rely on celebrity speakers, or worship leaders, to attract attendance, resulting in these individuals getting their names and faces emblazoned across posters and the internet. This is supplemented by competitions to find the "best" preacher, the "finest" worship leader, the "best" Christian song. We are setting too many up for a fall.

Ministers often fall into the temptation of becoming over-competitive about their churches, using arbitrary (rather than biblical) yardsticks for success: congregation or budget size, buildings, technical resources, and so on. We can feel threatened when others seem to do better than us. I vividly recall speaking to one denominational leader about a particular church that we both knew. I remarked that it must be one of the largest in the UK. He replied along the lines that it was the third largest in the denomination but that the minister was frustrated that it wasn't the largest.

Here is the problem. When we focus on personalities who crave success, popularity, and public acclaim, we easily (and perhaps inevitably) ignore more fundamental issues of integrity, godliness and humility.

Two of the biggest scandals to hit the secular world over the last ten or so years involved Jimmy Savile in Britain and Harvey Weinstein on both sides of the Atlantic.

Jimmy Savile died in 2011, having been a well-known DJ and TV presenter for many years, particularly noted for his charity work for children's and pioneering hospitals. However, amongst media insiders, he was notorious. As far back as 1978, Jonny Rotten (of Sex Pistols fame) was asked in an interview about public figures he (putting it politely!) disliked. He said that Jimmy Savile was "into all sorts of seediness. We all know about it but we're not allowed to talk about it. I know some rumors."

That part of the interview was never broadcast and it would take thirty-two years for the truth about Savile to become more widely known. During that period, Savile groomed and sexually abused dozens, if not hundreds, of young people, boys and girls. But insiders had known for years. Why did nobody intervene? It is not enough for people to claim that they had only "heard the rumors." Many knew perfectly well they were not simply rumors. Why were so few prepared to speak out? Or if they did, why did nobody act?

The answer of course is that people like Savile were regarded as untouchable, as if royalty.

The same was true of Harvey Weinstein, the film producer famously described by Meryl Streep at the 2012 Oscars as god. It took the bravery of one or two actresses, willing to risk their careers by telling the truth, to bring about Weinstein's exposure as the sexual predator many already knew him to be. He survived so long because he too was regarded as untouchable.

Much as we might assume or wish it otherwise, the Christian world can be no different. How does this culture arise? Here are some possible reasons.

Leading without Criticism

It is often the case that those who lead others astray are people with a high public profile, internationally respected, and thus seen as being beyond criticism.[3]

---

3. Eds. Though this is undoubtedly true, a leader does not need to have a high

Visitors to their churches are drawn from around the world because they appear to present a model of church to be emulated. They seem to be doing *something* right. Others are attracted by the leaders themselves and naturally want to serve them and their vision. Furthermore, members enjoy the status this brings, feeding the narrative that *belonging to*

> [this church is] something special, something blessed by God, something that could not be found in other churches. Young Christians were unlikely to challenge a leader who had a place on the global Christian stage.
>
> X had a global leadership role and this made him unchallengeable. He received major affirmation from global evangelical leaders."[4]

Consequently, they begin to believe their own publicity or global reputation as examples to the rest of the world for having captured the secret of real church. A member of the Crowded House Church in Sheffield wrote of their leadership:

> We have also suffered from cultural arrogance, a belief that our way is better than that of other churches, and that X is effectively infallible. This has never been preached (in fact the opposite has), but we have had a series of outsiders telling us how wonderful we are; how great a model we provide; how influential we (and X in particular) have been to the church globally. This leads to a position where it is very hard to address cultural flaws and learn deeply from others, and especially to question X's increasing "celebrity leader" status.[5]

The church-planting movement has brought great blessing to the church. It has rejuvenated dying churches, restored spiritual life to areas that have not heard the gospel for decades, and provided many with fantastic opportunities to develop gifts and ministries. But there is a downside. Many of the newly planted churches come from larger evangelical centers with their own idiosyncratic way of doing things. The plants can become part of a growing empire that sees itself, often unconsciously, as a spiritual elite, especially in terms of somehow being better than other, more mainstream or "middle of the road" churches. Henry Kriete, a leader in the London Church of Christ, was excoriating on where the church had gone so wrong.

---

public profile to behave as though they are above criticism.

4. Thirtyone: Eight, "Independent Learning Review," 29.
5. Thirtyone: Eight, "Independent Learning Review," 36.

We have taught that we alone are the "true kingdom," "true disciples," and the "One True Church." And not only do we believe these things, but we intensely advocate them—we know what we are doing, we have restored such and such, we are the remnant chosen by grace, we are the only church since the first century to . . .[6]

After all, how could any church with an international reputation for having discovered the true meaning of church possibly get things wrong?

Leading without Accountability

Many leaders of the largest churches function in practice (even if not on paper) with complete independence. They are law unto themselves, even when members of denominations with clear structures. To whom are they truly answerable? When things do begin to go wrong, who then has the responsibility for addressing them? Strong suspicions may abound, but people do not know what to do with them. When the truth does emerge, witnesses had invariably seen the warning signs but been at a loss regarding people to contact or action to take.

I recall only too well, some thirty years ago, attending a conference organized by an American megachurch on the subject of church growth. It was challenging and stimulating, but I was just a little disconcerted by the obviously close relationship between the church leader and one of his staff who had come to help with the conference. To this day I have no idea if there really was anything wrong at the time, but it came out recently that this same man—internationally known and respected—had been forced to resign because of an inappropriate relationship with a female member of staff. Should I have said anything at the time?

Many of these leaders do have an accountability group, people to whom they are supposed to be answerable. They are there ostensibly to stop the leader going astray, but they can degenerate into mere smokescreens, or shields from criticism. Such groups rarely seem to prevent the real problems.

Perhaps they are too distant (whether geographically or relationally) from the church situation to notice what is going on, or they only hear one side. They will then be too inclined to take the leader's word for whatever is going on. Alternatively, they are themselves part of the fellowship, thus creating a complex dynamic with the leader, especially if they owe their positions to the one whom they should be calling to account.

---

6. Kriete, "Honest to God," sec. "Our Shameful Arrogance."

Returning to the investigators' report about problems at Sheffield's Crowded House, one thing stood out. In contrast to how the leadership boasted about the effectiveness of their own accountability relationships in print, the reality was very different.

> I remember talking over lunch with two church leaders. At first, they expressed concern that we did not have an accountability structure over and outside of us. But, as I talked to them about the day-to-day accountability I enjoy from my congregation and from other congregational leaders with its opportunity to share heart struggles, their attitude changed. Soon they were saying, "I wish we had something like this; our accountability is so superficial; I feel alone most of the time." True accountability is more about relationships than hierarchies. It requires community more than structures.[7]

So much for the spin. What about members' lived experience?

> X was impossible to challenge. Anyone who attempted to challenge him was liable to end up apologizing to him. A challenge was seen as a personal attack, disloyalty, disobedience. There was only one way to leave well, with the blessing of the elders, to a church plant or an approved group.[8]

Instead of genuine accountability, there exists what C. S. Lewis described as an "inner ring"[9] of acolytes, too often a group of younger, inexperienced men, who make the important decisions and know all the important details. They are drawn into the leader's confidence precisely because they do not represent a threat to his dominance. Once in the "inner ring," they are perhaps fed morsels of gossip, salacious details about congregation members, which serves to enhance their sense of superiority and membership of the elite.

Another Christian leader, again highly respected and internationally known, would gather around him a group of younger men, who clearly looked to him for guidance and teaching. They would crave his approval and affirmation, something he clearly enjoyed. His strong personality meant that it was very hard to disagree with him, and he resented it if anyone did. Simultaneously, this individual could be withering about others and he loved to be the bearer of the latest bit of gossip. It intensified the sense of belonging to the privileged few.

7. Chester and Timmis, *Total Church*, 193.
8. Thirtyone: Eight, "Independent Learning Review," 39.
9. Lewis, *Weight of Glory*, 141–57.

But such belonging did not come cheap. So, for example, in the Crowded House Church,

> there was a price tag to being part of the inner core, unquestioned allegiance. A number of participants described how within this group "non-core people were talked about, dismissed in a word." They stated that this behavior was replicated by other leaders. . . . Later I just chose to sit silent. Increasingly I wanted to remove myself as I felt compromised to be hearing personal information and stories, questioning if it was gossip.[10]

Failure to obey or toe the line results in the speedy withdrawal of privileges. They might be made to feel ignored and given the cold shoulder or even publicly shamed. They become isolated, while any legitimate concerns about the culture in the fellowship get sidelined. Such treatment either leads to renewed compliance or departure. If the latter, remaining members are discouraged from making contact with them. The deserter is regarded as being disobedient, manifesting an evidently poor attitude. The problem is always with the one who leaves. Thus the leadership remains unchallenged for the next period until the cycle is repeated. Any criticism of the group is therefore effectively stifled or ignored. Henry Kriete again:

> We have seen almost all criticism of the movement to be sinful. We accuse people of having bad hearts or bad attitudes or independent spirits, when very often, they have every right to feel as they do . . . we have routinely humiliated and marginalized those members who speak out as "critical" and "disloyal." When anyone does leave the church, they are automatically categorized as a "fall away."[11]

No-one wants to be seen as disloyal, or risk losing friends and status. In addition people are aware of the way in which God has been seen to use the particular leader, and are extremely wary of attacking one seen as a real servant of God. Furthermore, it is unlikely that *everything* was or is bad. Many testify to the blessings received from their respective ministries—Bill Hybels had an international ministry and his seeker-friendly services have had an enormous impact upon the worldwide church. Steve Timmis and Jonathan Fletcher were fine preachers, appreciated across the world for their ministries.

But these individuals consistently managed to avoid being truly accountable.

---

10. Thirtyone: Eight, "Independent Learning Review," 34.
11. Kriete, "Honest to God," sec. "Our Corrupted Hierarchy."

What has become clearer as people have given their accounts is that apparently every alleged incident of abuse, bullying, harassment, control, was known about by somebody, but nobody was aware of them all . . . many people left quietly and took their stories and their questions with them. Often they were too bruised to speak out or take action until months or years later, when an online network of . . . "refugees" began to form, stories were shared, and their narrative began to gain traction.[12]

The Problem of a Gospel without Grace

A third issue that is often found in these churches concerns the central message—the gospel of grace mutates into a gospel of works. It will never be openly stated, but it becomes clear that members are judged for their failures to comply with the leadership's particular standards, rather than the Scriptures.

There may well be understandable reasons for this. There may have been a reaction to the prevailing atmosphere within the national church. For too long the church seems to have fallen into the trap of preaching a gospel without teeth, one of cheap grace, as Dietrich Bonhoeffer so devastatingly put it:

> Cheap grace means grace sold on the market like cheapjack's wares. The sacraments, the forgiveness of sins, and the consolations of religion are thrown away at cut prices. Grace without price; grace without cost! The essence of grace, we suppose, is that the account has been paid in advance; and, because it has been paid, everything can be had for nothing. . . . Cheap grace is the preaching of forgiveness without requiring repentance . . . grace without discipleship, grace without the cross, grace without Jesus Christ, living and incarnate.[13]

In response to a gospel of cheap grace, the highest standards are demanded of the membership, standards that can seem impossible to keep, and for which members are judged. But in the process grace becomes works.

> There was a widespread view expressed by participants that within [the church] culture there was an over-emphasis on sin and an under-emphasis on grace, although this was not universal. . . . At [the church] it was truth, truth, truth and no grace.[14]

12. Thirtyone: Eight, "Independent Learning Review," 45.
13. Bonhoeffer, *Cost of Discipleship*, 35–36.
14. Thirtyone: Eight, "Independent Learning Review," 53–54. See also Grant

A climate of insecurity and fear will invariably follow: "[we] were always striving to meet additional criteria; [we] felt [we] were always being monitored and were constantly anxious."[15]

A lack of knowledge of the Bible, an overdependence on unaccountable leaders, and a gospel that has lost its emphasis on grace. This has created a toxic cocktail that has left many believers vulnerable to leaders unwilling to face their own failings.

NECESSARY RESPONSES

So what should be our response?

First, we need a greater knowledge of the Bible. Secondly, we need to find a better way to hold Christian leaders properly accountable. And thirdly, we must be wary of ever allowing the gospel of grace to become a tyranny of works.

When I wrote the book, one thing that I had not been prepared for was the number of people who made contact to say that I had described perfectly their particular church, and then named a church I knew well. I thought I had been describing something out there, when all the time it was much closer to home. As Paul wrote in his farewell to the Ephesian elders:

> Keep watch over yourselves and all the flock of which the Holy Spirit has made you overseers. Be shepherds of the church of God, which he bought with his own blood. I know that after I leave, savage wolves will come in among you and will not spare the flock. Even from your own number men will arise and distort the truth in order to draw away disciples after them. So be on your guard! Remember that for three years I never stopped warning each of you night and day with tears. (Acts 20:28–31 NIV)

Questions to Consider

- How accountable are the leaders of our church? Are they untouchable? To whom do they have to give account? Who will tell them when their behavior is raising questions?

Macaskill's chapter 6 in this volume as well as Meynell, *Cross-Examined*.

15. Thirtyone: Eight, "Independent Learning Review," 54.

- Does your church have an inner circle who make all the decisions? If so, how are they chosen?
- Are dissenting voices in the church silenced or listened to? Does your church council consist of those who will go along with everything the leadership suggests or is it able to ask serious questions?
- How do we treat church members who leave either to join another church or leave altogether? With love or with judgement?

BIBLIOGRAPHY

Bonhoeffer, Dietrich. *The Cost of Discipleship*. Complete edition. London: SCM, 1986.

Chester, Tim, and Steve Timmis. *Total Church: A Radical Reshaping Around Gospel and Community*. 2007. Reprint, Nottingham: InterVarsity, 2010.

Kriete, Henry. "Honest to God." http://www.reveal.org/library/stories/people/hkriete.htm.

Lewis, C. S. *The Weight of Glory: A Collection of Lewis's Most Moving Addresses*. London: Collins, 2013.

Martin, Walter. *The Kingdom of the Cults: An Analysis of the Major Cult Systems in the Present Christian Era*. Rev. ed. Minneapolis: Bethany Fellowship, 1977.

Meynell, Mark. *Cross-Examined: The Life-Changing Power of the Death of Jesus*. Revised and expanded edition. Nottingham: InterVarsity, 2021.

Solzhenitsyn, Aleksandr Isaevich. *The Gulag Archipelago, 1918–56: An Experiment in Literary Investigation*. London: Harvill, 2003.

Thirtyone: Eight. "An Independent Learning Review: The Crowded House." https://thirtyoneeight.org/media/khzksimf/the-crowded-house-learning-review-full-report.pdf.

9

The Cost of Brokenness

Blythe Sizemore

INTRODUCTION

I never imagined I would be called a liar. Sure, as a child, my siblings would accuse me of lying and, of course, I can own up to telling the occasional "white lie," affirming a clothing choice I didn't actually care for or exaggerating the details of a story for maximum effect, but I never thought I would hear my boss calling me a liar. Following months of a difficult relationship with my supervisor, making note of many instances of his concerning behavior, and a horrific meeting behind closed doors in which I was accosted and belittled, I submitted a formal written complaint to the personnel committee at the church where I was employed. I was then shocked when the head of staff came to me and told me that my supervisor had said I lied. "What? Why would I lie? What was there for me to gain?" After lawyers were consulted, I was informed that it was a "he said/she said." "I'm sorry? I work at church, dedicating my life to act justly, to love mercy, and to walk humbly with God and you do not believe me?" I submitted my complaint to protect myself and others from someone I thought was dangerous. Yet, I was offered counseling and my supervisor was offered leadership training. I was supposed to carry on with my work. The months that followed were filled with meetings too numerous to remember, mandatory pastoral counseling, and the decline of my mental health. Panic attacks, anxiety, depression, and the many symptoms of PTSD became my normality. I wanted out of the situation and out of ministry all together. My story could have ended there when I was in the depths, but God provided a way out for me and led me to a new ministry context where I began to heal and eventually flourish again in ministry.

It is disheartening that my story of abuse is just one among so many, of varying degrees of severity, happening within our churches. Our churches seem broken and it is devastating to realize they are often far more broken than we could conceive. And, although facing this brokenness is upsetting, it should not be surprising. Sin reaches into every corner of creation and the church is no exception. "The sovereign and utterly good God created a good universe. We human beings rebelled; rebellion is now so much a part of our makeup that we are enmeshed in it."[1] Christians will continue to battle with indwelling sin this side of eternity. In 1 John, we are reminded of this reality and the hope of forgiveness and cleansing; "If we say we have no sin, we deceive ourselves, and the truth is not in us. If we confess our sins, he is faithful and just to forgive our sins and to cleanse us from all unrighteousness" (1 John 1:8–10). All believers experience this struggle with sin if they are pursuing Christlikeness. Yet, the fact we all share the same struggle with sin does not mean we should just give up the battle. Sin spoils and disfigures God's good gifts but it does not eradicate or overcome his glories, so there remains something to redeem. We are called to holiness. The Spirit is with us in our war against our flesh. "No temptation has overtaken you that is not common to man. God is faithful, and he will not let you be tempted beyond your ability, but with the temptation he will also provide the way of escape, that you may be able to endure it" (1 Cor 10:12–13).

We need to face the fact that evil and sin are still at work in our churches. Cornelius Plantinga writes,

> At its depths, sin corrupts religion itself, its public enemy. All of the turns and ironies of sin arise in some way from the fact that evil does not—indeed cannot—appear alone.... Evil always appears in tandem with good. Thus, in wartime espionage and in movements to harbor persecuted fugitives, the person likeliest to do well and to achieve a measure of justice is one who means well and who can also lie and cheat convincingly. In general, good and evil grow together, intertwine around each other, and grow out of each other in complicated ways.[2]

It does feel ironic that evil so easily thrives and causes harm within the very structures God has given us to serve his good purposes and to bring

1. Carson, *How Long, O Lord?*, 43.
2. Plantinga, *Not the Way*, 80.

him glory. But as Plantinga notes, sin is parasitic upon the good. It corrupts churches and church leaders, all too often manifesting as abuse of power, breaking the structures and the community as well as its victims. The damage done is incalculable.

DISORIENTED

To be a victim of abuse has an effect similar to that of the children's game where you put your head down on the top of a baseball bat, spin around it and then try to run in a straight line. The feelings of disorientation, confusion, and even nausea—such that you feel unable to reach the end of the race—are precisely how abuse victims feel as they attempt to process the hurt from those they trusted. One of the most devastating consequences of abuse in the church is the complete disorientation of its victims. They have been betrayed by the people to whom they have bared their souls, in the very place they were supposed to be able to share their sorrows and their joys. In the aftermath, it is only natural to question whether anything that ever happened with those people in that place was even real. "Am I just stupid?" "Were the relationships fake?" "Have I just been a pawn in some sort of game?" "Is the gospel even true?"

> Abuse is crazy making. It messes with a victims' mind because abusers are experts at deflecting responsibility and blaming their victims for their abuse. "If only you hadn't looked so pretty I wouldn't have done that," or "Why did you make me so angry? It's your fault I hit you."
> In addition, abusers are people we know. They can be charming and likeable people. They aren't always abusive. They don't look like monsters. They look like us.[3]

When abusers are our pastors, elders, or small group leaders, it is hard for victims to reconcile their abuse with the fact that those people do not often "look like" abusers. Because of the power imbalances between church leaders and the abused, victims are disorientated—where do they turn for help? "Again I saw all the oppressions that are done under the sun. And behold, the tears of the oppressed, and they had no one to comfort them! On the side of their oppressors there was power, and there was no one to comfort them" (Eccl 4:1). The victims of abuse in churches can find themselves in a tragically difficult place without comfort.

---

3. Hambrick, *Becoming a Church*, 19.

ASHAMED

"Shame is the intensely painful feeling or experience of believing that we are flawed and therefore unworthy of acceptance and belonging. . . . Shame creates feelings of fear, blame, and disconnection."[4] Following the disorientation that results from abuse, victims can become imprisoned in their own shame.

> People always think it's strange when I ask them where and how they physically feel shame. But for most of us, shame has a feeling—it's physical as well as emotional. This is why I often refer to shame as a full-contact emotion. Women have described various reactions to shame, including stomach tightening, nausea, shaking, waves of heat in their faces and chests, wincing and twinges of smallness.[5]

While it may seem strange to transition from being wronged by someone else to believing that we ourselves are the ones in the wrong, this is the way that evil works upon the wounded and vulnerable. "It is the emotional weapon that evil uses to corrupt our relationship with God and each other."[6] Our temptation as believers will be to think that evil exists "out there," but not really in our midst. Yet, those in positions of power in our churches, as a result of their own sin, do great harm to others through their abuse, not least because they impose the evil of shame on their victims. "Inflicted shame is when one human being uses, humiliates, and degrades another, leaving behind a profound and often lifelong sense of shame."[7]

Once trapped in this shame prison, even faithful Christ-followers have difficulty navigating their way to freedom. Tomkins defines shame:

> If distress is the affect of suffering, shame is the affect of indignity and alienation. Though terror speaks to life and death and distress makes the world a vale of tears, yet shame strikes deepest into the heart of man. . . . While terror and distress hurt, they are wounds inflicted from the outside which penetrate the smooth surface of the ego; but shame is felt as an inner torment, a sickness of the soul. It does not matter whether the humiliated one has been shamed by derisive laughter or whether he mocks

---

4. Brown, *I Thought It Was Just Me*, 30.
5. Brown, *I Thought It Was Just Me*, 69–70.
6. Thompson, *Soul of Shame*, 13.
7. Langberg, *Suffering and the Heart of God*, 133.

himself. In either event he feels himself naked, defeated, alienated, and lacking in dignity or worth.[8]

Though it can be immensely difficult, believers can find freedom from their shame. The author of Hebrews reminds us to look to Jesus, "the founder and perfecter of our faith, who for the joy that was set before him endured the cross, despising the shame, and is seated at the right hand of the throne of God" (Heb 12:2). Jesus suffered shame and he overcame it. Believers have the power of Christ within them to overcome their shame. But, the stakes are high when victims are captive to their shame, as evidenced when their disclosure of abuse does not go as planned.

> The lies a victim hears in her own mind—it's their fault, their shame, it's not that bad, they are overreacting—are so loud that if your response in any way reflects those lies, it is absolutely crushing. They are unlikely to speak to you again, they may even retract or soften their own allegations if your response indicates they are not safe and have not been believed. It often takes years for a victim to seek help after being crushed, even unintentionally.[9]

"Let us then with confidence draw near to the throne of grace, that we may receive mercy and find grace to help in time of need" (Heb 4:16).

BROKEN

"My soul is bereft of peace; I have forgotten what happiness is; so I say, 'My endurance has perished; so has my hope from the Lord'" (Lam 3:18). Sometimes victims of abuse find it too much to endure. Their minds cannot handle navigating the disorienting landscape, fighting their way through the shame, and they just break. "The word trauma comes from the Greek word for wound. PTSD is the result of a wound to your person. A traumatic event is one in which a person's ordinary coping skills are completely overwhelmed and useless."[10] This is why mental illness becomes a very real concern for those who have been abused. The evils people inflict upon one another may not result in physical death, but those sins can result in forms of death. The loss of hope that survivors experience is a death in their souls, another costly consequence of the abuser's sin. Yet, we know that Jesus has the power to resurrect the hope that has died. Paul prays "that I may know

---

8. Langberg, *Suffering and the Heart of God*, 124.
9. Hambrick, *Becoming a Church*, 19.
10. Langberg, *Threshold of Hope*, 53.

him and the power of his resurrection" (Phil 3:10). Our hope amidst abuse is that the power of the resurrection will bring life and healing to those who have suffered.

> Remember my affliction and my wanderings, the wormwood and the gall! My soul continually remembers it and is bowed down within me. But this I call to mind, and therefore have hope: The steadfast love of the Lord never ceases; his mercies never come to an end; they are new every morning; great is your faithfulness. "The Lord is my portion," says my soul, "therefore I will have hope in him." (Lam 3:19–24)

TOWARD HEALING

Following my experience of trauma in the church, I felt I had been left with a sunburn that just would not heal. Everything that touches sunburnt skin hurts to a degree. A scratchy shirt on burned arms might be mildly uncomfortable. But accidentally brush that arm against a bush with prickly leaves, and the pain is searing. My spiritual sunburn meant that it would require a great deal of healing before I felt less sensitive about church. Even in a healthy church work environment, if I was called into a meeting without a clearly communicated topic and purpose, the pain felt searing. In my previous abusive environment, I had found myself in many meetings in which I was cornered into having to discuss my shortcomings or other difficult topics. So despite now being in a much healthier environment, meetings still triggered me. Over time the pain shifted from searing to scratchy and eventually I could manage impromptu meetings on the majority of occasions. Occasionally, though, even many years later, I still feel that sunburn when I hear about a meeting I need to attend. I take those opportunities to thank the Lord for the healing he has given me and to trust him to provide for me as I face the meeting at hand.

Although the process varies between individuals, there is real hope for healing. The posture of fellow believers towards these wounded imagebearers is crucial. Jerram Barrs writes, "The Scripture calls us to love our neighbor as we love ourselves. To be made in the image of God means that we are crowned with glory and honor by God Himself. . . . In addition, God has set his love on us in his Son, and this means we are of infinite value to him."[11]

---

11. Barrs, *Heart of Evangelism*, 77.

As fellow believers receive those who are wounded, who may appear so very broken, they must keep in mind that these sons or daughters have been crowned with glory and honor. They are deeply loved by God. Christians are to imitate our Lord's demeanor towards them. "Bear one another's burdens, and so fulfill the law of Christ" (Gal 6:2). "Being abused is a devastating trauma that distorts how people see God and how they think God sees them. Victims carry with them the stubborn lies that they are abandoned, unlovable, and disgraced."[12] The ministry of reconciliation among brothers and sisters who have been wounded by the church, trusts God to use fellow believers to restore his hurting children to himself and his church. This requires great humility. "I have been crucified with Christ. It is no longer I who live, but Christ who lives in me" (Gal 2:20). "He who now stands at the right hand of the Father still has a body here on earth. We are that body of flesh, still called out of love and obedience to the Father to walk among others in their darkness."[13]

GIVING DIGNITY

"You represent God to the victim who asks for your help and justice. *Does God care about what's happened to me?* I know you want to represent him well. And the best place to start is with compassion and care so that the victim feels heard, believed, and loved."[14] It must be remembered that entering into the suffering of brothers and sisters is God's work. "If it is his work, the results are in his hands and you will not need to demand certain outcomes by a certain time, thereby pressuring hurting people to get better so that you feel successful."[15]

> The Lord is near the brokenhearted and saves the crushed in spirit. Many are the afflictions of the righteous, but the Lord delivers them out of them all. He keeps all his bones. Not one of them is broken. Affliction will slay the wicked, and those who hate the righteous will be condemned. The Lord redeems the life of his servants; none of those who take refuge in him will be condemned. (Ps 34:18–22)

Those seeking to love and help the victims of abuse need to trust to God to do the work as they give dignity by listening well, being patient

---

12. Hambrick, *Becoming a Church*, 134.
13. Langberg, *Suffering and the Heart of God*, 69.
14. Hambrick, *Becoming a Church*, 20.
15. Langberg, *Suffering and the Heart of God*, 116.

through the process of healing, and gently reminding the abused of God's eternal commitment to them in the midst of this broken world.

Listening means being present such that the person speaking to you does not feel abandoned and alone in their suffering. Listening is a significant ministry to anyone who has been trapped in their suffering for any period of time. Diane Langberg writes,

> The purpose of listening is to honor the teller in a safe place so that you may begin to grasp in some measure what it is like to be them. Let them know what they are doing is courageous and is the right thing to do. They are speaking truth and dragging darkness into the light. Abuse silences victims and renders them powerless. Listening makes room for their voice and restores dignity.[16]

In caring for the abused, it is essential not to feel pressured into giving immediate answers or solutions. It is entirely fitting, however, to express grief. "Let them know that you recognize the evil they have experienced, and it matters. 'I am so sorry. This is wrong. I am grieved to know you have suffered this way. This grieves the heart of God.'"[17] The experience of being seen and heard, being given dignity, is the starting point for restoration.

The healing process is rarely quick. Western culture tends to value quick fixes and the temptation is to avoid commitments as long-term as accompanying a survivor as they recover from abuse. Thankfully, this is not how God treats his people. "O Israel, hope in the Lord! For with the Lord there is steadfast love, and with him is plentiful redemption" (Ps 130:7). The Scriptures are filled with waiting and the reminders to endure, even as the Lord's love towards us is steadfast and enduring, with the hope of redemption.

> Neither prophets nor priests nor psalmists offer quick cures for the suffering: we don't find any of them telling us to take a vacation, use this drug, get a hobby. Nor do they ever engage in publicity cover-ups, the plastic-smile propaganda campaigns that hide trouble behind a billboard of positive thinking. None of that: the suffering is held up and proclaimed—and prayed.[18]

Langberg advises, "You will have to learn how to wait. . . . You will wait for truth to penetrate a dark mind. . . . You will wait while the Spirit of

---

16. Hambrick, *Becoming a Church*, 16.
17. Hambrick, *Becoming a Church*, 67.
18. Peterson, *Long Obedience*, 139–40.

God works internally in a life with no outward sign of growth. You will wait because God's timetable is not yours."[19]

Finally, and most importantly, those who have been abused in church need gentle and gracious reminders of the hope they have in Jesus. Even this may be painful because of the disorientation, shame, and brokenness resulting from their abuse, but God does use his truth to soften and heal. We can name and face the dark reality of this broken world and the evil among us, while simultaneously looking beyond to the suffering Christ, the one who truly understands our pain.

> He was despised and rejected by men; a man of sorrows, and acquainted with grief; and as one from whom men hide their faces he was despised and we esteemed him not. Surely he has borne our griefs and carried our sorrows; yet we esteemed him stricken, smitten by God, and afflicted. But he was pierced for our transgressions; he was crushed for our iniquities; upon him was the chastisement that brought us peace, and with his wounds we are healed. (Isa 53: 3–5)

With his wounds we are healed. Jesus knows suffering and he has secured eternal hope for us. While pain lingers during this earthly life, we can lean on Jesus's sustaining strength and final victory over evil. "In this world you will have tribulation. But take heart; I have overcome the world" (John 16:33). We cannot absorb or remove the pain of those among us who have been harmed, but we can listen, wait, and remind them of our present and future victory in Christ. "He will wipe away every tear from their eyes, and death shall be no more, neither shall there be mourning, nor crying, nor pain anymore" (Rev 21:4).

BIBLIOGRAPHY

Barrs, Jerram. *The Heart of Evangelism.* Wheaton, IL: Crossway, 2005.
Brown, Brené. *I Thought It Was Just Me (but It Isn't): Making the Journey from "What Will People Think?" to "I Am Enough."* New York: Avery, 2008.
Carson, D. A. *How Long, O Lord? Reflections on Suffering and Evil.* Leicester, UK: InterVarsity, 1990.
Hambrick, Brad. *Becoming a Church That Cares Well for the Abused: Handbook.* Nashville, TN: B & H, 2019.
Langberg, Diane. *On the Threshold of Hope: Opening the Door to Hope and Healing for Survivors of Sexual Abuse.* Carol Stream, IL: Tyndale, 1999.
———. *Suffering and the Heart of God: How Trauma Destroys and Christ Restores.* Greensboro, NC: New Growth, 2015.

19. Langberg, *Suffering and the Heart of God*, 110.

Peterson, Eugene H. *A Long Obedience in the Same Direction: Discipleship in an Instant Society*. London: InterVarsity, 2019.

Plantinga, Cornelius. *Not the Way It's Supposed to Be: A Breviary of Sin*. Leicester, UK: Apollos, 1995.

Thompson, Curt. *The Soul of Shame: Retelling the Stories We Believe about Ourselves*. Downers Grove, IL: InterVarsity, 2015.

10

Authoritative, *Not* Authoritarian

Sam Allberry

INTRODUCTION

I've never in my life been so eager to get away from a church. I'd been invited to come and preach for the weekend. I'd not met the pastor (I'd been liaising with a junior colleague of his) but he greeted me warmly and enthusiastically. I preached at the first couple of services (there were four in total that weekend) and we grabbed a quick meal afterwards with some of the church staff. I quickly realized his initial warmth hid a much darker personality. I could see that his colleagues were in fear of him. It became very apparent that he led his church through intimidation. By the end of the last service, I couldn't wait to get away.

His was a more overt example of something I've now seen a number of times; pastors who feel the need to be constantly asserting their authority, ensuring everyone knows who the top dog is. I've heard from junior colleagues who've been yelled and sworn at in meetings, to "put them in their place," and more recently a prominent and revered pastor in the UK has been exposed for many years of various forms of abuse of those he was meant to be pastoring. The phenomenon of the bully pastor is sadly not rare.

It may not be uncommon, but it is often unidentified. We have become accustomed to pastors having to leave the ministry because of adulterous behavior. Such stories sadly hit the news with regularity—the "vicar running off with the church secretary" scenario has even become a trope. Any time these things happen we will feel a mixture of deep grief that it has happened, together with a sense of gratitude that it has been brought into the light and that church discipline might now take place.

But the same Scriptures that tell us pastors must be above reproach when it comes to sexual misconduct are equally clear that pastors must not be domineering and bullying. They are to exercise God-given authority without being authoritarian. Writing to pastors in the first century, Peter exhorted them to

> Shepherd the flock of God that is among you, exercising oversight, not under compulsion, but willingly, as God would have you; not for shameful gain, but eagerly; not domineering over those in your charge, but being examples to the flock. (1 Pet 5:2–3)

There it is: pastors must not be domineering. And yet this form of behavior can often go on for years before it is even recognized, let alone brought into disciplinary light.

We do, thankfully, hear of this sin being dealt with more often than we used to. The #MeToo and #ChurchToo movements have shed much light on various kinds of abuse. We're more conscious of the issue of bullying than we might have been a decade ago. And so, here and there, we are at last hearing stories of pastors being dismissed for being domineering.

But the fact remains, even then, that the behavior has often gone on for many years without being challenged. That may be because of unbearable pressure placed on victims not to question or challenge what is going on. Alternatively, it will be because we do not notice bullying behavior even when it takes place in front of our eyes. We know what bullying is, we know it exists, and yet we can sometimes be oblivious to its very presence in our churches. Which raises some important questions: What leadership virtue are we mistaking bullying for?

AUTHORITATIVE LEADERSHIP: TWO TRANSATLANTIC MODELS

Over the past several years I've had the opportunity to visit many churches and ministries in both the US and UK. My observation is that authoritarianism plays out in slightly different ways on either side of the Atlantic. It is common in American churches to borrow leadership wisdom from the business world. The pastor is the CEO. His role is to bring success, often measured in numerical terms. The church needs him in order to grow its membership and giving. The UK scene is slightly different. Churches can tend toward a military model. The pastor is the general who directs everyone to do the right things. He's the one with the battle plan. The church needs him to lead them to victory.[1]

There is obviously much to be learned from both successful CEOs and also great generals, but both models can quickly become toxic in church life. When either becomes the primary model for Christian leadership, is it any wonder that domineering pastors result? The pastor-as-CEO approach might foster entrepreneurialism and risk-taking, but it easily becomes results-oriented. The pastor-as-general approach might foster perseverance and grit, but it easily becomes task-oriented. One produces swagger: Their word is law because they're economically indispensable to the church. The other produces presumption: Orders must be followed because only the general really knows what is best for every person—they're strategically indispensable to the church. In each case we either tolerate or fail to see traits of bullying. Ministry ends are used to justify ministry means.

This must not be. Paul warns us about even superlative gifting wielded without love:

> If I have prophetic powers, and understand all mysteries and all knowledge, and if I have all faith, so as to remove mountains, but have not love, I am nothing. (1 Cor 13:2)

Paul doesn't simply say that loveless giftedness is "compromised" or "diminished in effectiveness." He doesn't even talk about ministry "results"—only the person exercising the gifts—and he says they are nothing. Giftedness at the expense of character is never finally effective. No matter how dazzling in the eyes of men, loveless pastors vanish into nothingness in the sight of God.

PROBLEMS WITH AUTHORITARIAN LEADERSHIP

We need to look closely again at what Peter says:

> Shepherd the flock of God that is among you, exercising oversight, not under compulsion, but willingly, as God would have you; not for shameful gain, but eagerly; not domineering over those in your charge, but being examples to the flock. (1 Pet 5:2–3)

---

1. Eds. The point Sam makes here generally holds true, though it's important to add that there are further differences in different parts of the UK as well as in churches of different theological and cultural flavors.

Here Peter sets out three pairs of contrasting features of an elder's work and heart: there must be willingness, not compulsion; service, not greed; and he must lead by example, not by coercion.

1. Authoritarians Pursue Compliance by Force

In the context of pastoral ministry, it happens when the flock assents to things by human compulsion rather than by the work of the Spirit in their hearts. It involves the use of intimidation, threats, or bullying. There may be some connection with the previous contrasts Peter has just made: being domineering is a form of greed ("shameful gain")—greed for power over others. And just as Peter has already said that an elder must serve willingly (v. 2), so too those who follow must follow willingly.

Paul gives us a wonderful example of how to do this well. In his letter to Philemon, Paul is wanting him to receive back his runaway slave Onesimus, "no longer as a slave but. . . as a beloved brother" (v. 16). But notice how Paul frames this desire:

> Though I am bold enough in Christ to command you to so what is required, yet for love's sake I prefer to appeal to you. . . .
> I preferred to do nothing without your consent in order that your goodness might not be from compulsion but of your own free will. (1 Cor 13:8–9, 14)

Paul could have simply played the "apostle card" and pulled rank. There were certainly times when that was necessary (e.g., 1 Cor 14:37). But, for Paul, that seemed to be the nuclear option, when his gentle appeals were never going to result in their freely consented obedience. His clear preference is not for there to be compliance by force.

2. Authoritarians Misunderstand the Pastor's Role

There is a genuine authority derived from the office of pastor, as we shall see. God means for this to be so: Hebrews tells us to "obey your leaders and submit to them" (Heb 13:17). But it continues: "For they are keeping watch over your souls, as those who will have to give an account." The first part guards against anticlericalism on the part of the congregation, the second guards against authoritarianism on the part of the leadership. Ideally, the pastor is to serve joyfully, just as the flock is to follow willingly. Although the pastor is set over the flock (see 1 Thess 5:12), that is not his only relationship to it. The flock is not only "under" him in this sense (reflecting genuine authority, under God, over the church); but, as Peter reminds us, the flock is also "among you." The pastor can only be over the flock as someone who is also a fellow member of it. While Peter is happy to describe pastors as shepherds, he makes it very clear that Christ is the "Chief Shepherd." The pastor's authority is never absolute nor ever final but only derived from God. We might say the pastor's authority, in common with all forms of human authority, is not his at all—it is given by God, to whom he will give account for his use of it.

3. Authoritarians Are Worldly

Jesus said, "You know that those who are considered rulers of the Gentiles lord it over them" (Mark 10:42). That is the way of the world around us, but it shouldn't be true of the local church—"it shall not be so among you" (v. 43). Secular insights into leadership have much to teach us, but there must also be clear contrasts between how leadership is exercised in the secular world and how it is exercised in the church. We can learn from CEOs and generals, but pastors are not meant to be CEOs and generals. It is in the secular world that leaders "lord it over" those under them. That is Jesus's expectation and we see it all around us. Because this is the way of the world, it will inevitably be the way of the church unless we consciously work for it to be otherwise. The cultural current will always take us in this domineering direction unless we actively swim against it.

4. Authoritarians Flout New Testament Teaching on Church Governance

Christians have differing convictions about precisely how churches should be structured, but one thing seems incontrovertible from the Scriptures: Churches are to be led by plural eldership. The New Testament does not speak of a church elder in the singular. The church may have a lead pastor, but there is to be a plurality of those who share leadership responsibility. No one person is meant to be in charge. Of course, it is easy to have plural eldership in theory and yet still have a pastor who rules the roost. The key is whether there is clear accountability and correction, and whether that can be—and actually is—executed.

5. Authoritarians Risk Spiritually Shipwrecking a Flock

Strong and controlling leadership might seem effective in the short term—it gets things done—but it is disastrous in the long term. What Paul says to the Romans about dealing with those "weak in faith" is instructive here. Those weak in faith (Rom 14:1) abstain from certain foods or observe certain days even though God doesn't require them to.[2] But if this has become a conscience issue, they shouldn't be coerced into changing their practice:

> Whoever has doubts is condemned if he eats, because the eating is not from faith. For whatever does not proceed from faith is sin. (Rom 14:23)

Paul is highlighting a broad principle that applies beyond the immediate discussion about food and special days. *Whatever* does not proceed from faith is sin.

A major way in which pastoral authority is abused is when pastors impose their views on secondary issues on their congregations. This is seen either in beliefs on certain issues or in behavioral codes. If a believer has certain doctrinal views or behaves in certain ways simply because a domineering pastor has coerced them to, then those views or actions are not proceeding from faith. It is not the Spirit of Christ who has brought them about, but the forcefulness of a leader. This is catastrophic because the believer isn't being led by the Lord, but by man. Believing even the right things is no good if it is for the wrong reason.

I've seen this play out a number of times. I think of one student-ministry context where the pastor was highly prescriptive. He told people what the "line" was on every issue, without demonstrating it from Scripture or providing space for questions or pushback. You believed as you were told. It was a disaster. As these students graduated and moved to other places, they were, in effect, moving away from what had become the basis of their faith—their pastor's forceful personality. Many saw their faith crumble. Others wreaked havoc in other churches by exporting the pastor's "line." To what extent was their faith in Christ and his word, and to what extent was it in their pastor? The calling of a pastor is to strengthen the flock's faith in Christ, not in their own ministry.

In all these ways, we see how serious domineering leadership is in the church. There is good reason Peter forbids it. It is not an unfortunate

---

2. Eds. It is ironic that "weak in faith" therefore may look "stronger" as a result of conscience decisions giving the impression someone "takes their faith seriously." However, in the context of Rom 14, the "strong in faith" are those who are more relaxed on these matters of conscience.

character trait that can be overlooked or justified just because there seems to be growth in the church. It is just as disqualifying as marital infidelity.

PREVENTING AUTHORITARIAN LEADERSHIP

The best way to prevent this kind of dangerous leadership is to cultivate the sort of leadership ethos and culture given to us in the New Testament.

It is important to recognize that churches need authority. The problem of authoritarianism is not authority, but authority turned in on itself and exploited to give the leader a sense of justification and importance. Leadership is part of the God-given way that human relationships and communities function. Paul can therefore say,

> We ask you, brothers, to respect those who labor among you and are over you in the Lord and admonish you. (1 Thess 5:12)

Authority, rightly exercised, is a good thing. God has put people over us for the sake of our spiritual protection and growth; to be human vehicles of Christ's divine shepherding—to bring us under his voice so that he can lead us to green pastures and beside still water.

This being so, healthy leadership will not just seek to be faithful to his word, but equally faithful to his character and demeanor. Christ himself summed it up in these astonishing words: "I am among you as the one who serves" (Luke 22:27). He calls those who would lead in his name to do likewise. Therefore, there is no place for grandiosity and self-promotion. Whatever authority we possess is only to be expressed in service, not superiority. Paul reflects this so commonly that we tend not to even notice him doing it. He almost always introduces himself as "Paul, a servant [or slave, bondservant] of God and apostle of Jesus Christ" (e.g., Titus 1:1). His very apostleship is seen in his servitude. All that Christ has given him in terms of his influence and authority is to be exercised for the sake of others, not himself. So it is to be with pastors.

There are two particular ways to exercise authority in a healthy way.

Leading by Sharing Authority

Authoritarian leadership treats power as a zero-sum game. For me to have power, others must be denied it. Healthy leadership takes the opposite approach. It seeks the honor of others rather than self. In fact, Paul tells us to "outdo one another in showing honor" (Rom 12:10). This competition to "out-love" one another is one in which everyone wins.

For example, a pastor may constantly seek opportunities to share authority with others. Jonathan Leeman writes that "exercising authority and giving away authority are two sides of the same coin." He continues,

> If a person leads . . . from a posture of humility, he will exercise authority while also giving away authority. After all, he seeks not his own ends but the ends of the One who has put him in office. So he will strive to equip and empower more people for the work.[3]

Leeman offers suggestions of what this can look like, such as giving other people opportunities to preach, not dominating elders' meetings, and being willing to lose elder votes. This last point I found especially striking. I've met two leaders of very large and influential megachurches in America. In both cases, as I spent time with their staff teams, it became apparent that they had gone to considerable lengths to make sure their own authority was limited and counterbalanced by that of other elders or pastors at the church. Each told me of significant moments where the other elders had voted against them at key decision points. Both these men said they found that reassuring (if a little frustrating, at the time), as it showed them that they really were accountable to others and under authority themselves. This is one of the reasons, of course, the Bible commends plural eldership to us.

Leading by Example

At the very point Peter insists pastors not be domineering, he shows us the alternative:

> Not domineering over those in your charge but being examples to the flock. (1 Pet 5:3)

This, then, is the antidote to authoritarian leadership: leading by example rather than by coercion.

I think of two pastors who embody these alternatives. The first can be very forceful. He is an intimidating man, and at times uses that in leading others. He can make people do things just by force of personality. I remember him talking about some lay leaders whom he wanted to involve in some pastoral reorganization, but who had not wanted to. In the end they gave in. "I made them do it," he told me afterwards.

The second pastor is also someone who certainly had the opportunity to make his presence felt and intimidate others but chooses not to. He told

---

3. Dever, *Discipling*, 106.

me once that the most overlooked component in church leadership was gentleness. There is little sense of ego with him. He loves promoting others and not himself. His closest colleagues tell me they would gladly follow him into any battle.

Both these men are compelling individuals. In one case, it is as a result of forcefulness; in the other it arises from example and character. One is authoritarian; the other leads with a far more Christlike character. The first can compel behavior, but only the second can compel hearts.

Flocks do need to be led. Leadership should never be by force of personality; instead it should only be by the beauty of example. Being domineering is bad leadership; and the answer to bad leadership is not no leadership but the right kind of leadership.

Again, there is meant to be authority in the office of an elder (Heb 13:7). There will be times when a pastor needs to call for that office to be respected and honored. But too often, that practical requirement gets abused by authoritarians. The people should be obedient to their leaders not because they're terrified of them, but because they're inspired and encouraged by them. Ultimately, it should be because the leaders point them to Christ by their example and spur them to their own love and good deeds.

BIBLIOGRAPHY

Dever, Mark. *Discipling: How to Help Others Follow Jesus*. Wheaton, IL: Crossway, 2016.

11

When Our First Love Is Loving to Be First

Chris Green

INTRODUCTION

I CAN STILL SEE them in my mind: a young couple in my living room, in tears. It was a desperately sad story of starting work in a church, but their early optimism being soured by the pastor's insistence on having his own way, playing politics with agendas and meetings, and making constant loyalty calls. A few years into that ministry, they were close to leaving.

I thought about disguising the story, but I haven't, apart from leaving out the names. I have had too many conversations over the years, about too many churches, to make it necessary. I taught in a seminary for over a decade, so I have plenty of contacts with younger pastors. Too many will read that first paragraph and wonder if I'm telling their story.

Everyone's case seems plausible until you hear the other's explanation (Prov 18:17), but in the cases I have in mind, the pastors were abusing their power, as confirmed by multiple sources. To reassure you, yes, in each case the issue was referred to the relevant church authorities, and none of them involved criminality or sexual immorality.

The stories share a pattern of a clear Bible teacher exerting increasing control over the loyalties of staff and members, to the point where there is a clear in/out delineation; some do leave, but many remain, unhappy yet wondering if they are seeing things clearly. When a Bible teacher is so highly regarded, their suspicions must be wrong, mustn't they?

The reasons and excuses lie easily to hand. To be an effective Bible teacher, you have to be strong and clear. Leadership requires definite direction. No one wants to be in a church where there is gossip, back-chat, or second-guessing the elders.

One consistent element is how hard the issue is to make sense of or believe, even for those actually involved. Victims can need help to see what has happened, to make a better sense of what they have experienced, to stop seeing their being abused as normal, way before they can find the courage to speak. Individual observers may see only part of a picture, and because the wider context seems a good one, they gave the benefit of the doubt to a troubling thought. Which inadvertently makes other individuals question what they have seen, too.

And one of the most difficult elements to be clear on is the extent to which the perpetrator might be blind to the damage that is being caused. Can you be a bully without knowing it? Can you simply not notice that culture has so changed that what might have been tolerated in the past is so no longer? One popular term for what abusers do to victims is to "gaslight" them. It comes from a 1938 stage play, *Gas Light*, where a villain persuades a victim she is going mad by consistently varying the lights at home but telling he her hasn't. It's become a standard way to describe how abusers distort reality and rework the narrative around their victims. But as Christians we know that sin deceives us, even as we sin (Heb 3:13). Is it not possible for a perpetrator to convince himself he is innocent—in effect, to gaslight himself?

I say "Bible teacher" because the part of God's church where I work is evangelical. I'm an Anglican, but I have many friends who are not, and I know the problems straddle that divide. I'm English, but the problems are present in all cultures. In the light of constant news stories across the Church of England, and across the denominational spectrum, it's unnecessary to point out that this problem exists all over; nevertheless, as an evangelical, I am minded to ask about how we keep our own house in order.

One central problem is cultural accommodation. Chuck DeGroat is a Christian therapist and author, who has spent over twenty years helping pastors and churches to face the pain this issue has caused, and assessing potential church planters for this flaw. He calls the problem "Narcissistic Personality Disorder."[1] Narcissus was the beautiful youth in Greek mythology with whom many fell in love, but who fell in love with his own reflection and died through self-neglect. In his case the harm done is to himself, although some

---

1. DeGroat, *Narcissism*.

versions of the myth have others harmed as well. Reflecting on this, DeGroat asks to what extent Christians and churches love and celebrate the very kind of pastors who, by their vanity and self-regard, do the most damage to others.

DeGroat is no pessimist, and his book contains powerful stories of slow redemption from the problem, both for perpetrators and victims. But he is no fool, and knows these are facets of a bigger, more damaging problem. He too has felt rage and a longing for revenge at the pain he has seen. He writes, "We swim in the cultural waters of narcissism, and churches are not immune. Western culture is a *narcissistic culture*."[2] In other words, the church is in danger of unconsciously adopting, and even applauding, something enormously damaging from the wider culture. We don't see the danger because we think it is a strength. When it damages us, we cannot describe the problem.

Mulling this over with troubled church members and pastoral staff, the New Testament book I keep returning to is the scarcely noticed 3 John. It's the shortest book, a mere twelve verses in all, taking about a minute and a half to read, but I'm persuaded no biblical text has more relevance to this issue of the abuse of power in the service of self-love, under the guise of serving the Lord and his church.[3]

THE CAST

There is a lot of activity in such a short letter, so we need first to meet the principal characters, in order to get a feel for the issues at stake.

a. John[4]

Although we are in the dark about time and place of his letters, we can infer why John wrote. He saw his addressees as his children (v. 4), maybe because he was their founding missionary, and so he felt ongoing responsibility for

---

2. DeGroat, *Narcissism*, 4, his italics.
3. For a fuller exposition of 3 John, see Green, *Message of the Church*, 259–75.
4. In what follows, I'm going to follow the line that the same author lies behind the Fourth Gospel; 1, 2, and 3 John; and Revelation and that internal evidence points to that being the apostle John. Even though 3 John simply comes from "The Elder," I will refer to him as "John." Numerous complicated solutions for the relationship between 1, 2, and 3 John have been proposed, but the simplest remains the most plausible, namely, "that 1 John was written first as a circular letter to address theological issues that were causing problems in various local churches, and was followed by the writing of 2 John to one of those churches and 3 John to an individual." See Kruse, *Letters of John*, 36–40, 42–43. See too Yarbrough, *1–3 John*, 5–21.

them. This is why he was keen to gather information (v. 3), wrote more than once (I wrote to the church [v. 9] implies the existence of an earlier letter) and intended to visit (v. 10). More, he expected that church to recognize his apostolic authority, and seems rather startled that they did not (vv. 9–10a).

John was collaborative. He had evidently made two or three informal visits to the church (vv. 3, 5,10), during which he noted the disturbing lack of any welcome for the visitors (see below on who they might have been). He drew on a wider circle of friends as he wrote: we, verses 8 (twice), 12; our, verses 9, 12; us, verses 9, 10. One highlight of his future visit would be friendship and fellowship with Gaius (v. 14).

b. Gaius

Gaius was the first to receive the letter (v. 1), which suggests that John saw him as an established and loved Christian with deep roots in the faith (vv. 1–3, 5) who would be loyal—Gaius had previously demonstrated this at some cost (vv. 5–8) and John expected the same again—and who had influence and would therefore be able to lead others in the work of discipline (Anyone . . . anyone, v. 11).

c. Diotrophes

Diotrephes was the damaging cause of the letter, summed up in the sharp observation, that he was "the one who loved-to-be-first."

d. Demetrius

Demetrius was another of the loyalists and perhaps the letter bearer (v. 12). John's use of authority is subtle: yes, Demetrius had a good character-reference from John, but he also had one from the truth (v. 12). This may be a veiled reference to the Lord Jesus himself, thus providing his perspective on the scandal. If so, then it is hardly surprising that John avoided trying to negotiate with the cult and its leaders to find common ground. This was no less than a battle between good and evil (v. 11).

e. The Churches

John and Gaius are members of Christian communities, although the contrasts are stark. Both are called a church (vv. 6, 9), but where John's was clearly thriving with activity and visitors, news and prayer (vv. 3, 14b), the other was scarred by factionalism, bullying and secrecy (vv. 9–10).

It appears that John was supporting the church as it experienced a power play. By repeated connection (two visits by The Brothers, two letters, his own plans), he sought to counter the isolationism that arises from leaders' cultish behavior and practices. He relativized the dominance of Diotrephes by exposing his behavior, naming it as ugly and egocentric, and insisting it should be addressed. He gave the members an alternative model of love (vv. 1, 6), friendship (vv. 2, 5, 11, 14), and collaboration (vv. 5–8). Rather than trading insults (v. 10), he repeatedly affirmed others (vv. 2–4, 5–8, 12, 14) publicly.

f. The Brothers

A quick comparison of two leading translations of 3 John shows a marked difference. Where ESV has consistent references to the brothers (vv. 3, 5, 10), the NIV has, variously, "believers," "brothers and sisters," and "other believers." Both use a footnote to clarify that although the undergirding word is "brothers," it should be understood in a gender-inclusive sense.

The difficulty with this approach is that it misdirects a reader away from a significant plot element in the letter, and where we need to be clear.

The NT uses the word "brothers" in at least four ways, and so we must take care to identify which it is on each occasion.

Obviously, first, it means a male sibling, as we use the word today (Acts 1:14). Second, by extension, it was a standard way for Jews to address one another (Acts 2:29, 37; 3:17, 22), and translators decide whether the group would most likely have been mixed or single sex.

Third, it was used for all Christians, male and female, and is a synonym for believers, or the saints (Acts 1:15, 16). Hebrews, for example, uses the word to build out from Jesus's self-chosen similarity to his people (Heb 2:11, 12, 17; 3:1, 12), and the argument fails if he doesn't mean all Christians. So on those many occasions where the NT writers uses the word without any specific teaching, translating to underline the inclusivity is wise, maybe with footnotes to help with any nuances.

However, there is also a fourth category. There are unambiguous cases, including the three in 3 John, and a wider group of possible cases, where "brothers" refers to a labeled group of itinerant, commissioned and recognized missionaries and leaders. For example, 1 Cor 16:11–12 sees two references to brothers, and one to our brother Apollos, and 2 Cor 8:23 mentions our brothers who are messengers of the churches. Multiple interconnections between the churches were made by these people, giving the term "the brothers" a semi-technical sense, and one that interlopers might claim to their advantage. This is what necessitated their unmasking (false brothers, in Gal 2:4, or 2 Cor 11:26).

Once that grouping is identified, a wider set of passages come into view. There are repeated mentions of brothers in Acts, for instance (e.g., Acts 18:18, 27; 21:7, 17), and glossing them as "all the Christians" rather than "the (traveling) workers" makes an interpretative decision; minor, maybe, but important at each point. I put the word "traveling" in brackets because some of those verses might refer to a more settled leadership, whether equivalent to elders or overseers, or deacons, or something else.

Using the term for settled leadership is more tentative, but it is well established for itinerant workers. So despite the NIV, this in some way needs to be acknowledged in 3 John, because of the issues surrounding them. I will not use "worker" because John uses it in verse 8; the NLT translates them traveling teachers in all three occasions, but perhaps we can simply use a convention not open to John and capitalize them: The Brothers.

Why all that fuss? Because it was Diotrephes's orchestration of a hostile reception for The Brothers and the wider churches they represented, which prompted John to write.

THE CHURCH AND THE CULT

As best as we can reconstruct it, here is the sequence leading to 3 John being written.

John, and the church of which he was part, had a practice of sending out traveling missionaries, known as The Brothers, for evangelism, apologetics, church planting, and teaching, who would return with news and fuel for prayer. This seems to have been a pattern common in the early church, plausibly based on the template of the mission-hub of Antioch (Acts 11:19–30; 13:1–3; 14:24–28).

One such group returned with the good news about a church of growing Christians, becoming mature and stable in their faith. But alongside that, they had a disturbing report: rather than being welcomed by that church, they were ostracized by its leader. While some individuals had been hospitable, the church itself was closed to them. John's letters, presumably of introduction, had been ignored, and his character had been publicly discredited. Anyone who showed any concern about the issue had also been removed from church membership. Diotrephes had thus made the church into a personality cult, with what we would recognize as the key features of unaccountability, isolation, disconnectedness, rejection of criticism and narcissism.

Third John is John's personal response to this situation, written to the loyal Gaius and conveyed in person by a faithful messenger, Demetrius, traveling in the company of other Brothers. All of them would need hospitality on their arrival, as would John himself when he made a personal visit to address leadership issues. Third John is therefore a test of whether Gaius would prove his loyalty to John by welcoming Demetrius and The Brothers, and thus publicly committing himself to the wider church? To do so would incur Diotrephes's malice and exclusion. The alternative would be for Gaius to remain "safe" within the inner circle of the cult, controlled by Diotrephes's ego and avoiding his censure. To choose that alternative, however, would be to distance himself from the apostle John, the wider Christian community of churches, and the global Christian mission. It would be to join a cult.

FIRST WITHOUT EQUALS

It is often rightly observed that those who have responsibilities in and for New Testament churches do so within a plurality. There were *elders, overseers, deacons, shepherds,* and *leaders* and *brothers*.[5] Though for example 1 Tim 3:1–13 refers to individual elders, this concerns their character and qualifications to work in a group or team: *The elders who direct the work of the church well are worthy of double honor, especially those whose work is preaching and teaching* (1 Tim 5:17, emphasis added; see too Titus 1:5–9).

Most biblically minded churches through the centuries have sought to express this plurality in their structures: a Congregational system may or may not have a pastor, but they normally have elders and deacons; a Presbyterian system assumes a Presbytery, or connection of fellow elders, as well as elders and deacons from the congregation; an Episcopal system looks the most hierarchical, but even so the most senior will be called only "first among equals," however much that phrase may have been misused.

Against this background, Diotrephes *loved to be first*—not "first among equals," but an unqualified "first." He was not challengeable; any challenger was driven away. Diotrophes was first—with a loyal team around him—but first nevertheless.

This example in 3 John helps us examine contemporary ministry dysfunction and identify whether a leader is a modern-day Diotrophes. As I recall several cases to mind, I can see both how clear the "Diotrophes marks" are in hindsight, and how extraordinarily hard they are to spot in real time. I've seen dominance in a leader masked by charm and social grace, alongside

---

5. E.g., "elders," Acts 14:23; "overseers and deacons," Phil 1:1; "shepherds (or pastors)," Eph. 4:11; "leaders," Heb 13:7, 17.

a stated and modeled willingness to be accountable and held in check. Reflecting now, I saw, and believed, the illusion. Once the illusion is exposed, a wider public often wonders why no-one noticed, and questions about a cover-up are inevitable. The reality is often simpler. Diotrophes-like leaders are skilled manipulators whose behaviors are deliberately performed in order to be seen; they are stage-managed. A good conjuror can make you gasp at magic tricks on a grand, theatrical scale, but also fool you inches from your nose. But the conjuror always controls the angles and sight lines. So too with a Diotrephes. Who doesn't want to be seen as humble and charming and self-deprecating? What we don't see is what happens behind closed doors, in the one-to-ones, the staff appraisals, the elders' meetings. There, the mask is dropped. As was said to me recently concerning a high-profile minister: "He believes in the plurality of elders until he walks into the elders' meeting." Third John is a letter written about what happens behind closed doors.

BLINDSIDED

The second reason we may not spot a Diotrephes is that he passes the "teaching" test. It is striking that there is no accusation of wrong teaching. False doctrine, and false teachers, which are such an issue in both 1 and 2 John (1 John 2:19; 4:2–3; 2 John 7, 9), are notably absent. Third John teaches us to be alert on another front altogether. Those of us who are rightly concerned with doctrine can be blindsided. In thinking that doctrine is the only test which matters, we may allow a Diotrephes to flourish.

There is ample evidence that people who teach error can do so plausibly. The New Testament letters show how frequently churches fell for a false gospel, or a convenient gospel, or a culturally trimmed gospel, and church history shows how every generation must relearn the lesson. Every pastor knows that the church needs to be taught discernment, a task that is never complete. Our bookshelves are loaded with accounts of controversies past and outlines of controversies present. We must never relax our guard. We long to say, as John could in this letter, *I have no greater joy than to hear that my children are walking in the truth* (v. 4).

But not even all of that would protect us from a Diotrephes.

Here was a man who was in open breach with one of Jesus' appointed apostles, the "disciple Jesus loved," and yet there isn't a hint in this letter that he was doctrinally unsound.

How should we then frame this problem? Abusive power, bullying, self-willed leadership, all characteristic of Diotrephes, are evidently as aberrant to John as flat denial of the incarnation. He had addressed that doctrinal issue in 1 John, where false teaching had led in an awful logical chain (1 John 2:22–23; 4:19–21; 5:3) to lovelessness and disobedience. Here, though, while John portrays Diotrophes's power play as the stark difference between evil (v. 11, twice) and good (v. 11, twice), it is happening without any doctrinal deviation.

Diotrephes, thoroughly orthodox, loved to be first, and by that simple false step, wrecked a church.

In John's mind it is possible to be relationally wrong (evil, v. 11), while yet being doctrinally right. As I cast my mind over some evangelical abuses of power I have seen, some high profile and some much more local, they share the common pattern of having a clear, authoritative Bible teacher at the core. It seems to be a fault line, a persistent weakness, a genetic vulnerability in our churches.[6]

To meet the obvious rejoinder, yes, I do know plenty of clear, authoritative Bible teachers who have not been abusers of power. In my experience, they have been, thank God, the majority. This is as it should be, because from the outset Paul had laid out how those two criteria sit together closely, in a wider character set: an elder must be able to teach, not given to drunkenness, not violent but gentle, not quarrelsome (1 Tim 3:2–3). Paul required elders to be good teachers, and to be self-aware enough that they would not abuse the social power their position brings.

My late colleague Mike Ovey would also insist at this point that to teach false doctrine is itself an abuse of power (he labeled that "tyranny"), as is a refusal to correct it (he labeled that "anarchy," while pointing out that it too is a form of "tyranny").[7]

But none of those poisonous fruits which grow in the presence of false teaching, should stop us seeing the poisonous fruit of Diotrephes, which grows in the presence of true teaching, in an abusive leader.

God has designed his church to be led by faithful Bible teachers, and his people know that they need to be led and fed well. Yet that healthy symbiosis between teacher and taught, shepherd and sheep, lays us wide open to an almost imperceptible abuse of trust (we might wonder if even Diotrephes was aware at first) when the teacher/leader makes requirements that lie outside the loving shepherding of Jesus.

We cannot psychoanalyze Diotrephes. Had he always been a charismatic, domineering bully? Did he start to realize that he could gently use the power of inclusion and exclusion to get his way? Was he just a powerful

---

6. For obvious reasons, these tend to have been men, although biblically neither false teaching nor abusive leadership is a uniquely male sin (Rev 2:20–23).

7. Ovey, *Goldilocks Zone*. I recommend starting with the essays on Isaiah Berlin.

man, unaware of the impact of his personality? Was he a fraud, or self-deluded? He might have been any of those, and more. All we know is that he loved to be first.

We can go deeper still. While this is not a description of Diotrephes, it is a plausible application of the pattern. There have always been doctrinally orthodox Christians who love to pick a fight, whether with a surrounding culture, or other Christians. They are only happy when they have found something in another position with which to disagree or from which to distance themselves. They are professional denouncers, distinguishers, and heresy hunters. Some do so with a sad smile, showing their disappointment with the foolishness of error, others do so with glee, apparently relishing the punishment of the slightest slip of the tongue.

The proliferation of Christian publishing on and offline has only exacerbated the problem. False teaching is ubiquitous—it always has been—but now it is delivered straight onto our screens. More distressingly, in order to get a hearing amidst the white noise of the internet, it is necessary to be different, to stand out, to shout louder. It's a platform that favors the noisy, the populist, the aggressive soundbite.

Again, we must be on the guard against false teaching—but that is not the point at issue. Rather, this issue is more subtle. People use the banner of doctrinal correctness as a means of gathering a group around them, with themselves as its only safe guardian.

Diotrephes's way of working was to cut anyone and everyone down to below his level, regardless of their common beliefs. He needed to stand out, and he needed others to acknowledge that he stood out. He would never be a team player, let alone a loyal follower; his only way of working was to be first, and he would dismiss anyone—John included—who refused to acquiesce. No one could even be a respected equal. Certainly no one could hold him to account. No one could even bring good news from another church. If you did not let him lead, you would be excommunicated.

CONTRAST

Here, then, is the contrast, between collaborative, connected John, and domineering, controlling Diotrephes. As so often, the one with the right to the authority exercises a quiet command, where the one who has seized it, does so viciously. And Gaius stands in between, working out who was right, and what the price of loyalty to each would cost.

The close of the letter is full of John's genuine warmth of Christian fellowship: *I have much to write to you, but I do not want to do so with pen and ink. I hope to see you soon, and we will talk face to face* (literally, "mouth to mouth"). *Peace to you. The friends here send their greetings. Greet the friends there by name* (v. 13). There is individual closeness (*I . . . you . . . I . . . you . . . we . . .*), but also a general atmosphere of kindness: *The friends here . . . the friends there. . . .* Contrast the atmosphere in the church: *Diotrephes, who loves to be first, will not welcome us . . . spreading malicious nonsense about us. Not satisfied with that, he even refuses to welcome other believers. He also stops those who want to do so and puts them out of the church* (vv. 9–10).

APPLICATION QUESTIONS

Perhaps, for pastors, we could propose three tests from this letter, one from each of the three main characters:

1. *John*—Is my ministry marked by friendship and love, or am I aloof and distant? How do I react when my best intentions are rebuffed or misread? What is my attitude towards those who are hostile to my ministry?

2. *Gaius*—Am I willing to make a stand on principle, or am I swayed by those around me? How would I choose between John and Diotrephes, or would I try to find a middle way? Would I risk Diotrephes's anger as I tried to rescue people from his influence?

3. *Diotrephes*—Do I love to be first? How do I react when others have the success, the platform, the spotlight I crave? How do I react when I'm challenged?

BIBLIOGRAPHY

DeGroat, Chuck. *When Narcissism Comes to Church: Healing Your Community from Emotional and Spiritual Abuse*. Downers Grove, IL: InterVarsity, 2020.

Green, Christopher. *The Message of the Church: Assemble the People Before Me*. Downers Grove, IL: InterVarsity, 2013.

Kruse, Colin G. *The Letters of John*. The Pillar New Testament Commentary. Leicester, UK: Apollos, 2000.

Ovey, Michael. *The Goldilocks Zone: Collected Writings of Michael J. Ovey*. Edited by Christopher Green. London: InterVarsity, 2018.

Yarbrough, Robert W. *1–3 John*. Baker Exegetical Commentary on the New Testament. Grand Rapids, MI: Baker Academic, 2008.

12

Mentors, Not Masters

Marcus Honeysett

> How do we prevent healthy, discipling relationships that bear a good concern for a person's wellbeing from descending into those that control, domineer, and abuse?
>
> *And Saul's son Jonathan went to David at Horesh and helped him to find strength in God.* (1 Sam 23:16)

INTRODUCTION—WHAT IS MENTORING?

THE AIM OF CHRISTIAN mentoring is to help a person grow in their relationship with Jesus, the chief shepherd. Mentors are merely under-shepherds strengthening people in their union with Christ and helping them to work out that union in their lives. Our job is not to point them to us or to replicate ourselves in them, but to help them know, love, and submit to the Lord, and to participate in his purposes for their lives and for the world. The purpose is that mentees become mature disciples.

Mentoring is a fluid, vague, and nebulous term in both secular practice and the Christian world. Even if it carries a clear set of connotations and expectations in, say, teaching or the world of business mentoring, those assumptions are rarely exactly mirrored in other spheres.

Here, then, are several scriptural verses that contribute to a biblical foundation for the task of specifically Christian mentoring.

- Paul tells the Philippian church that he wants to work with them for their progress and joy in the faith. The aim of his relationship with them is that their "joy in Christ Jesus will overflow on account of him" (Phil 1:25–26).

- Paul takes this a step further with the Corinthian church, writing that he works with them for their joy in God, and that this joy produces firm and secure faith. Faith that endures through trials is firmly founded on joy in God (2 Cor 1:24).

- Paul's best example of this working in practice is perhaps his reminder to Timothy of all he has shared with him: the gospel teaching, his way of life, his purpose, faith, patience, love, endurance, persecutions, sufferings, not to mention the events that occurred in various cities (2 Tim 3:10). He took Timothy under his wing and immersed him in whatever he did, as a father would for his son in the gospel.

Mentoring, here, is a deliberate, personal relationship to help another person grow in God, enjoy God in his grace, and grow in participating in the mission of God. The Bible, however, never uses the word mentoring. The better biblical idea is discipling or spiritual parenting. It is an intentional connection to foster growth, with the foundation being the grace and joy of the Lord.

MENTORING AND POWER DYNAMICS

There are essentially two kinds of power dynamics in ministry church relationships:

- Formal, legitimated power. This is authority granted by a legitimizing body—for our purposes typically a church or Christian organization—to carry out delegated responsibilities. Formal power and authority is, theoretically at least, accountable to agreed principles and oversight, normally plural or collegial, and is readily transparent to scrutiny.

- Informal, relational power. This is the authority that a person carries by dint of relational credibility and trustworthiness, as well as greater life experience. It is a vital and valuable component without which much Christian ministry simply would not happen. It might well be legitimated by the same body that legitimates formal authority but with the notable difference of being far less transparent. Positively, this can foster the safety needed for exploring confidential issues. Negatively, it is less open to accountability.

How might Christian mentoring fit within this scheme?

Scenario 1: Discipling another believer for their spiritual growth. A friendly advisory relationship with encouragement, support, role modeling, reflection on the gospel, and on being a disciple of Jesus.

Scenario 2: A leader who is discipling another believer for their spiritual growth (just as in scenario 1), but with the additional factor of being an employee of the church or organization.

In the first scenario, mentoring occurs entirely within the sphere of informal relational authority. In the second, however, the mentor works within structures of formal supervision, line management, training, communication, evaluation, and review. The interplay between formal and informal power dynamics at play is thus more complex. Any church leader who has had to remove a junior team member after a period of mentoring knows the pain and conflict that results from this interplay, creating a tension between pastoral care for the individual and a formal responsibility to the church.

It is useful to tease out some of the differences between these two mentoring scenarios, because the power dynamics are not the same.

1. Mentoring as Part of Informal Ministry

The aim of discipling is that a person is delighted with the Lord, enjoying his word, and participating in his great purposes. There are few things more enjoyable in ministry than a healthy discipling relationship on the lines of the one Paul had with Timothy.

I had the privilege of discipling a young believer. Simon started with very few obvious skills, but the light in his eyes when he talked about Jesus was utterly infectious. He was incredibly teachable—including when he thought of questions about the Lord at 3:00 a.m. and thought nothing of picking up the phone! He was impetuous and did what he thought God was telling him to do regardless of whether I thought it was wise. Thankfully he was also good at repenting! What Simon most needed was a person to take him under their wing, provide a gentle on-ramp to try things out and to cover his back when things went wrong.

It is easy for the person in the discipling role to assume that because no formal power is at play in the relationship, there is little or no power imbalance. But there always is. Power imbalances are inevitable, and not necessarily bad. An apprentice should not have equal authority with their trainer if they want to learn anything. There may well be a high degree of influence born of trust, which itself is a non-transparent form of power and can be misused. For example, I do not report to the formal church authority structures of leaders whom I mentor. Were I to encourage one of them to do something that would be considered illegitimate by their church they don't have to do what I suggest, but it would still be a misuse of power on my part because I have influence with them. Where power imbalances exist in informal relationships it is important to clarify mutual expectations of what the relationship provides and where any boundaries lie.

Even when a mentor is oblivious to power imbalances, the mentee may be all too aware of them. The combination of experience, personality, credibility, gifting, and personal investment means a junior (or even a peer) is susceptible to taking on trust what the more experienced person says. It can be a small step from this to a relationship of unhealthy codependency in which the more junior enjoys the company, investment, and patronage of the more senior, and the senior values the appreciation and respect of someone who acts on their advice.

The possibilities for subtle manipulation are obvious. Mark Stirling notes how easy it is to tip from leading a person to grow in maturity in their own right, to influencing them to do what I think they should do. Additionally, the slightest hint of damage to, or even termination of, the relationship if the mentee rejects advice, then informal, nontransparent influence risks degenerating into manipulation. The key principle, in Stirling's words, is that:

> People need to be free to make their own bad decisions rather than my good decisions. While I might be right, I can influence you to make a decision against conscience. And I might be wrong. And you just doing what I think is right doesn't lead to your growth in maturity.

Those with a greater degree of relational power and influence therefore need to be fully aware of our influence in order to take every possible step not to abuse it, intentionally or unwittingly. The point of mentoring is never to empower ourselves but always to empower others. It is a supportive relationship where the support goes one way. It is critical for Scenario 1 mentees to grasp clearly that if they decide to act differently from what we suggest, it is not relationship-ending.

2. Mentoring in a Formal Ministry Context

The second type of mentoring relationship occurs within a formal structure. Ministry supervision typically contains the elements of spiritual formation and encouragement as a disciple, as per any other discipling relationship, but is supplemented with a variety of training, coaching, and line management elements, often in the same meeting.

There are advantages to mentoring in a formal context. There is often greater clarity about the provision of formal training and development outcomes, for example. It is also more transparent and accountable to checks, balances, and scrutiny. On the downside, the power imbalances are often greater. A bishop once told me, "I took the job as bishop assuming it would allow me to exercise my gift of encouraging and caring for clergy. In fact, it has done the exact opposite. They no longer seek me out when they are in need because of the power imbalance. I want to care for them, but they see me as the person with the power of hire-and-fire." Mentees can feel that there is only a certain degree to which the relationship can ever be completely safe, especially if it involves record-keeping. A group of clergy said, "we can't talk to our bishop if we are struggling with sin even if they are a good, helpful, safe person. While we might trust them, we don't want those conversations on our records to be read later by whoever eventually replaces the bishop."

A tension arises because the mentor in formal mentoring situations has multiple responsibilities: to the organization and its goals as well as to the individual. When these are all lined up and progressing in the same direction there is no difficulty. But when pastoral care for the individual conflicts with the needs of the organization, power imbalances are inevitable. And just because they are legitimized by the organization doesn't mean they are publicly transparent or easy to navigate.

"David" was radically underperforming in his ministry role. Worse, he was actively, privately dismissive of the team leader, his supervisor, and other team members. After extensive efforts to help him change, it became obvious that he lacked a teachable spirit, with the only remaining option being to remove him from the team. The difficulty was that David was popular in the church and had a public image that belied what was going on in private. The supervisor and team leader had to tease out their various responsibilities to David, the wider team, the church, and the mission and decided the appropriate thing was to dismiss David but not reveal the extent of his character flaws to the church. David, by contrast, drummed up support by presenting himself as the powerless victim of powerful leaders.

The leaders were legitimized by the church to mentor David and, finally, to remove him. Strictly speaking they could legitimately have revealed the reasons for dismissal and saved themselves some heartache, but it was pastorally wiser not to and to absorb the resulting flack. The only thing the mentors had to protect them in this situation was the legitimizing structure and the good process and policies that were followed. Those who had the authority to scrutinize the process were content that all had been done well and could publicly defend both the process and the leaders.

The combination of mentoring for spiritual growth and line management is complicated. At any point the role might be: boss, kingdom colleague, point of accountability, pastoral support, servant, shepherd, example and role model, trainer, reviewer, and a host of other things. Few other organizational roles are as complex, and the elements don't always fit well together.

Under normal circumstances there should not be much conflict and discipling of a team member for their spiritual walk will be an easy and frictionless part of wider ministry supervision. Jesus was primarily a person-oriented mentor rather than a task- or organization-oriented one. The disciples learned by being with him, being formed by him, and then being sent out to imitate him. He gave them practical opportunities to rely on God. That is the way workers still learn best. The primary task of supervisor-mentors, therefore, is similar: to help team members walk with Jesus and be sent out with him, doing what he did, with practical opportunities to rely on God.

Supervisor-mentors may often wonder whether a person's prayer life, Bible habits, church relationships, struggles with sin or marriages fall inside or outside their purview. This is trickier in the formal setting than in informal relationships. It is easy for team members to think that churches want to own their entire life, as is common in vision- and values-driven organizations. Good mentors wish to disciple, knowing that is a whole-life category, but do not wish to be invasive. It is no longer just about one person helping another to walk with Jesus, but about an organization having access to—and possibly power over—highly personal areas of life.

Once again, clarity of mutual expectation is crucial. What one person sees as a desire for accountability, another may read as inappropriate and unwanted intrusion or "heavy shepherding." Such intrusion may be sincerely motivated but is easily open to abuse. Different team members may have different desires and expectations. Mentor-supervisors should not necessarily expect new team members to be open to a high degree of life-on-life involvement just because that is the expected norm among existing team members.

A (different) bishop remarked to me, "I realized when I became bishop that there were certain things a vicar could talk to me about before, that now were off-limits. However, I wanted to make sure they still had access to help and counsel in those areas so I appointed a chaplain for them who was outside the line management structure, did not report to me, and thus was safe." This is often a good compromise, albeit a hard one to accept for those who, thanks to increasing seniority, have much wisdom and experience to share. They have to recognize that they can no longer enjoy the same kind of relationship with juniors that they once enjoyed when they were peers.

It is equally important to have clear process for when organizational relationships go wrong. Christians can be remarkably naïve, assuming that discipline, grievance, and whistleblowing processes are less necessary in the church because everyone will act Christianly. It is common for churches to have far less-well-developed protections than secular organizations such as ACAS, for example, on the innocent assumption they will never be needed.

But we are foolish to assume that abuse of power and position will never happen in our church, or that we ourselves are immune. Nobody ever imagines they will become an abuser, but that's exactly what happens to some. Supervisor-mentor relationships are an obvious place where it can happen. Where organizational power differentials exist, leaders do have opportunities to dominate, intimidate, or exploit, even justifying their behavior with claims to God-given authority or implicit threats of using organizational leverage in the worst cases. We are wise to make ourselves as accountable as possible and never to assume it cannot happen to us.

A Mentoring Process

As an aside, while mentoring is a life-on-life exercise and by definition flexible, it can also be useful to have a standard procedure in mind when approaching intentional mentoring sessions. Mine consists of reminding myself beforehand of 1 Sam 23:16 quoted at the head of this chapter and then trying to help a person using this process:

- Pray
- Listen
- Explore
- Decide
- Act
- Review
- Encourage

I also keep a list of helpful (if blindingly obvious!) exploratory questions to hand, including:

- What would you like to discuss?
- What do you see?

- What do you think about that?
- What questions do you have?
- What would improve the current situation?
- What interrupts things for you?
- What does the Bible say?
- What ideas do you have?
- What might some good approaches be?
- Who could help you?
- What help, resources, support, and encouragement do you need?
- What do you recommend?
- What have you learned?
- How can I support you?

Mentoring and Wisdom

Policies and procedures, mutual expectations and clarity provide a degree of protection from misuse of power in mentoring relationships. They enable scrutiny and accountability if things go wrong, but they aren't infallible. It is impossible to legislate for wisdom, and the greater the potential for power imbalance the greater the need for wisdom becomes.

Thankfully, the way discipling relationships work between adults and minors is now carefully and comprehensively determined by safeguarding legislation and policies. One reason for this volume is that in the last few years historical abuse by powerful evangelical church leaders against minors over whom they held a huge power advantage has come to light. Safeguarding procedures in churches and organizations make that much harder today—though not impossible—by ensuring that adult-minor relationships happen transparently and publicly, governed by principles and policies, whereby those in positions of authority are regularly, legally scrutinized.

What policies cannot do is legislate for our hearts and emotions. A lesson from the safeguarding of children is to set the safeguards a long way back from danger. Two places in which there are obvious power issues at play are the formal ministry context already discussed and discipling relationships between men and women.

In the latter case it is often less clear how to act wisely. One approach is to legislate a blanket ban on cross-sex mentoring relationships, deeming the potential for emotional dependency or manipulation (either way) to present too great a risk. Most people who have been in ministry for a while know what it is like to have someone find them attractive simply because of their role. Moreover, when ministers do fall into adultery it is common to find that they worked for an intensive period with little relief from pressure or criticism and then someone offered affection and a listening ear. It is not hard to see how a mentoring relationship can provide a context where such emotional vulnerability can override better judgement. The downside of the blanket ban, however, is that it can mean, in some types of churches, that women have far less access to mentoring than do men. It just might also indicate a church culture in which women's perspectives and voices are rarely, if ever, heard.

In general, I am not in favor of blanket-banning things that Scripture doesn't. But I am in favor of recognizing where Scripture tells us our hearts are vulnerable to self-deception, or where there might be any hint of immorality that might cast a stain on the gospel. Moreover, there is often a paradox in which the more experienced a leader becomes the less self-aware they may become about the emotional affects they have on other people. They can see themselves as just one disciple trying to help another, and not as anything special. While this is true, of course, it is easy to become unconscious and unmindful to the fact that they occupy a more powerful position in the power dynamic. It is when leaders become unmindful that they can cross boundaries unknowingly and unintentionally .

How do we set boundaries not according to law but according to wisdom? Some answer the cross-sex mentoring question by insisting their spouse is also present or at least nearby. But that doesn't work in all situations, not least when the mentor isn't married.

While every situation is different, we should carefully apply the same wise principles of transparency, visibility, and scrutiny. Once again, few people set out expecting to manipulate and control others, or to be manipulated ourselves (because the temptation can go both ways). However, we are never our own best arbiters of wisdom. The heart is deceitful; nobody is immune from temptation. So, good practice for everyone's good might include the following.

1. Protective policies that are easily understood, readily accessible, simple to use, and corporately overseen.
2. Well-communicated, mutually understood boundaries, expectations, timescales, and purpose.

3. Visible, and perhaps public, settings for mentoring relationships. A coffee shop is better than a private house and several people meeting together may be preferable to one-to-one.

4. Agreement and scrutiny of our practice by other people, with clear processes if mentee, mentor, or third parties sense anything is out of order. Other pastoral professions insist (even legally) on the provision of third-party scrutiny through professional pastoral supervision. It is rarely possible to provide this professionally in Christian mentoring settings, but it is nevertheless wise to create equivalent scrutinizing mechanisms.

5. A collegial approach to resolving gaps in mentoring and pastoral provision if wisdom dictates that we should not personally mentor a particular individual or group. Titus 2, in particular, seems to suggest that women are best mentored by more mature women (and not by Titus). If there is a gap in provision for the discipling of women it may be revealing that we need to give more attention to equipping and releasing more women to do it.

We do not want to be so cautious that some individuals or groups are left unable to access provision that would be helpful for their growth. But neither do we want to dance near an indeterminate cliff edge, as if testing our own moral and emotional resilience were a sensible thing to do. It is far better to have fences some way back from the top of a cliff than an ambulance down in the valley.

DANGER SIGNS

Relational power is usually invisible to those who wield it. Leaders can think we are just being ourselves, unaware of the power differentials that others perceive or are affected by. We rarely stop to consider what it would look like to abuse our power.

In conclusion, then, here is a list of telltale signs of being on an unhealthy trajectory with respect to power. They are not limited to mentoring relationships, and inevitably it is easier to see these things in others than in ourselves. Therefore, it is vitally important to consider whether we have trusted people who are close enough and with the necessary responsibility to point out these things in us. Or have we instead grown used to acting unilaterally, independent from legitimate structures of oversight and scrutiny?

There are no foolproof means of avoiding or arresting a healthy discipling relationship sliding into control or domination, especially if someone is determined. However, the surest protections come from ensuring that collegiality, transparency, and accountability are foundational to mentoring, both in principle and in practice.

1. Character

- I see everything in black and white terms. Questioning my judgement or decisionmaking is disloyalty.
- I retreat easily into aggressive defensiveness and find it hard to apologize sincerely.
- I have a sense of personal leadership entitlement or that I am the most important person in the organization.
- I have a sense of insecurity, feeling threatened or intimidated by talented people.
- I struggle to trust others and therefore find it difficult to listen to or release others to exceed me.

2. Indispensability

- I have a God-given mission; *therefore* disagreeing with me is disagreeing with God.
- I am gifted and experienced at this; *therefore* nobody else can legitimately hold me accountable because they don't understand my job. E.g., only professional, paid ministers can really understand so others cannot legitimately question them or have authority in their areas of competence.
- I can see what needs to be done more clearly than others; *therefore* I should be the one who defines reality, the mission, the ends.
- The church needs strong and decisive leadership; *therefore* I need to deliver that even if others vacillate or oppose it.
- I am confident that my intentions are good and have no concerns about my own integrity; *therefore* I am justified in using unaccountable means.

- I am a loving person, dedicated to service, conforming myself to the word of God. I never ask of anyone else what I am unprepared to do. In fact, I make greater sacrifices than most; *therefore* people should follow me out of respect for my greater sacrifice

- I am the smartest person in the room; I am the (best/only) trained one; *therefore* others should listen to me, not the other way round

- In a worldly career, I would have had status and compensations like many of my contemporaries. However, in Christian ministry I frequently feel taken for granted, abused, and uncared for. People expect me and my family to make sacrifices for the gospel that they themselves would not make; *therefore* I should have some status in this community to compensate for what I have sacrificed.

3. Leadership

These are beliefs and behaviors that concern a leader's relationship with the church, organization, or team. They are all concerned with control, the avoidance of oversight or the undermining of legitimate means of scrutiny. They reveal leaders' temptations to override structures of collegiality or to presume they are owed unconditional loyalty.

A. Control.

- I should have the most powerful or decisive voice on all issues.
- I should exercise control over all decision-making.
- I have the right to communicate on behalf of team members things they have not agreed, on the assumption that they will fall into line under a duty of corporate accountability and personal loyalty.

B. Avoidance.

- Oversight structures are a hindrance to my ministry, so it is fair I try to evade, avoid, ignore, neutralize, or control them.
- Negligence, grievance, or whistleblowing policies are unnecessary and do not apply to me.

- Standard conflict of interest protocols are unnecessary and do not apply to me.
- I ensure that any accountability structures which are in place rely on people with less influence than me, in some way dependent on me, or who can easily be manipulated, ignored, or dismissed.

4. Defensiveness

The following is a range of responses when a leader's overarching concern is for survival in the job or the fulfillment of a personal vision for accomplishing the mission.

A. *Subtle, self-protective behaviors.*

- I create dependency upon myself within the organization or community.
- I gather around me an inner ring guaranteed to support me and back my plans.
- I assume that those without my experience or position lack the necessary insight to evaluate my ministry decisions.
- I employ *"faux-vulnerability"*[1] (defined as "domination camouflaged as meekness") to get my way.

B. *Overt controlling behaviors.*

- This manifests as the deliberate control, subversion, or corruption of systems, along with evasion of standard protocols and oversight systems. Leaders become their own referees.
- Leadership may be plural constitutionally or on paper, but does not function as such in practice.
- Frequent use of divine calling to confer an exclusive or unassailable right of command.
- Turning privacy into secrecy, especially to conceal decisions from legitimate accountability.

---

1. See DeGroat, "Fauxnerability."

- Actively covering tracks through lies, dishonesty, or deceit.
- Hypersensitivity in areas where we may have made mistake and inability to admit failure (for a variety of reasons, but often out of fear of reputational damage).
- Deliberate isolation and making accessibility difficult for all but the inner ring.

C. Aggressive behaviors.

- Public disempowerment of others, especially if perceived as threats (e.g., due to gifting).
- Victim-blaming transference: "I am disappointed you would think that"; i.e., it's you, not me. You misunderstand the situation or misunderstand me, or lack the necessary facts or judgement.
- Silencing opposition, ensuring those who raise concerns about me, my behavior or decisions are ignored or discredited. Encouraging people to self-censor or using others to censor them on my behalf.
- The use of nondisclosure agreements (NDAs).
- Characterizing those who question or reject the leader's vision as showing a lack of commitment or possessing character flaws.
- Expressing anger, frustration, or disappointment so as to demean or diminish others.
- Resorting to intimidation, threats, coercion, and moral blackmail.

5. Exploitation

These indicate that leaders have become more concerned with their mission goals than the people involved in achieving them. People are treated as tools, a means to an end.

- The use of nepotism or favoritism to create a vanguard of ready defenders, especially by gathering younger leaders who are dependent on the leader's patronage for advancement.
- Lobbying for support outside the organization or through private appeals to some individuals within it, in order to subvert or overrule

legitimate structures. Mentees may be particularly vulnerable to such requests. The use of soft, relational power beyond the constraints on formal authority is itself an abuse of position and trust.

- The offer, whether implicit or explicit, of advancement, access, influence, or status in order to advance the leader's agenda. This can degenerate into a "purity spiral" whereby greater acquiescence to the leader's vision and values is rewarded.

- Once people cease to be useful, they are ignored, dropped, or excluded from the inner ring.

Reflection Questions.

- What power do you have in mentoring situations: Formally? By dint of trust or personality?
- What would constitute overuse of that power? Where are the points at which you have to take care not to manipulate?
- How would you know if you were doing so? Who could (and would) challenge you if the need arose?
- Which, if any, of the danger signs listed in this chapter most resonate with you? Who can you talk to about these?
- How can you bring as great a degree of transparency as possible to your mentoring relationships?

BIBLIOGRAPHY

DeGroat, Chuck. "Fauxnerability in the Church: What Is It? What Do We Do About It?" *Chuck DeGroat* (blog), June 11, 2018. https://www.chuckdegroat.net/chuck-degroat-blog/2018/06/11/fauxnerability-in-the-church-what-is-it-what-do-we-do-about-it.

13

Of God and God-Men

Sushila Ailawadi

SHILPA[1] AND HER SISTER *were a part of a congregation of believers along with their parents. The church was under the leadership of a pastor deeply venerated by his simple flock. When she was in her early teens, he had rented out the small room above his apartment to her family. Her father did not have a job and was a harsh abusive man. Her mother was the only earning family member. Before long, the pastor befriended Shilpa and groomed her to believe in the sanctity of his demands. He began to rape her at every opportunity. The family was dependent on his goodwill for the roof over their heads. He exploited this fully and kept Shilpa fearful of what he could do should she divulge anything. He went on later to abuse the younger sister as well.*

INTRODUCTION

As a woman growing up in a country deeply rooted in a male-dominated worldview, I have often felt at complete odds with myself. Made in God's image, created as a counterpart, set free through his precious blood and yet so bound, trapped in a world that denies my equal worth.

Modern India is full of ambiguities. It has a colonial past, an expanding urban population with a growing, insistent demand for recognition of its place in the new global order, alongside a rural population with an unchanged, ancient mindset. New and old exist side-by-side, apparently incompatible, but nevertheless in one nation.

1. All names are changed throughout this chapter.

The church too, steeped in the contradictions between the natural and the redeemed, is fragmented by its inability to see itself as called out from its cultural setting. It is therefore more shaped by that culture than it realizes. There is much to unlearn and reimagine, immersed in the dominant culture of the nation, yet attempting to live counter culturally.

In Indian patriarchal culture, it seems impossible for us as women to be equally yoked with our brothers in ministry. It is an insurmountable task for women to engage in any kind of public or private discourse and be received. At the core, we are a species divided within itself and there seems to be no difference between the church and the world outside.

Power abuse can thrive in an environment of such imbalance. Wherever power is concentrated exclusively in the hands of one group over the other, oppression and exploitation are a constant danger.

Jesus threatened the powers of his day simply because he did not play by their rules. He did not cater to their thinking and denounced unequivocally what they stood for. He had not come to be served, but to serve (Mark 10:45). His ways have always been to wrap a towel around his waist and wash the feet of those who follow him (John 13:5). The power on the throne of heaven is that of the slain Lamb (Rev 5:6).

Born in poverty and vulnerability, far from the courts of the kings of his time, he became a servant and "poured himself out" (Phil 2:7). Jesus' attitude does not give a competitive advantage in a world where leadership brings all sorts of privileges and perks. With 1.3 billion people in my country, one learns to compete from an early age.

At every level and in all our relationships, the politics of the power-play corrupts us. This profoundly affects us in our relationships as men and women. Something needs to be recovered in the way we follow God. We have forgotten how to be good stewards of position and authority, forgotten about servant leadership and the priesthood of all believers. This article explores male abuse of power against women in my context, and its effect on the believing community.[2]

---

2. Eds. Throughout this essay, Sushila clearly refers to the term "patriarchy" as shorthand for the abuse of power by men in their treatment of women. In multiple other places in this volume the point is made that power imbalance in and of itself is not necessarily wrong, but the exercise of power must be redeemed and conformed to the pattern set out in Phil 2:5–11 (see chap. 1).

CONTEXT

Social wealth[3] is a commodity that depends largely upon social connectivity and social status. Both connectivity and status are measures of power: the greater the connections, the greater the status, the greater the power, and social wealth of a person in any community.

Various factors contribute to social wealth: the color of our skin, our looks, our nationality, our ethnicity, our education, our bank balance, our skills, amongst other things. Our ability to capitalize on these gives us ascendancy over others.

In a traditional patriarchal society, maleness is the single most defining factor of social wealth. The man has indelible status by virtue of being male; the man has greater physical, economic, and social mobility; he has the connections, he is confident, he represents the family, he controls the finances. He has exposure to the workings of the outside world where the woman may not. Such sharp imbalance creates the potential for a high degree of gender power abuse.

The male generally in such a culture learns to believe his maleness makes him superior. He *"internalizes his dominance."*[4] The woman is subordinate and must serve the man. Women and children are owned by the men in the family. He is indulged and pampered and, in some cases, even worshiped by his female siblings and offered all the devotion due to a deity.[5] The women, if the family is economically constrained, get the leftovers and will even do without at mealtimes. A family that has only girls keeps on trying for a boy. A wife redeems her status by having a son, the preferred child.

In such a context, to be born a female is a crime. It is seen as a shame and a blot on the woman to give birth to a girl.[6] This is enacted many times in delivery wards in hospitals: joy, celebration, and euphoria when a boy is

---

3. Social wealth must be distinguished from social capital. Social capital is good will, fellowship, sympathy, and social intercourse among the individuals and families who make up a social unit (Putnam, *Bowling Alone*). Since wealth is associated with power, social wealth of an individual or community is the dominance an individual or community has over others by virtue of possessions that are perceived as socially valuable. This could take several forms including color, nationality, ethnicity, caste, and class, normally a mixture of two or more of these.

4. Internalized Dominance: Where individuals are unconsciously conditioned to believe they are superior or inferior in status, affecting social interaction. Internalized domination or dominance is likely to involve feelings of superiority, normalcy, and self-righteousness, together with guilt, fear, projection, and denial of demonstrated inequity.

5. From much counseling experience in my context.

6. *It's a Girl: The Three Deadliest Words in the World* is a 2012 documentary film which explores the practice of female infanticide. This is a must-see for all those who would like some insight into what happens in India and China to the girl child.

born, whereas deep dismay, disappointment, and shame when the child is a girl. A girl is in danger from the moment she is conceived and identified as a female in the womb. Someone has well said, *the three most dangerous words in the world are, It's a girl!* Sex selective abortions have led to highly skewed male female ratios in many parts of India.[7, 8] A girl is in danger of being bought and sold and considered a drain on a family's resources. A female child in traditional families will be fed less than her brother and may even be starved to death. In some cases, local midwives have been paid to kill a girl child. Nobel Laureate Amartya Sen estimated in 1992 a hundred million missing women because of these practices worldwide, thirty-seven million of whom were in India alone.

Families often have double standards for how boys and girls are raised. They smile benignly when their sons get drunk and mess around with women. Boys are allowed all kinds of freedom and can do pretty much as they please. Girls, on the other hand, are curtailed in all kinds of ways, from their mobility to educational opportunities and will even often be blamed for crimes committed against them. Many rapes have resulted from just such a mindset. Listen to these comments in response to rape and rape laws:

> "Boys are boys, they make mistakes."
> "Rape is a social crime which depends on men and women. Sometimes it is right, sometimes it is wrong."[9]

The above are examples of indifference to women, who are perceived as inferior beings, while perpetrators of crimes against women are treated with gentle benevolence, just because they are male. It is no wonder that the Thomson Reuters Foundation voted India as the most unsafe country for women in the world, surpassing war-torn Syria and Afghanistan.[10]

Patriarchy is not confined to gender alone; a patriarchal culture is founded on the principles of power and dominance, and so naturally leads to societies built on oppression, exploitation, injustice, and conflict, the likes of which have been sadly common in human history.

Part of this narcissistic heritage is that

---

7. "India's sex ratio, or the number of females per 1,000 males, declined to 896 in 2015–17 from 898 in 2014–16, according to a government survey" (Tripathi, "Declining Sex Ratio," para. 1).

8. "In 2011, male to female ratio for Daman & Diu was 618 females per 1000 males. Male to female ratio of Daman & Diu fell gradually from 1,143 females per 1000 males in 1921 to 618 females per 1000 males in 2011" (see https://knoema.com/atlas/India/Daman-and-Diu/Male-to-female-ratio).

9. Madan, "'Boys Will Be Boys,'" paras. 4, 5.

10. Goldsmith and Beresford, "Exclusive: India Most Dangerous Country for Women with Sexual Violence Rife—Global Poll."

a person's self-worth is almost exclusively determined by the rank he occupies in the profoundly hierarchical nature of society. If the perception of another person has first to do with gender ("Is this individual male or female?"), followed by age ("Is he/she young or old?") and by other such markers of identity, then in India the determination of relative rank ("Is this person superior or inferior to me?") remains very near the top of subconscious questions evoked in an interpersonal encounter.[11]

So a patriarchal culture is, by the above definition, also an oppressive and exploitative culture, desensitized to its marginalized, as well as dehumanising in its treatment of them. Such cultures do not understand the notion of rights when applied to women and children.

One of the first girls who came to our home for those rescued from abuse and exploitation, was seventeen-year old Seema. She was pregnant with the child of her grandfather. It took her a long time to open up about what had happened to her. There was also some confusion about which one of the other men in her family was the father. She had to flee the family just to stay alive.

Basanthi, another girl, was not so fortunate. Someone in the village raced to our house to request us to take a burn victim to the hospital in our vehicle. She was already dead by the time we reached her house. Her weeping, grief-stricken family had seen this as their only recourse, rather than face the shame of an unmarried, pregnant daughter.

These stories are repeated in thousands of lives. Some girls who have been raped are given in marriage to the first old man who fancies a young wife. They have no say in who they marry anyway, but once publicly disgraced, they are viewed as damaged goods and fit only to be discarded, though they may have already been victims of incest and rape within their households, used and abused till the day they marry.

Victims of sex abuse end up paying the price for the crime of another many times over. They are often killed with no questions asked, or survive deeply scarred and tormented by what they have suffered. The shame and the blame is theirs alone. The punishment heaped on them is so unendurable that suicide is often seen as a way out. Domestic violence, rape as a form of revenge, rape as a way of subjugation and control is not an occasional aberration. It is a daily horror faced by many.

Vimla, another woman, came to us for counseling after she was raped and threatened by the local landowners in her village. The tiny hut where she lived with her young son and daughter was snatched from her and she

---

11. Kakar and Poggendorf-Kakar, *Indians*, 8.

was driven from her home. Men in her village had eyed her small land holding the moment her husband died. She was too scared to go back and fight for her rights. Fear for her life and that of her children forced her to relocate and seek a livelihood elsewhere. She lost her husband, and with him, the right to keep what belonged to her.

Honor killings of girls who have been raped have led to no consequences for men in most of the cases.[12] There is no recognition of the rights of children and women, no rights for the weak and the vulnerable. Instead, there is a "might is right" mindset that eventually leads to no clear understanding of what is moral and what is not. This leads to greater oppression and injustice. Patriarchy has deep spiritual consequences.

THE CHURCH

What of the church in India? Does the church subscribe to this treatment of women? Is the church also oppressive, or is the church free of the shackles of such practices?

"There are six beliefs present within traditional Christian thinking that have aided perpetrators in rationalizing their behavior when it comes to abuse:

- The first belief is that God intends for men to dominate and for women and children to submit
- The second belief is that because of her role in the Fall, woman is morally inferior to man
- The third belief is that children are inherently evil and must have their wills broken
- The fourth belief is that marriage is to be preserved at all costs
- The fifth belief is that suffering is a Christian virtue
- The final belief is that Christians must promptly forgive those who sin against them."[13]

In a traditional context, though perhaps not uniquely so, I would add a few more beliefs and practices:

- A woman is created solely to serve men.

---

12. See Xavier, "Honour Killings."
13. Franz, "Power, Patriarchy and Sexual Abuse," 6–7.

- Good wives look after their husbands and never complain about their behavior, just modify their own to suit their context.
- A girl born into a family is someone else's property, as she will leave one day to marry another. She is the property of a future husband and his family, who are to be paid to take her away. As such she is a liability and does not deserve the same care as the male who remains with the family.
- Women are objects owned by men, the symbol of honor in a family. One way to assert ascendancy over and humiliate a man is to publicly rape the women in his household.
- Domestic abuse is the norm, to be expected in any family. Where this is not present, the man is weak, has no control over his woman, and is scorned by others.
- It is usually the woman's fault when men pass lewd comments at her or molest her, because of her manner of dress, or her having spurred him on in some way.
- The highest call for a woman is to nurture her family. It is her responsibility even if she's working in a job to supplement the family income.
- Single women are therefore inferior to married women for they do not subscribe to this call and have no man or children to serve.
- Children have no rights, they are the property of the man in the family

The more traditional the society, the more fixed a belief system. In a culture where patriarchy is the norm, these beliefs taken together wreak havoc among the vulnerable. Unfortunately, all the above beliefs are present in most circles, including Christian.[14]

The deep-seated conviction in parts of the church in India that it was the woman who led the man astray in that primordial past has also led in many churches to viewing women as weaker, not just physically, but morally and emotionally as well.

This belief goes on to suggest that because God cursed Eve, all women must suffer the pain of childbirth. An indignant pastor was filled with wrath at the thought of any escape from such pain. He was convinced that a Caesarean operation was disobeying God's intentions for the woman to go through a painful labor. Any epidural process to make it easier for the woman was flagrant disobedience. When I spoke to him about Jesus

---

14. Eds. It is vital that Western Christian readers are not too quick to condemn what seems obvious to them as outsiders before they have examined their own churches for similar capitulations to unbiblical aspects of the dominant culture.

becoming the curse so that we would all no longer be under the curse, he spluttered in speechless wrath. This same pastor shared about how he had brought an illiterate widow suffering with AIDS to display to his class of (all male) theology students. She was humiliated, gawked at, and subjected to intrusive questioning with no Savior to say, *he who is without sin cast the first stone* (John 8:7). She had forfeited all rights to be respected and treated with dignity by virtue of being a woman, poor, a widow, and one who now had AIDS.

Pastors are revered in India and exercise immense power in a society where God-men are widely worshipped. In her article on "Power Abuse and Theologies of Sexuality in the Church," Nancy Hopkins says that an imbalance of power and unequal relationships will lead to an abuse of power.[15] Though not inevitable (see other essays in this volume), it is sadly often the case. From our own experience we have found just how easy it is for a leader to believe in his "inalienable rights" by virtue of just being a leader to be heard and listened to, and in some cases obeyed without question. According to Hopkins, "*Females and children, long viewed as the property of males, have been socialized to be victims, males to be offenders.*"[16] So, a clergyman has even greater power as a man, and in addition, one who has spiritual authority.

In a workshop with twenty pastors over three days, my husband was speaking on the issue of church engaging with social evils in the city. On the second day, having some idea of the kind of attitudes prevalent amongst some in the church, my husband asked the question, "*How many of you think it is right to discipline our wives?*" All agreed. The answer to the next question, "*How many of you have beaten your wives, in order to discipline them?*" was dismaying. Nineteen of twenty raised their hands.

Made in his image? What part of the image of God do women bear? Is it sacrilege to think of God being female in any way? What kind of partnership did God mean for women to have with their male counterparts to serve him? Patriarchy leads to a misogyny which will resist the rights of others. It is a hierarchical mindset that leads to inequality and injustice. To completely deny one half of the human race the right to a shared humanity, to being fellow image bearers of the great Creator.

Every local church reflects in some part the wider culture within which it exists. When the same attitudes and perspectives, the same goals and aspirations as shape the wider culture, are allowed uncritically to influence and shape the church, something is terribly amiss. When the church

---

15. Hopkins, "Power Abuse."
16. Hopkins, "Power Abuse," 360.

is not at odds with the dominant culture, it is deeply influenced by it. *To be friends with the world is enmity with God* (Jas 4:4). Such a body has parted company with the paths of life that the church is meant to live by and ceased to be the salt and light.

RECOVERY

How can we return to a place where what influences us is our kingdom mandate? As the ecclesia we must discover how to create that environment that nurtures godly community in which all are equally valued. The business world is sadly often ahead of the church in this, incorporating biblical values of, e.g., servant leadership and fair treatment of minorities as aspects of strategy.[17] We, on the other hand, have lost our way, and are now seeking to learn from them, running our church organizations on marketing strategies instead, forgetting where these originate and defining success on the world's terms, rather than God's.

The deeper issue is not the disagreement on roles, the arguments on complementarianism or egalitarianism, or on female and male representation in church leadership, or even on the way the family is ordered. Hot debates around these issues have divided the church, alienated the genders, destroyed our unity. The deeper issue concerns loving, faithful, sensitive, considerate relationships, forged in the unity of the blood of Jesus.

Elaine Storkey writes:

> We can be greatly in danger of getting some themes way out of perspective. Even those who take (wrongly in my view) an authoritarian view of the relation between men and women need also to recognize that in the light of other biblical truths this is insignificant anyway. Far deeper issues about the relationship between men and women are at stake than that of who makes the (somewhat mythical) "final decision." Far more crucial is the teaching on truth in relationships, on faithfulness, justice, truth, forgiveness and reconciliation. The way others will know that we are Christ's disciples is in the way we love one another.[18]

Defining a problem rightly is part of the solution: without right definitions we cannot find real solutions. Jeremiah defined the problem that the community of God had left God: *For My people have committed two evils:*

---

17. Of course, in the case of business, this is often motivated by profit, rather than purely the well-being of individuals.

18. Storkey, *What's Right with Feminism*, 152.

they have forsaken Me, the fountain of living waters, and hewn themselves cisterns—broken cisterns that can hold no water (Jer 2:13). The problem of forsaking God and his ways leads us to follow patterns that are broken and cannot produce life. Any evils found in the church or the world have their root in the forsaking of God.

In forsaking God, we are no longer imitators of God: "Therefore be imitators of God as dear children. And walk in love, as Christ also has loved us and given Himself for us, an offering and a sacrifice to God for a sweet-smelling aroma" (Eph 5:1–2). This verse is the foundation of what comes later in the same chapter, in the covenant relationship between us and God and between each other. This, I believe, is the basis for a marriage covenant which then makes sense of Eph 5:22–33. There can be no submission without imitating God, which means sacrificial love patterned after Christ's love for us. Likewise, there is no exercise of authority without the same kind of love. Because we have not imitated God, we have perverted authority to be authoritarian and twisted submission to become the bullying rule of men over women. This has led to power abuse in the church, breakdown of authentic community, loss of intimate relationship, loss of vulnerability and sacrifice.

Without revelation, there can be no conviction, and no hope for change. Revelation comes when we seek God. When together, from a place of unity, our hearts cry out to him, seeking to be founded on his love and his word, things begin to change.

The book of Malachi summarizes the essence of the entire Old Testament: God in pursuit of man, the tormented plea of a divine Lover for his Beloved. *I have loved you!* (Mal 1:2) Our human relationships have been given us to understand God's heart. We know in some measure God's deep, wondrous love for us as we experience the love of fathers, mothers, spouses, siblings, and friends.

When these are distorted, our experiences become the filters through which we view God. We project onto him, who is perfection, our human failings, thinking wrong thoughts about this awesome, loving King. We lose sight of God's love and ask the question: *"In what way have You loved us?"* (Mal 1:2). Malachi sought to restore a lost people to God, his love, and to a right appraisal of their circumstances: they were in captivity because they no longer loved God, not because he no longer loved them. What a responsibility church leaders carry not to distort the picture of who God is.

"Esau I have hated" (Mal 1:3). How strange that sounds coming from God. Esau despised his inheritance and in so doing, despised his father and God from whom all blessings ultimately come. Though he lamented and pled later (Heb 12:17), he was unable to get back what he lost. He was slave

to his appetites, yearning for immediate gratification. God despises indifferent, shallow, fleshly responses.

The worshipping community had begun to go through the motions, offering what was blemished, half-heartedly, devoid of faith. Their priests had departed from the way, causing many to stumble. They had covenanted themselves to spouses who did not follow God. The men had dealt treacherously with their wives, their children no longer had role models who would lead them to God. They did evil and called it good. Systems of exploitation and injustice flourished, they did not consider the marginalized and the vulnerable. They had robbed God, and so were under a curse. Perhaps it is time to examine whether we too have gone wrong in a similar manner?

Solutions are not found in tweaking our existing systems, these are discovered when we entirely reject the essence of all that is evil and return to God in love, beginning from there, male or female, young and old, whoever we are. We have lost a sense of community with him, therefore with one another. We have forgotten how to live lives that are accountable to his word.

God wants to restore us to a place of purity and fidelity where out of fear of God, we live lives that are considerate, loving, and full of integrity. We are not our own, we belong to him.

In these days, I believe God is refining and purifying (Mal 3:2) so that our offerings are once again pleasing to him. Perhaps it is time for us to entreat God's favor once more, that he may be gracious to us (Mal 1:9), that we may take to heart what God desires; truth in the inward parts, so that what we do and say reflects our love for him.

Without a commitment and prayer for change, there will be no change. History has shown such a prayer arises from the oppressed, the outcry of the oppressed in Sodom and Gomorrah,[19] or the Israelites in the land of the Pharaoh.

Paulo Freire writes:

> For . . . struggle to have meaning, the oppressed must not, in seeking to regain their humanity become in turn oppressors of the oppressors, but rather restorers of the humanity of both. This, then, is the great . . . task of the oppressed: to liberate themselves and their oppressors as well. The oppressors, who oppress, exploit, and rape by virtue of their power, cannot find in this power the strength to liberate either the oppressed or

---

19. Ezekiel tells us the sin of Sodom and Gomorrah was that they used oppression, exercised robbery, and vexed the poor. God responded to the ensuing outcry (Ezek 22:29–31; 16:48–50).

themselves. Only power that springs from the weakness of the oppressed will be sufficiently strong to free both.[20]

The initiative for change comes from the cry of the oppressed before God. It does not lie in militant, aggressive responses; for those too dehumanize, as much as any oppression does. It does not lie in formulating new rules, laws, or strategies; for these do not change our heart but may just affect our behavior. It lies in the loving restoration of both the oppressor and the oppressed, but the initiative lies with those who have conviction born from the revelation of who God is through his Son Jesus, the vision of what he wants to create and the longing to be the authentic community of the living God.

BIBLIOGRAPHY

Franz, Thaeda. "Power, Patriarchy and Sexual Abuse in Churches of Christian Denomination." *Traumatology* 8 (2002) 4–17.
Friere, Paulo. *Pedagogy of the Oppressed*. New York: Continuum, 1993.
Goldsmith, Belinda, and Meka Beresford. "Exclusive: India Most Dangerous Country for Women with Sexual Violence Rife—Global Poll." *Reuters*, June 25, 2018. https://www.reuters.com/article/us-women-dangerous-poll-exclusive-idUSKBN1JM01X.
Hopkins, Nancy Myer. "Power Abuse and Theologies of Sexuality in the Church." *Sexual Addiction and Compulsivity* 1 (1994) 357–61.
Kakar, Sudhir, and Katharina Poggendorf-Kakar. *The Indians: Portrait of a People*. New Delhi: Penguin, 2009.
Madan, Karuna. "'Boys Will Be Boys': Outrageous Rape Comments by India Politicians." *Gulf News*, June 15, 2014. https://gulfnews.com/world/asia/india/boys-will-be-boys-outrageous-rape-comments-by-india-politicians-1.1347378.
Putnam, Robert D. *Bowling Alone: The Collapse and Revival of American Community*. New York: Simon & Schuster, 2000.
Storkey, Elaine. *What's Right with Feminism*. London: SPCK, 1985.
Tripathi, Dhirendra. "Why the Declining Sex Ratio in India Is a Cause for Worry." *LiveMint*, July 22, 2019. https://www.livemint.com/news/india/why-the-declining-sex-ratio-in-india-is-a-cause-for-worry-1563816826590.html.
Xavier, M. Sreedevi. "Honour Killings: A Global Concern." *Paripex—Indian Journal of Research* 4 (2015) 6–9.

---

20. Friere, *Pedagogy of the Oppressed*, 44.

14

Pastors Empowering Women to Flourish

Tasha Chapman

INTRODUCTION

Throughout Scripture, God calls his people to lead and to use power in uniquely countercultural ways. We are to love our neighbors, pray for our enemies, and lead by serving. Our biblical priorities include providing advocacy and care to those who are most vulnerable. Ministry leaders also bear the responsibility of equipping and empowering others for fruitfulness in good works, together as the body of Christ, as part of God's mission in redeeming his whole creation.

In sharp contrast to humble service, however, our secular societies expect leaders to pursue power over others, to be nonpersonal and lacking empathy, to impose decisions, to give directions, to control resources, and to set the rules. These cultural assumptions about leadership pressure us to act in ways that are contrary to Scripture. They also blind us to the damage caused by that kind of cultural leader.

The purpose of this chapter is to consider how, especially in church contexts with majority male leaders, they can and should empower women to flourish.

LEARNING TO SEE POWER

"Change the language; change the culture." A common leadership motto, this expression is actually solid, research-based advice for leaders. The words we choose for naming the world matter. When we attach language to our experience, we influence how we will perceive and respond to similar events in the future. Like wearing new corrective glasses, renaming can be a significant way to learn. By rethinking the term "power," we increase our awareness of how we use it.

What images and feelings does the word "power" evoke? Probably negative ones. Perhaps many of us think of physical strength. Simply put, men usually have more physical strength than women. This makes women more vulnerable to harm. It also makes men more vulnerable to the sin of dominating over women. Historically, in human brokenness, most cultures developed around those with the most power, the men, and women tended to suffer the most abuse.

To take a step in changing this cultural trend, try reassigning power a neutral description, without assuming sinfulness: power as the human capacity, as image bearers of God, to act and to influence others.[1] We all unconsciously leverage power to negotiate with each other. With God-honoring desires, our power leads to innovation, stewardship, redemption, and blessing. Power-as-capacity is a gift to be stewarded for the redemptive work of God's mission. Consider what power you have in your household and in your ministry. What are your capacities to act? How much influence do you have? With whom and in what contexts?

Andy Crouch employs "power" with this neutral meaning, painting an expansive vision of what wise stewardship of power can do. "When power is used well, people and the whole cosmos come more alive to what they were meant to be. . . . Flourishing [for all creation] is the test of power."[2] Helping others gain power this way does not diminish our own power, as some fear. Instead, all benefit and become more fruitful and power multiplies. To what degree are women flourishing under our leadership? How would we even know?

The church should be a place of deep personal belonging, worthiness, respect, and purpose. We can dream of the covenant community being the

---

1. Friere, *Pedagogy of the Oppressed*, 19 Burns, Chapman, and Guthrie, *Politics of Ministry*, 19. Several concepts in this chapter were first published in *The Politics of Ministry*, which provides an in depth, research-based study exploring what 21st Century grace-based, Kingdom-oriented ministry leadership might look like. It includes reflection and discussion questions for contextual application.

2. Crouch, *Playing God*, 13. Also recommended: Langberg, *Redeeming Power*.

most psychologically and physically safe place to be. Women would say to their neighbor, "The clergy at my church care about me and understand me. They understand that women are often oppressed in this broken world. I can count on them to look out for me. We learn to follow Jesus together as siblings, listening and supporting each other and forgiving each other when we fail. I feel so encouraged and fulfilled when I use my talents to serve there."

Account for Many Types and Amounts of Power

Although all human beings are created with power, our capacities and strengths vary. Even the toddlers in our Sunday gatherings have power; they have the capacity to cause bedlam and the influence to make us laugh with joy. When considering the world's most powerful people, the first to come to mind tend to be the military dictators, presidents, CEOs, and billionaires. Did any use their power to help others flourish? How many are women? How many wielded great influence for good without military command or riches? We might then consider those like Sacagawea,[3] Anne Frank, Rosa Parks, Mother Theresa, and Malala Yousavzai. These renowned women represent very different types of power.

People are unique in gifts, experiences, personalities, strengths, struggles, and cognition. Two individuals are rarely equal in power. Power inequalities are inevitable and not innately bad. Society depends on them for structure and stability. Many power differences reflect God's good design for diversity. But when corrupted by sin, our power differences lead to injustice and the abuse of the less powerful. God's people have the gospel imperative to care for and to empower those who are less powerful.

Contexts also determine a person's power and its uses. Formal power is a type of power derived from organizational position and job responsibilities. For example, pastors might have great influence over the beliefs of their church members but very little influence over the views of their dentist.

In contrast to formal power, relational power derives from the quality and quantity of human relationships. It grows over time as an individual gains credibility, trust, and respect with others. Perhaps unexpectedly, it is most often stronger than formal power. For example, a pastor is unlikely to have as much influence over congregants involved in the children's ministry

---

3. See "Sacagawea." She was a native American woman of the Shoshone tribe who served as interpreter to explorers Meriwether Lewis and William Clark on their US military expedition (1804–6). They traveled thousands of wilderness miles across the Northwest US to the Pacific Ocean and back.

as the children's ministry leader, even if she is a volunteer. Her relational power will be stronger than the pastor's if she built deep trust with parents and volunteers over many years. If the pastor crosses her, the parents and workers will side with the director.

Account for Many Types of Interest, Which Direct the Power

It is natural to use the power available to us to gain desired outcomes according to our own interests. Interests are the matters in which we are invested, in which we have something to gain or to lose. An ounce of reflection on this could lead to a pound of wisdom for how to get things done with others. Instead, leaders tend to operate with their interests hidden, assuming others agree with their goals and will work to reach them. Studies show that those with the most power in an organization tend to be the least aware that others have less power, and those in power are the least informed about where others' interests conflict with their own.

Ministry leaders probably have little idea how powerless staff colleagues and lay leaders feel and little idea of what matters most to them. They do not understand that those serving under them do not often feel seen, heard, or valued. Therefore, leaders need to be intentional about identifying power and interest differences with those they work with. In most Western countries, white male pastors must make extra effort since they are from the dominant culture profile. This accords them more power than they realize, making them more prone to be blind to the differences in power and interests of those around them. Enabling the flourishing of others will be impossible without such intentional efforts.

LEADING HEALING FOR THE LESS POWERFUL

Pastors and male ministry leaders can use their power to bring healing to women. They can provide empathetic listening and deepening awareness of power inequalities, injuries from injustices, and resulting suffering. Church leaders can use their power to shine gospel light on the darkness of injustice and abuse. They must not remain silent. Instead, they should model how power can be used to bless others. The following seven actions will help pastors use their power to help women thrive.

1. Lament Injustices Suffered by Women

Western societies are riven by inequalities, whether economic, political, or social. This brings a heavy burden for women to bear. Every week, the women in our ministries probably hear of horrendous abuse of women from the global news. Do they also see this mourned and prayed about in the church? In Christian ministry, where verbal power is highly valued and influential, pastors can lead the congregation in lamenting these injustices before the Lord, in the sure and certain hope of God's presence and ultimate justice. Together with the laity, they can and should work for women's safety, equality, and respect in the local context. Church boards and councils should remedy gender inequalities of honor, title, pay, and benefits within their churches. They may be surprised to learn that the unmarried, female children's director has the same training and experience as the married, male youth worker while receiving substantially lower remuneration, despite bearing responsibility for more people and working longer hours.

2. Pray for Unity while Celebrating Diversity

Gender is a foundational aspect of difference in the unity of the body of Christ. We need to admit humbly that even with advancements in science and Bible exegesis, gender differences remain a mysterious part of our image bearing as male and female. People rejoice when their gifts and talents are welcomed and shepherded to serve God's mission. The church grows together toward maturity in Christ, as our sanctification is a corporate as well as an individual process. Role distinctions do not need to prevent this. The Lord is redeeming all his creation, and he provides good work for all to join in. Male ministry leaders bless women when they speak of gender with respect and refrain from cliches. We should not buy into cultural gender stereotypes when thinking about roles in church.

3. Confess and Repent Personally and Corporately

Despite some change, Western cultures still tend to socialize boys to be "real men": strong, tough, commanding, hypersexualized, and objectifying of women. All are quite contrary to the fruit of the Spirit. In response, male leaders can mentor boys toward holiness and model repentance for participating in these cultural evils. Train children collectively about their identity in Christ, as brothers and sisters, so they can practice actions counter to the cultural norms. The congregation can corporately repent of participating in the culture's godless pressures on both genders. We can lead our people to pray against wife battery, bullying, and sexual harassment, and to pray for courage to be salt and light in the areas of gender injustice that they encounter during the week.

4. Invite Sisters onto the Team

True joy and satisfaction come from serving with the body of Christ and partnering in God's redemptive work. Our cultures make empty promises of gain via competitive performance. How beautiful it is when all work together with our God-given gifts (Rom 12:3–8; 1 Cor 12:4–18; Eph 4:1–16)! In a broken world, the biblical ideal is still radically unique—that all are created with equal worth, dignity, and value. It takes intentional leadership to strive for our calling of being a unified family in Christ. Research continues to show that women usually provide most of the volunteer work in the church and society.[4] Leaders can eagerly recruit these women to work alongside brothers, with honor and dignity. Ministry teams are fruitful and fulfilled when appropriately gifted women and men serve together.[5]

Gender power inequality and abuse do not necessarily correlate to beliefs about roles, despite the varying views on the issue. The way a male ministry leader treats women has much more to do with the man's character than his theology of role distinctions. By God's grace, women can experience significant healing by serving alongside godly brothers in Christ.

5. Honor Women Who Serve

The church should be a place of active thanksgiving for, and honor to, the women who serve as employees and volunteers. When women serve in the more hidden roles (such as cleaners, secretaries, child-care workers, or cooks), they should receive the church's corporate thanks and prayers. How encouraging it is to have an appropriate title to go with one's responsibilities. It also eases church communication. Leaders should review titles and responsibilities annually and publish them to avoid confusion in the body. Publicly celebrate and regularly thank women who have served well, and especially when they step down or move away.

---

4. E.g., Babcock et al., "Why Women Volunteer," and the summary of the 2016 US Bureau of Labor Stastics at Lifeway—Gibson, "Who Volunteers in America?"

5. For excellent research from the marketplace on teamwork in our culture, see Edmondson, *Teaming*.

6. Prize Relational Skills

For most of us, our best bosses were those who excelled at the "soft skills" of trust building and communication. These people skills largely correlate to emotional intelligence (EQ). EQ is the self-awareness and self-control to quickly name and respond to one's own emotions, combined with the ability to perceive correctly and respond calmly and wisely to others' emotions. The health of relationships in our work and ministry contexts largely determines the degree of well-being and success. Marketplace leadership research shows it even impacts profitability.[6] Building trusting relationships and healthy communication with EQ are biblical priorities, as seen in the Great Commandment to love God and our neighbor.

However, Western culture tends to ascribe leadership skills to performance and to competitive individualism, while demoting relational skill as something less valuable and more feminine. Marketplace organizations demonstrate this by celebrating the things that matter less to human flourishing. Raises and advancement often go only to individuals who get the most tasks done efficiently, no matter how damaging their behavior was to relationships and teamwork.

Ministry leaders need to work on their own EQ, to model empathetic listening, and to encourage the sharing of emotions and conflicting ideas with respect and honesty. Those with less power need extra affirmation and thankful feedback for their work since they will usually feel hidden. Otherwise, women feel the need to overperform to prove their worth. Be intentional to acknowledge work done by women, and take extra time to understand their contributions.

7. Serve alongside Sisters with Holy Discernment

Fear has no place in a church pursuing love. Wise clergy, who have their identity firmly rooted in Christ, can serve with, invest in, and mentor women nearly much as they do the men. Ministry leaders often create many rules about how to work with those of the opposite gender. But rules alone do not protect us from sin and can be injurious to women. Pastors' fears of sexual temptation should not be used as an excuse to diminish discipling,

---

6. "A leader's emotional intelligence creates a certain culture or work environment. High levels of emotional intelligence, our research showed, create climates in which information sharing, trust, healthy risk-taking, and learning flourish. Low levels of emotional intelligence create climates rife with fear and anxiety. Because tense or terrified employees can be very productive in the short term, their organizations may post good results, but they never last." Goleman et al., "Primal Leadership," 2.

equipping, or teaming with one's sisters. Each situation requires wise discernment. Pray against temptation, and discuss best practices and guidelines together, as brothers and sisters in Christ. The open communication and reliance on God will help the team move toward holiness much more than restrictive rules, suspicion, and avoidance.

TEAM MEETINGS: A PLACE TO PRACTICE POWER FOR FLOURISHING

Team meetings provide an essential forum for many of these practices to be played out. By helping women to flourish through the way meetings are led, the culture of an entire church can be changed. Power that raises others up benefits everyone. Meetings provide a clear window into the health of a ministry culture. How leaders perceive their own power and employ it to negotiate their interests is on display.

Observe the power dynamics and the lack of trust and psychological safely in this meeting story.

> The church board chairman is short in stature. He was teased about it as a teenager. Unconsciously, he sits in the most prominent chair and spreads his papers out on the conference table. The anxious, new Assistant Pastor speaks out at every pause in the discussion. The Senior Pastor, who had a father whom he could never please, has little patience for ideas that counter his own. He uses most of the meeting time explaining his own thinking and judgments. He interrupts others to correct their ideas. The children's director is the only woman at the meeting. She sits in the corner farthest from the Senior Pastor. She stays quiet and takes lots of notes. She nods enthusiastically in response to the Senior Pastor. She hopes to prove she is on his side and worthy to be at the table. She is not fully conscious of how threatened she feels by his size, loud voice, strong influence over the congregation, and quick temper. At the end of the meeting, the Senior Pastor congratulates the team on making a solid decision. The rest breathe a sigh of relief that they have survived another power struggle. They continue the real collaboration work in the hallways and nearby offices.

Meeting habits frequently embed systemic injustices, poor communication patterns, and harmful uses of power. Therefore, consider inviting your team to try new ways to do meetings. Try small intentional changes each week. After a month, reflect on what has happened, focusing on what worked or what needs more tweaking. Here are some suggestions for before, during, and after meetings.

Before the Meeting

Pray against cultural norms

How do we talk to ourselves and to God about our ministry leadership? Our cultures pressure us relentlessly to dominate, to be efficient, and to control others and circumstances out of fear. We can push back intentionally through prayer. Pray for humility. Pray for those who might feel they do not have a voice at the meeting. Pray for courage to listen well, to learn from others, to ask good questions, and to welcome help. Ask for wisdom to steward power well to equip and empower others. Thank God that in Christ, we have nothing to fear, nothing to lose, and nothing to prove; we can freely serve others. We can use our power to help others feel seen, heard, and valued during meetings.

Reflect on power

Prayerfully consider the varying capacities and influence of the meeting's participants, especially as they compare with the one leading. Identify the interests at stake in the meeting topics for each attendee. This reflection work is challenging and perhaps even counterintuitive. Anthropologists describe Western cultures as "low power distance" cultures.[7] This means that people expect to be treated as equals and that obvious power markers are discouraged. It manifests in casual dress, informal communication, and hidden agendas. Actual power differences between people are hidden, easily ignored, and, therefore, power use can have much less accountability.

Remember that women often enter meetings feeling powerless or unsafe. They might assume that men's trust and respect can only be gained through performance. Prove them wrong. They probably are more aware of how others use power during meetings, a hyperawareness derived from the personal experience of historic injustice and abuse as well as ongoing gender inequalities. By no means do these burdens result from self-imposed victimhood or false humility or a lack of maturity.

---

7. Hofstede, *Culture's Consequences*, or "Power Distance Index."

Invite women to participate more

Those with more power usually decide on meeting attendance, the perspectives to be considered, and the decision-making process. Consider how many formal and chance meetings you have in a week. How many involve women? Statistics suggest that most of the adults involved in churches are women. How is this majority group (with minority status) being represented at the meetings and by whom? Who helps you know how your leadership and preaching is impacting the church's women?

Equip women and men together

Though some discipleship rightly happens in single-gender groups, church unity is greatly strengthened by training men and women together. Our people need more practice being one body while valuing their individual diversity. When pastors boldly encourage women to serve or lead in areas in which the women are more talented, they make powerful statements to the men in the fellowship. To what extent do your women's and children's ministries seem to function independently of the rest of the church? Try welcoming these leaders to other meetings to integrate groups toward the church's vision.

Pastors could consider more carefully how much ministry responsibility women are bearing and their needs for training. For example, if your church regularly has the pastor train men to be elders or board members, consider having the spouses participate as well so that marriage partnerships are strengthened, even when the responsibilities and calling to serve are not identical. When a ministry internship program includes both men and women learning together, all gain from deepened relational skills, insights, and the appreciation of differences.

The meeting's agenda

Those with less power are easily injured in meetings with hidden agendas. The agenda should be drafted and communicated in advance, with participants invited to give feedback on it. What issues do others think are priorities for face-to-face discussion? After gaining input, set clear goals for the meeting and resend the agenda. Provide a topic-relevant relational goal, to grow in trust and understanding of each other. Consider how the meeting can be empowering to others such that they feel seen, heard, valued, and resourced to take action.

Encourage preparation

Encourage attendees to prepare by distributing necessary information in advance. When dealing with challenging topics, those with less power will find it highly challenging to offer clear and thorough comments spontaneously, as they are already burdened with the emotional challenges of being present. Instead, help people come prepared to have differences of opinions and conflicts and to collaborate and learn from each other. Seek to work the hard conversations for tough challenges together. Otherwise, why meet face-to-face? Hope and trust grow when leaders share information openly, without manipulating decisions or the creative process. Increased trust improves future communication and productivity.[8] Leaders should use their power to keep meetings honest, caring, and focused. However, the process collapses if people come unprepared or are fearful to bring their unique perspectives.

Design good questions to ask

Good leadership facilitates a team to solve tough challenges together. Good questions require thoughtful wording that invite honest contributions from all, especially those with less power. Closed questions requiring single "right" answers tend to result from anxious or unprepared leaders, and they hinder discussion and problem-solving. Instead, ask for multiple answers, drawing out different perspectives or possibilities. Have the team create lists. What do people know about the history of the challenge at hand? What groups in the church might have concerns and interests regarding the challenge? Rely on the Spirit for the necessary courage and confidence in Christian identity to avoid defensiveness or anger at opposing contributions.

During the Meeting

Celebrate the diversity of the team

Identifying diversity involves neither ignoring issues of culture, race, and gender, nor treating individuals as representatives (for example, "As a woman, what do you think?") This merely reinforces a person's outsider status (here because of her gender). Instead, respect individuals by their individual and unique perspectives. Gather as many relevant perspectives as possible for the group to consider.

---

8. For more on leadership and trust, see the marketplace leadership book Covey and Merrill, *Speed of Trust*, and Edmondson, *Fearless Organization*.

Invite individual contributions

Invite the woman to contribute specifically. Sincere welcome can help heal the wounds of having no voice. Give space to those who are quieter to share thoughts if they wish. Welcome contrary ideas with respect. Model honesty and curiosity about the challenge at hand. Be open with phrases such as "I don't know. Let's create a list of possibilities. Can you say more to help me understand? I'm eager to listen well to your concerns about this. You seem pensive; I'd like to hear what you're thinking." The silence of those with less power may well indicate a lack of healthy collaboration and trust.

Represent women's interests in the planning process

To advocate for those with less power, compile two lists for any major planning meeting. Use a whiteboard or flipchart to provide structure and a learning climate for the process.

- Which people groups will probably be impacted by the meeting's decisions? Make sure to list the various ages and stages of the women affected.
- For each people group, what are their probable interests in the decisions? Consider their potential gains and losses.

Deeper understandings and wiser decisions will result from this process of considering how others will be impacted by the results of the meeting, especially those with less power.

Make complicated discussions visible

Capture the discussion on a whiteboard or flipchart. This allows all to keep track of the topic's complexity and varying perspectives. This method helps all to listen to one another better, to contribute more succinctly, to feel heard, to keep discussions more focused and objective, and to feel calmer. It slows the process down, allowing for needed reflection and collaboration for emotive issues. Even if one person must ultimately make the decision, this process builds more mutual trust and support for that decision.

Give emotions a respected place at the table

Emotions are constantly present; they faithfully show us what we care about. Our brains respond to input with emotion much faster than with logical reasoning, in part because emotions tend to be linked to identity and ministry purpose. This makes all who serve in the church more vulnerable to each other relationally and emotionally than might be the case in a secular organization. Welcome the tears and frustrations of others, naming the emotions with respect. Cultural pressures likely make observable emotions a source of shame for women. Try placing a tissue box on the conference table and reminding the team to respect emotions. Good meetings often are emotional meetings because the work matters deeply. Leaders can name their emotions to the group to model good EQ.

Pause an intense discussion to ask people how they are feeling. Ask for reflection on the meeting process itself. Are there concerns about how decisions are being made? Are there some unwritten rules on "how stuff gets done around here" that are surfacing and need to be addressed? What outcomes from the meeting are people fearing? Honor what people dare to share with empathy. Empathy acknowledges the truth of the emotions, even if one does not agree with the content. Empathy does not jump to fix the problem but lets people know they are not alone in that painful place. Model repentance by asking for forgiveness for hurtful behavior that has already happened during the meeting.

Openly advocate for women

Give honest, positive feedback to women at meetings. Look for ways to affirm each member of the team. Women, and all those who feel they have significantly less power, need to know that the leaders consider them worthy of respect and are thankful for their participation and contributions. They need to hear that the leader heard their comments and concerns.

Openly discuss post-meeting expectations

What expectations do participants have for the outworking of the meeting? Communication and trust grow when these are openly discussed. Unspoken or unclear expectations are toxic to relationships and create communication havoc. When those with less power feel they must guess what the leader expects, fear and feelings of being manipulated result. Expectations need to be discussed to gain assessment and mutual agreement. Then people will be accountable to each other for the agreed upon work.

End with mutual, transparent accountability

At the end of meetings, try having everyone state something they learned from the meeting and the next steps they will work on. This simple exercise establishes clarity and division of tasks across the team. Healthy accountability works across roles and power differences. If misunderstandings are still present, they will surface now, before causing real damage. Open accountability by clergy provides a healing antidote to the women's experiences of manipulation, control, blame, and shame. It also invites people to collaborate further, giving feedback to each other as the work progresses. Leaders, we desperately need more accountability in our ministry work simply because we have more power.

CONCLUSION

Pastors minister from a place of great power and responsibility in the church. From this position, even simple miscommunication potentially harms those with less power. Whether admitted or not, women tend to have significantly less power than men in modern societies and churches. Ministry leaders must use their power to help heal and support women to thrive. Even simple changes in how we lead meetings can help change our churches to be the most encouraging and safe places for women in society. God's church can and should be a place where women belong and serve according to their talents, where they have a voice, and where their agency is respected. The result will be fruitful ministry and growth toward Christ for all.

BIBLIOGRAPHY

Babcock, Linda, et al. "Why Women Volunteer for Tasks That Don't Lead to Promotions." *Harvard Business Review* (blog), July 16, 2018. https://hbr.org/2018/07/why-women-volunteer-for-tasks-that-dont-lead-to-promotions.

Buckley, Jay H. "Sacagawea." https://www.britannica.com/biography/Sacagawea.

Burns, Bob, et al. *The Politics of Ministry: Navigating Power Dynamics and Negotiating Interests*. Downers Grove, IL: InterVarsity, 2019.

Covey, Stephen M. R., and Rebecca R. Merrill. *The Speed of Trust: The One Thing That Changes Everything*. New York: Free Press, 2008.

Crouch, Andy. *Playing God: Redeeming the Gift of Power*. Downers Grove, IL: InterVarsity, 2013.

Edmondson, Amy C. *The Fearless Organization: Creating Psychological Safety in the Workplace for Learning, Innovation, and Growth*. Hoboken, NJ: Wiley, 2019.

———. *Teaming: How Organizations Learn, Innovate, and Compete in the Knowledge Economy*. Boston: Harvard Business School, n.d.

Friere, Paulo. *Pedagogy of the Oppressed*. New York: Continuum, 1993.

Gibson, Helen. "Who Volunteers in America?" *Lifeway Research* (blog), July 26, 2018. https://research.lifeway.com/2018/07/26/data-paints-a-picture-of-volunteerism-across-the-nation/.

Goleman, Daniel, et al. "Primal Leadership: The Hidden Driver of Great Performance." *Harvard Business Review* 79 (2001) 42–51.

Hofstede, Geert. *Culture's Consequences: Comparing Values, Behaviors, Institutions, and Organizations across Nations*. Thousand Oaks, CA: Sage, 2013.

Langberg, Diane. *Redeeming Power: Understanding Authority and Abuse in the Church*. Grand Rapids, MI: Brazos, 2020.

"Power Distance Index." https://clearlycultural.com/geert-hofstede-cultural-dimensions/power-distance-index/.

15

Signs and Symptoms of Unhealthy Leaders and Their Systems

Mark Stirling

INTRODUCTION

IT IS A TRAGEDY for the church that this book is necessary.[1] Addressing the abuse of power in the church is not simply a matter of modifying harmful behaviors in a few bad leaders. Rather, this is a fundamentally theological problem; underlying abuse of power by Christian leaders is a wrong view of God and the gospel, a misunderstanding of the purpose of Christian leadership, a deficient doctrine of humanity and a superficial understanding of sin. When leaders do things in the name of Jesus that misrepresent Jesus, they are guilty of bearing his name in vain. This is much more the burden of the Third Commandment (Exod 20:7) than the mere use of wrong vocabulary.

Misrepresenting God's character is a sin of such magnitude as to exclude even Moses from the promised land (Num 20:2–13). The structure of the passage (the people grumble to Moses; Moses speaks to God on behalf of the people; God speaks to Moses; Moses speaks to the people on behalf of God) clarifies that Moses' responsibility is to represent the people to God and God to the people. In this case, he is to reflect God's kindness in providing water for the grumblers from the rock. He fails to do so, and, instead of speaking to the rock, communicates anger to the people by striking it. He

---

1. I will use "church" as shorthand for any "Christian organization."

SIGNS AND SYMPTOMS OF UNHEALTHY LEADERS AND THEIR SYSTEMS

is condemned for failing to trust God (v. 12) and uphold him as holy before the people. In communicating harshness instead of God's kindness, Moses had misrepresented the character of God.

The punchline, is that, even though Moses had acted sinfully and had misrepresented God's character, the water still flowed. To use contemporary terminology, despite his sin, Moses' ministry was still successful and people were still being blessed.

Moses illustrates the danger of allowing apparent results to rationalize away bad behavior or bad character in leaders. Good "results" are possible even in the midst of egregious misrepresentations of God, which is why success in itself is an unreliable indicator of a ministry's health. Because we cannot afford to ignore or be complacent about the issue, we must be able to recognize possible symptoms and ask hard questions. That is the burden of this chapter.

HOW DOES THIS CHURCH FEEL?

A common theme in this chapter is that abuse of power flourishes in the dark, so leaders must be willing to speak truth and churches must become more conducive to truth-speaking if they are to be healthy. This chapter therefore seeks to shine light on the manifold, subtle outworkings of leaders using their power for selfish gain instead of self-giving love (see chapter 1).

This is not an exhaustive list and none of what follows is necessarily "proof" that abuse of power is taking place. But all of what follows suggests unhealthy dysfunction alerting us to the possibility of misuse of power.

This first section is a reflection on the ethos of a church and what observations might point towards something being wrong.

"I Can't Say That."

The feeling that there is something wrong but we're not allowed to say so is almost universally a sign of sickness. It is not that lack of criticism is always diagnostic of abuse, but it is an essential ingredient in an environment where abuse can happen. A church in which people feel they cannot or should not criticize can allow leaders to operate without proper accountability and their behaviors may go unchecked. The feelings and ambitions of leaders become more important than the growth to maturity of members.

That this sort of organizational culture can develop in churches reflects the subtlety of power abuse. Just like Moses and the rock, the water still flows, and people's thirst may still be satisfied. God still graciously provides for his people even through the worst sorts of leaders, and, in the face of apparent blessing, it becomes very difficult to raise questions. So, a common reaction to recent scandals in the UK has been disbelief in view of an abusive leader's wonderful preaching. If a man gave good sermons and so many experienced blessing, how could he possibly be guilty of abusing power and harming people? The reality, however, is that ministry is always mixed, but people don't want to face the possibility that the leader through whom God blessed them could have a darker side.

Culture and Ethos of a Leader

The character and behavior of a leader profoundly shapes the culture of their organization. Though a leader will rarely explicitly forbid criticism, people quickly detect whether there is genuine openness to feedback and criticism. Insecurity in leaders (see chap 1), who may misuse their leadership to compensate for what they lack, may manifest subtly in apparently contradictory ways. The leader who looks strong may be masking fear and insecurity with a display that communicates "don't challenge me." Alternatively, apparently humble self-criticism may be a strategy to preempt and shut down criticism before it happens. The implicit message either way is that this leader cannot be criticized, either because they are strong or because they are fragile. The result is an unhealthy environment in which necessary feedback is shut down.

Is Feedback Ever Actively Sought? Defensiveness Is Indefensible

A simple diagnostic question is whether a church actively solicits feedback and is seen to act upon it. Are there mechanisms for people to give feedback safely? How does the leader respond to feedback? Defensiveness is indefensible and a key measure of a leader's use of power is how they respond to challenge or disagreement—in fact, this may be the principle way a leader's character is revealed. Defensiveness, *ad hominem* attack, excuses, anger, or self-pity may all be unhealthy signs of a leader who cares more about their own reputation and feelings than about the health of God's people.

Of course, there are times when church leaders are wrongly accused or criticized and that can be extremely wearing. However, avoiding unjust criticism by allowing no criticism is bad for everyone. A church leader must be prepared to receive feedback, appreciate the courage it often takes for someone to give it, consider it prayerfully, and deal with the person gently.

There is nothing to lose and everything to gain from listening and taking concerns seriously—even if the concerns prove unfounded.

Related to defensiveness is the "red-flag" sign of a leader talking about their own authority. Regular reminders of who is in charge are a worrying sign, especially when used to support a particular course of action or directive counsel. "As your pastor . . . ," or "God told me that . . . ," or "I've prayed about this and we have to . . . " or "I'm exercising my pastoral authority . . . ," can all shut down questions and enforce compliance.

Ask Questions and Become the Problem

A key diagnostic sign of unhealthy organizations is when those who ask questions become a problem to be managed. This can be utterly destabilizing and even traumatizing for the questioner. It is most damaging because it most affects those who actually care about the organization. It is therefore all the more surprising to them when honest and well-intended questions cause them to be treated as a villain. An unhealthy system cannot cope with questions and those who ask them must be persuaded of their wrongness, or convicted of the ungodliness that would cause them to ask these sorts of questions at all. Failing that, they will be marginalized or excluded.[2]

Competitiveness—We're the Best!

Leaders set the tone publicly in any church and there is little that discourages feedback or criticism more quickly than an atmosphere of self-congratulation or self-satisfaction. A congregation that constantly hears how blessed they are that they can come to this "true Gospel church" where there is "sound biblical teaching" unlike many churches out there that are "compromising with the culture,"[3] is also receiving a not-so-subtle message that if you don't appreciate how great we are, it's because there is something wrong with you. A leader must make an intentional effort to create an environment in which people are free to feedback and criticize, or risk sowing seeds of abuse by setting themselves up as unchallengeable.

Competitiveness in church leaders towards other leaders, churches, or organizations is so common, I wonder whether we no longer think of

---

2. I need to balance this point. Not all question asking is innocent or constructive and we're not the best judges of our own motivation. There is a way of question asking that can be undermining and be more of a reflection of the questioner working out their own issues. Great wisdom is required. I am grateful to Jared Michelson for this insight.

3. Insert here whatever measure of status applies in your church culture.

it as sin. A narrative that we are better than others and that we don't colabor with "inferior" churches clashes with a theology of the body of Christ. Ephesians 2:11–22 describes Christ's peacemaking work on the cross creating "one new humanity," whose unity believers are to strive to maintain by "walking with humility, meekness, long-suffering and bearing with one another in love" (Eph 4:1–2). Unity is evidence of the efficacy of the cross that reconciles us both to Christ and to each other. Disunity declares to the world that the cross does not work. Any church that is competing with others not only denies the reality of this "one new humanity," but has also embraced an attitude antithetical to Jesus' example and teachings.

Competitiveness may arise from insecurity, fear, lack of confidence in God, or unchecked pride. Members of the church become resources deployed by a leader to achieve "victory." Jesus rebukes the disciples when they want him to stop someone who is successfully casting out demons (something the disciples had just failed to do) because he "does not follow with us" (Luke 9:49–50). Such party spiritedness has no place in the body of Christ. It denies our equal dependence upon God's grace and is therefore a denial of the Gospel. Positively, a test of the degree to which a leader has really grasped the generosity of God in the Gospel is their willingness to share or even give away their best resources and people to serve others' ministries.

Public self-congratulation and explicit or implicit criticism of the "competition" is a worrying sign. Anyone who leads God's people in these sorts of attitudes is misusing power in pursuit of self-serving goals—and that could hardly be more serious.

How Does This Church Treat People Who Leave and How Does It Speak about Them?

Every leader faces a decision about how to respond when someone in whom they have invested and for whom they have high hopes wants to leave. They may want to go and serve in another church or organization, or move geographically, or they just don't enjoy the church any longer. Whatever the reason (and regardless of whether it is a good or bad decision), the leader's response reveals their heart and will shape their future ministry. In this moment of disappointment, even of feelings of betrayal, will the leader bless and release a person, entrusting them to their Lord? Or will the leader use power to persuade the person to stay? How many have been made to feel guilty when they want to leave a church, or flattered or manipulated to stay? Alternatively, how many have been reminded of the character flaws that alone explain their desire to leave? These well-worn playbooks are as sinful as they are predictable; a child of God is made to serve a leader's insecurity, disappointment or hurt feelings.

Similarly, people who have left an unhealthy church may be bewildered when their character is attacked and criticized. But how else can those who remain justify staying? If our church really is better than others, then it makes no sense for someone to leave unless there is something wrong with them. Criticism and attack are inevitable. A person who leaves after failed attempts to address what is wrong will be even more viciously attacked. Alternatively, but just as viciously, a leaver may simply be erased—friendships cease, phone calls and contact stop, their names are never mentioned. Leavers' stories don't usually end up on newsletters or church websites.

Making Right Decisions or Making Decisions Rightly?

My maxim is that in matters of guidance (not in clear moral issues) it is better for people to make their own bad decisions than to make my good ones. Guidance and decision-making are a matter of relationship and trust and a godly leader's aim is to strengthen people's trust in the Lord. If leaders make decisions for people, then the people's faith will be stunted because they are not exercising faith in Christ; they are exercising faith in the leader's decision making. Furthermore, the leader has placed himself as mediator between the person and God—and they don't need another mediator.

Many leaders do not realize how much influence they have and how easily and quickly (and unintentionally) they can override a person's conscience. I have observed an extraordinarily charismatic leader who always assured people "It's your decision and you need to trust God for it," but who also left them in no doubt what he believed to be the right decision. Praise or criticism—often publicly or to others in conversations—would follow the "right" or "wrong" decision. People quickly learned how to avoid becoming another illustration of bad or ungodly decision making.

Some may object that there are times when a leader must challenge bad decisions. This is true, but requires caution. A leader must first address potentially manipulative emotions like disappointment or disapproval in their own heart, before challenging a decision. The question must not be how to persuade someone to do what the leader thinks is right, but how to help someone make a decision that starts and finishes with reference to God's character, will, and ways. The aim is not so much to help people make right decisions as to help people make decisions rightly—and a key cost of this for leaders is bearing the pain of loving people through their bad decisions.

Institutional Idolatry

Much of what I've discussed this far may reflect a deeper underlying problem of institutional idolatry. This is one of the more subtle sins and good churches are most at risk. It is remarkably easy for people to cross an almost-invisible line between trusting in God himself and trusting in this church or organization that is serving God. Institutional idolatry seems almost a spring-loaded default in human hearts. It is so much easier to derive joy, security, and a sense of identity from the organization of which I am a member than it is to derive these from God himself. An element of this is right and proper—we are members of a body and the stability and security that comes from that is genuine and deep. However, it is the best gifts that have the greatest idolatrous potential. The way people are treated who question, criticize, or leave may be evidence of institutional idolatry. It is up to leaders to recognize this potential and take steps in their preaching, teaching, and pastoring to mitigate it.

The Price of Success

When a church is closed to critique or feedback, it suggests its leaders may be using power to build their own organization rather than to serve God's kingdom purposes. The trail of bodies behind an organization is very revealing. This seems a particular problem where strong, visionary leaders are organizational founders. A succession of traumatized individuals who have been discarded by an organization in its pursuit of "success" is not a good sign!

The last point under this heading is a more positive pointer towards some signs of organizational health. They may be inferred from above, but it is useful to list them: a healthy church with godly leadership should treat people with generosity, encourage feedback, speak well of other churches—especially those that may be seen as "the competition"—should positively and publicly bless those who leave and should demonstrate evidence of practically blessing and serving other members of the body of Christ, even and especially at cost to themselves. Finally, a healthy church that helps people make their own faith decisions should be gloriously messy and inefficient (see below on "neatness").

IDEOLOGY AND IDEOLOGUES

This isn't so much a diagnostic sign as a helpful explanatory framework.[4] The issue is ideology in pursuit of utopia. Leaders point out what is currently wrong (in a church, state or economic system) and paint a picture of what could be. If they can then persuade people that they have the ideology and the plan to get to the promised utopia, all that is required is for the leader (the ideologue, if you will) to be given the power, money, and resources necessary. The problem with utopian visions is that they do not sufficiently account for sin. Ideological plans and programs never survive contact with reality and only ever work in part. But when power, money, and resources (and, of course, people) have been committed to the program, how does the ideologue deal with the increasing cognitive dissonance as people realize it's not delivering as promised and begin to ask questions or point out the failure? The response of ideologues through history has been to punish, silence, marginalize, exclude, and exile those who question or disagree. In extreme cases, this is literal—of course in churches we don't torture people in the Lubyanka or send them to the Gulag, but we have "Christian" equivalents.

There are two contributing factors to this problem: first a superficial view of sin allows over-promising in the present; secondly, the Good News is reduced from the person of Jesus to an ideological methodology or program. Whether this results in a program for the "right" kind of expository preaching, the best way to train young people in a church, the right kind of missional communities, the ideal evangelistic strategy, the best kind of small groups, the most impactful church music, etc . . . , the dynamics and potential for abuse are the same. Though none of these is necessarily bad, when combined with the dynamics of ideology and a leader with the power to make it happen, God's people are consistently misused as the raw material to make a leader's plan for "utopia" a reality—and the irony is that the shepherd demands the sheep sacrifice themselves for his vision. Leaders must guard against viewing people as the raw material means towards the end of a leader's "success."

No program or method of ours can ever deal with the problem of sin. Progress in sanctification, though real and substantial, is nevertheless usually slow, partial, messy and sometimes barely detectable. In fact, progress (and therefore "success," on which, see further below) is rarely what we want or imagine it to be, and does not conform to our timetable.

The reduction of sanctification to program or methodology is problematic not just because Christ may be excluded from the process, but also

---

4. Somewhat darkly, this became clear to me when reading a biography of Stalin.

because it doesn't work—sin and its devastating effects cannot be managed behaviorally. Any program or methodology implemented by a church risks misrepresenting sanctification and spiritual growth as mere behavioral change. The problem is that it is relatively easy to change people's behavior through programmatic means and the application of appropriate reward or punishment. In fact, the attraction of ideologies and the methodological programs they generate (whether "missional" or "ministry methods" or "discipleship") is that it is so much easier to conform people's behaviors than it is to "labor to see Christ formed" in them.

Ministry that serves the strengthening and outworking of people's union and communion with Christ (see Phil 2:12), trusts that with healthy roots, fruit will grow and ripen naturally. Such ministry leadership must inevitably tolerate the slow and messy process of organic spiritual growth. By contrast, ministry that is ideologically flavored will usually be focused more on approved behaviors or stated beliefs that constitute short-term, measurable results. This is far easier to produce, enforce, and police and leaders who work hard and become good at producing this sort of conformity are celebrated in many Christian circles—they are "successful." This leads us naturally to a discussion of Grant Macaskill's concept of symbolic capital and how it operates in leadership in churches.

In summary, ideologues and their systems will tend to emphasize behaviors over character. They will place a high value on conformity and uniformity and will pride themselves on "getting it right" when others haven't. Disagreement or question-asking will be discouraged and those who persist in questioning will be treated as a problem. Leavers will be criticized or cut off. Young leaders will tend to copy the behaviors of their heroic senior leaders. Cynics will accuse them of being clones. Bad behavior and bad character will be excused by an appeal to "results." Reading lists are narrow and authors who are not "ideologically pure" are blacklisted. All these may be signs we are dealing with an abusive system and should encourage us to ask hard questions.

SYMBOLIC CAPITAL

Grant Macaskill suggests that leaders must become aware of the dynamic of symbolic capital accrual in order to subvert it with "capital" derived from Christ alone as gift.

In a church centered on accruing symbolic capital apart from Christ, people will focus on performing certain identity and boundary markers/behaviors that establish their membership and good standing within the social group. This is reflected in what is rewarded and celebrated, or punished and criticized, and is therefore intimately related to definitions of success.

Newcomers to any social environment (and churches are no different) ask, either consciously or subconsciously, what the rules are—what do I need to do to be accepted here? Leaders play a crucial role in shaping how that question is answered. What stories are told from the front? Who is spoken about? What successes are celebrated? What or who is criticized? Who gets to be at the front? Who gets to preach? These sorts of questions can quickly reveal what constitutes symbolic capital in a church and leaders must become aware of this dynamic. If they are not, then by default they will reinforce exactly what Paul rejects as antithetical to the righteousness of Christ in Phil 3. Leaders who are self-aware can take intentional steps to subvert this issue, considering their own accrued capital and the status it confers as "rubbish" compared to knowing Christ, and teaching and helping others to do the same. Leaders who are not self-aware risk using their power to encourage others to work hard at accumulating symbolic capital—"rubbish"—that ultimately moves them further away from Christ and has them serving the leader and his expectations rather than the Lord himself.[5]

THE CLOSED CIRCLE

Toxic groups tend to close the social circle. There is something attractive about a group of people who get on well and enjoy spending time together. In an age of endemic loneliness and isolation, existing paradoxically alongside the most sophisticated communications technologies ever devised, "community" is enormously attractive. However, community is not always healthy. In unhealthy community, boundaries are carefully policed and behavioral conformity is highly prized. A telltale sign of a community being or becoming unhealthy is the closing of the social circle when a community derives all its social and educational needs internally. Members spend all their social time with each other, only "our" speakers get to teach, and there is usually a list of approved authors or books. In more extreme cases, members are discouraged from spending too much time with those outside of the group, or even with family members if they are not part of the group. At this point a group may become cultish.

Thus, a church in which people are so busy with church activity and social gatherings that they have fewer and fewer real friendships outside

---

5. C. S. Lewis discusses something very similar to this in his essay "The Inner Ring." One question any church leader can ask in order to address what Paul critiques in Phil 3 is, "Who are the cool people here?" See Lewis, *Weight of Glory*.

that circle, should be a concerning sign. This is a danger in any church. Recognizing it and acting to mitigate its unhealthy effects is vital for leaders.[6]

LACK OF HUMILITY

Unfortunately, the obvious needs to be said; lack of humility in Christian leaders is not a good sign! Yet pride, hubris, even downright arrogance are often tolerated or rationalized because a leader is gifted in some valued task—usually preaching. My country of Scotland has a long history of church ministers who can give a "good sermon" on a Sunday, but are excused all sorts of bad behavior the rest of the time. A tradesman who worked in my house told me of a famous preacher who subsequently fell morally, describing him as "an arrogant man" who had looked down on him and his colleague, treating them with disrespect. The signs were there for those outside the church to see, but the church ignored them.[7]

This can only happen with the active collusion of congregations who want a minister who performs well more than they want one who demonstrates Christlike humility.

While humility is a key marker, lack of it does not always manifest as overt arrogance or pride. There is also a self-deprecation that remains just as self-centered and invites the comment, "You seem very proud of your humility."[8] Our capacity for self-deception seems limitless and leaders will hide their pride in manifold subtle ways. One clear implication is that leaders need to be known—if they are to be safe and healthy leaders, they must have relationships that do not allow them to hide. The sadness for many church leaders is that they are isolated and unaccountable in any meaningful way.

---

6. I recognized this potential when I was working with a parachurch organization and addressed it by intentionally seeking out speakers and teachers from outside the organization for friendship, mentoring, and teaching. Another way of tackling this is simply to reduce the amount of church-based activity so that people actually have time to form and build real friendships with people who are not part of their church. This, of course, is also the most human of missional strategies.

7. The sentence "He's a great preacher, but . . ." should be banned.

8. This was once said to me in all seriousness by a friend when I was in my twenties. I've never forgotten it.

LEADERS ON PEDESTALS AND WEAKNESS NEVER SHOWN—THE FALSE VIEW OF MATURITY

Humility is difficult when a church puts a minister on a pedestal, and some ministers are all too willing to allow it to happen.[9] This damages both the people and the minister who is set up for failure or even abuse.

Such elevation of leaders encourages them to lie, promoting a false view of maturity in which weakness, struggle, or sin dare not be shown lest the respect of the church members is lost. This is highly problematic, not least because of the example it sets for a congregation. Instead of modeling the life of grace that (one hopes) is being preached, it models a life that has reached a point where less grace is needed. Leaders effectively say, "Let me tell you about how much you need Jesus, while I demonstrate how little I need him myself." This false view of maturity contributes to a misunderstanding of the gospel and a failure to grasp the reality of grace and live by it. Furthermore, this places unbearable pressure on church leaders, since they feel unable to share genuine struggles with anyone, becoming increasingly isolated and vulnerable to temptation. Alternatively, the occupation of a pedestal can pamper a minister's ego and may generate the misuse of people as the means towards their ends of ministry "success."

By contrast, growing maturity in Christ requires not simply hearing about grace, but witnessing lived-out examples of grace. And if people are going to see what living by grace looks like in practice, then a leader's appropriate self-disclosure is essential. This cannot happen if leaders conceal the realities of their inner lives, pretending to a holiness that is not theirs. Grace must be both preached and demonstrated. Paul clearly did so which was why the Corinthians despised him. They wanted him to play the "pedestal" game (1 Cor 2:1–5). He refused because he wanted them to trust in Christ, not in Paul.

Church leaders who seek both to preach grace and model it, will have to relinquish the desire for a good reputation. Why should they think they can follow a crucified Lord who was shamed, betrayed, and rejected, and avoid these things?

Many will object that for a leader to make himself thus vulnerable before a congregation is emotional and, perhaps, career suicide. This indicates how far from biblical principle we have strayed in our conception of Christian leadership. What is required is "appropriate" vulnerability and honesty. There is no neat formula for this, but it starts simply with the question of what will best serve the spiritual growth of those we lead. The

---

9. Some homes in the Highlands of Scotland still have a photograph of the minister on the mantelpiece.

indiscriminate sharing of every detail in one's life is unlikely to do that and may, in fact, be self-indulgent. However, it does mean that every detail of our lives is surrendered to the Lord so that he might direct its use for the blessing and benefit of his people.

To summarize, putting leaders on pedestals and expecting them to be what they are not, nor ever can be, contributes to abuses of power. Leaders cease to be honest with themselves and others, they become isolated and can begin to see the members of a church as the raw material means towards their own "success." Leaders who don't appear to have any struggles any more are playing a dangerous game.

NEATNESS, ORDER AND SUCCESS

A community nurse once shared with me that a red flag for her was a home with very young children that was immaculately tidy. Children can't grow if the priority is order and neatness—they can't learn to feed themselves without making a mess. In a similar way to parents who insist on good behavior in their children because of how that reflects on the parents, rather than because of what's best for the children, church leaders may insist on certain behavioral and organizational standards. Unaddressed and externalized perfectionism in a church leader can result in subtle pressure on members of a church to behave in ways that the leader has decided constitute "a good witness." This is another way of creating an environment in which symbolic capital is accrued and the righteousness of Christ neglected. Again, it is easier to shape behavioral conformity than to labor to see Christ formed in people.

But what gain is there for leaders in fostering such an environment? Like parents wanting their children to behave well in public, how things look to others may be a significant motivation. A congregation that looks good and behaves well reflects on the pastor. It's also a visible, achievable "success measure." One of the greatest pressures on Christian leaders is that there are few short-term, measurable outcomes that confirm we're doing a good job, and the temptation to create some is hard to resist.

The attempt to define and measure outcomes is, however, problematic. "Success" in the church must be defined carefully, since people adjust their behaviors towards whatever "success measures" are adopted (implicitly or explicitly). But what are legitimate "success" measures in a church? Can spiritual growth be measured? Not all that counts can be counted and not all that can be counted counts. In other words, the desire to have measurable outcomes often means measuring things that aren't centrally important.

We must be so careful about what "success measures" we encourage. Behaviors will change towards what is rewarded, often to the detriment of what is centrally important, and we may end up treasuring the "rubbish" of Phil 3 and missing out on the righteousness of faith. In all of this, we must also confront what Os Guinness refers to as evangelicalism's "capitulation to late modernity," expressed most in our devotion to program and technique.[10] Proxy outcome measures together with an unthinking modernist mindset and devotion to program lead very quickly to churches that can be very busy and apparently very "successful." The problem is that all of that can be accomplished without Jesus and at the cost of God's people. We ought to be thoroughly suspicious of "efficient" and "successful" Christian ministry.

USELESS PEOPLE?

The concept of "efficiency" presupposes means and ends and leads to an unsettling question about how "useless" or "little" people are treated in a church. A pastor or leader motivated by a certain view of "successful" church will evaluate and rank people according to how useful they are in contributing to this "success." So, who is celebrated and rewarded, ignored, provokes a roll of the eyes by leaders, or is left with no one talking to them after a service?

Francis Schaeffer spoke of there being no "little people" in the body of Christ.[11] For the church to do what God has made it to do and be what God has made it to be requires every member to grow to maturity in Christ, finding their place and making their unique contribution, using the gifts God has given them. There really are no "little people"—every member of the body is indispensable to its health and functioning.

Thus, if we see a church in which some people are treated as being less important because they don't contribute as much to our "success," then we can infer that success has been wrongly defined and the functioning body of Christ is neglected. It is infinitely sad to hear of brothers and sisters who have felt themselves to be either useless to the church or a drain on resources. An environment that makes one of God's children feel this way is, by definition, dysfunctional, even abusive. How dare anyone treat "one of the least of these" differently to the way Jesus himself treats them?

---

10. See Guinness, *Gravedigger File*.
11. Schaeffer, *No Little People*.

HOW ARE WOMEN TREATED? HOW DO WOMEN FEEL—REALLY?

Closely following the previous point, but worthy of a separate heading, is the question of how women are treated. Regardless of one's views on specific roles of women and men in the church, it is uncontroversial to say that the Spirit has gifted every member of the body of Christ for the benefit of the whole, so it is a marker of ill health when members are not being genuinely equipped to use their God-given gifts to build up the body (Eph 4:11–16). Thus, any functional neglect of the contribution of women is a denial of a key biblical principle. In practice, sadly, many churches have neglected the contribution of women, relegating them to gender-stereotypical roles like childcare or catering. Leaders should not assume they know the answer to the question of how women are treated in their church; they need to ask the women how they actually feel.

MONEY AND PATRONAGE

Another sign of the way power is used by leaders in churches is how money is used. In the UK it is tempting to think this is not much of an issue as there isn't nearly as much money in the church as there is in the US. However, the issues are the same. Is money used to serve or control? Is it used to advance God's kingdom purposes or to advance the dominance of my particular tribe? Does any money flow out from this church or organization to bless and benefit others in different—even competing—churches or organizations?

Closely connected with this is the issue of patronage. A lot of young men starting out in ministry hope that someone senior will act on their behalf and help them to get the position or platform they are hoping for. The dynamics of control and manipulation (even of baptized empire building) inherent in this are deeply concerning. A church leader, whose job offer I had declined, commented to a mutual friend that "The problem with Mark Stirling is that he doesn't need my money." Something has gone badly wrong when a church leader thinks it is a problem that someone cannot be bought. How should churches handle the power of "hiring and firing" and the temptation that comes with it to direct and control individuals?

The idea that large amounts of money will enable us to do lots of good things, quickly and subtly crosses a line to become the belief and practice that my financial resources can be used to overcome opposition and ensure that I get my way—and, since my way is clearly God's way, the end always justifies the means. It is challenging to reflect on the example of Francis and Edith Schaeffer who founded L'Abri. They believed in "inbuilt institutional weakness" whereby their organization was financially only ever a couple of months away from collapse and failure. The only way it could continue would be if God were clearly supplying their needs. The presence of ample financial resources, though potentially a blessing, may also allow us to continue with particular work long after God has finished with it. It also exposes a leader to temptation to use those resources to accomplish their own will rather than God's.

Leaders urgently need to become more self-aware. Rigorous mechanisms of accountability will also help, but awareness of the issue and repentance for all the ways we have made money and the power it gives us into an idol is a start.

LIFELONG LEARNING—IS THERE EVIDENCE OF TEACHABILITY OR DO WE KNOW IT ALL ALREADY?

A final point in this long, but far-from-comprehensive list is the issue of teachability. To be publicly, humbly teachable is one antidote to the abuse of power. Sadly, the opposite is often the case; leaders can communicate that they already know everything they need to know and have nothing to learn from anyone—not even from God! Especially in churches in which leadership is defined in terms of possession and delivery of knowledge, for a leader to maintain his power, he must also defend his position of knowing more than others. The authoritative pastor, with the keys of knowledge and right interpretation of Scripture, has great power and may feel they cannot admit to not knowing or understanding things. How often does a church leader feel threatened by the presence of academics or theology students in his congregation? Criticism of the academy or of academic theology voiced from the pulpit is, sadly, all too common.

Pastors and ministers who know it all and have nothing to learn from anyone is another concerning sign. Their power is based on being the authoritative dispenser of knowledge and they will react defensively and sometimes aggressively to anyone who questions, or to anyone who reads widely and may know more than they do.

CONCLUSIONS

In this chapter I have reflected on some features of either individuals or systems that should cause us to ask critical questions about whether power is being used well or badly. To be clear, there is no single one of these that "proves" the presence of abuse.[12] Rather, these are all observations that invite further questions. It is possible for us to observe some of the features in this chapter and for there not to be abuse present. It can be subtle, and I am urging caution that we do not jump to diagnostic conclusions.

Where do we go from here? By now it should be obvious that character matters, and at the heart of character is the quality of humility.

Is There a Test for Humility?

So much of what has been discussed in this chapter and in the wider book relates to simple lack of humility on the part of Christian leaders. Yet humility is such a central quality, grounded in a response to Jesus' call to deny self, take up cross and follow. This call to discipleship necessitates the dethroning of the sovereign self. The core posture of a life that may meaningfully be called "Christian" must be one of submission to the sovereign of the universe, recognizing that we are not in charge, the world does not revolve around us and the story is about God's glory, not ours. If this is so, we may ask why lack of humility goes unaddressed so frequently? I've discussed this earlier in this chapter, but a consistent observation is that churches really do value competence and gifting more highly than they value character. It is amazing what people are willing to excuse or put up with for the sake of an entertaining (or reliably orthodox) sermon every Sunday. If abuse of power in our churches is ever to be addressed, then humility in leaders must be the starting point. It is something that congregations must pay more attention to in their leaders and should be close to the top of the list of assessment criteria for those who are involved in selection for ministerial training.

The bottom line, however, is remarkably simple; where there is misuse of power by leaders, there is misunderstanding and misrepresentation of God and of the gospel. Such leaders are themselves failing to follow Jesus whilst claiming to act with the authority of his name. This is a time when repentance is required of the shepherds who have fed themselves on God's sheep instead of feeding the sheep.

We cannot and must not do Jesus' work in non-Jesus ways.

---

12. Proving abuse is extraordinarily difficult and is one reason some abusive leaders have seemed to get away with it for so long.

BIBLIOGRAPHY

Guinness, Os. *The Gravedigger File*. London: Hodder & Stoughton, 1987.
Lewis, C. S. *The Weight of Glory*. Grand Rapids, MI: Eerdmans, 1949.
Schaeffer, Francis A. *No Little People*. Wheaton, IL: Crossway, 2021.

Conclusion

That No Bruised Reed Is Ever Broken

Mark Meynell

INTRODUCTION

THE CURRENT DALAI LAMA (the fourteenth) has occupied a place on the world stage for an astonishing length of time. Born in 1935, he was formally recognized as the fourteenth Dalai Lama not long before his fifth birthday. When Chairman Mao's China annexed Tibet in 1950, he and his administration tried to continue with their new constraints, but it became impossible, especially with the Tibetan uprising of 1959. So, with his community, the Dalai Lama fled to northern India, from where he has functioned as figurehead and led the people ever since. In the 1970s, he developed a different tactic with China, the so-called Middle Way Approach from around 1974. The idea was to negotiate a Tibetan acceptance of China's political sovereignty over its territories, which included Tibet, while committing China to preserve the culture, religion, and national identity of Tibet. However, as he noted in his speech on the fiftieth anniversary of the uprising in 2009, their nearly two decades of talks "did not bear any concrete results" and formal contacts eventually broke off in 1993.[1] China clearly held all the cards and every time an agreement seemed close, the terms would shift and the Tibetans' hopes slip away.

---

1. Mullin, "Dalai Lama Seeks Peking Accord."

In an interview in 1980, the Dalai Lama was unable to conceal his frustration, letting his true feelings known to the British journalist and later politician, Chris Mullin.

> Frankly speaking, it is difficult to believe or trust the Chinese [government]. Once bitten by a snake, you feel suspicious even when you see a piece of rope.[2]

In such circumstances, it is remarkable that he and his team persevered for another thirteen years. Nobody could accuse them of half-heartedness or unwillingness to find solutions. But the decades-long pattern of slippery tactics took its toll. The legacy was suspicion bordering on paranoia. And who can blame him?

1. On Spiritual Abuse

Contemporary discourse in the public square, in whatever field, has become contentious in part because of the fluidity, and occasionally the deliberate garbling, of meaning. Terms too often seem to be selected more for their rhetorical force than their semantic precision. This is hardly a new phenomenon, for it has been a standard tool in the demagogue's armory ever since the forum speeches of Roman tribunes seeking to rouse the mob. However, when it is a feature both of social media campaigning and of pastoral testimony, the situation is fraught. For survivors who must process deep wounds and confused paranoia as it is, the situation can become perilous for all involved. Accusations made without method, precision, or proportion can have devastating, unintended consequences. For example, what results from semantic blurring? Through the marshalling of rhetorical force, it may well elicit immediate victories, but the subsequent witness of abuse victims (especially when more extreme) is tragically undermined. A heedless application of terms tends to erase any distinctions between levels of genuine suffering. Furthermore, it lends credence to the contention that calling out abuse is merely the appropriation of a cultural or political bandwagon.

So, for the protection of all victims, not to mention those unfairly accused, it is vital that great care is taken over vocabulary.

---

2. Mullin, "Dalai Lama Seeks Peking Accord."

Contentious terms.

As several contributors have noted, the public exposure of abuses has become much more prevalent and supported in recent years. For all the complexities brought about by this cultural shift, it is hard to see any justification for its opposite, namely the concealment of abuse. When abuses take place within the frame of unequal power dynamics (whether derived from formal or informal power), victims need and deserve everything they can get to compensate for their inherent vulnerability. As Chuck DeGroat rightly notes:

> When pastors and churches deny the impact of emotional abuse, they retraumatize the victim. When we defer to suspicion of a victim and support of a potential abuser, we run the risk of doing irreparable harm. Victims may shut down or return to their abuser. They may blame themselves for being too much trouble.[3]

But there has been disquiet in some circles about how to describe such abuses when occurring within a Christian context. For example, the Theology Advisory Group of the UK's Evangelical Alliance (chaired by David Hilborn) published a report in 2018 questioning the value of the term "spiritual abuse." Far from dismissing the reality of abuses by Christian leaders, the report was clear that it "in no way downplays the harmful actions and effects of Emotional and Psychological Abuse in religious contexts."[4] Its underlying concern was the difficulty of adjudicating within a secular context precisely the nature of "spiritual" abuse as opposed to other forms. Furthermore, it maintains that within the British context at least, the legislation is easily sufficient for dealing with such breaches.

> While religious organizations might say that sexual or any other sort of abuse committed by their adherents is particularly heinous because religions generally hold those adherents to higher moral standards than the secular law, the actual prosecution of such abuse in criminal court cannot realistically pay significant heed to those higher moral claims of religion, since that would once more require lawmakers, barristers and judges to make theological as well as legal determinations, which as we have established, is unfeasible in a modern secular democracy. It is enough that a religious sexual abuser be tried for sexual abuse; by the same token, it is enough that a religious emotional or psychological abuser be tried for Emotional or Psychological Abuse.

3. DeGroat, *Narcissism*, 124.
4. Hilborn, "Reviewing the Discourse," 1.

It would be both unnecessary and unworkable for such abusers also to be tried for a separate offence of "spiritual abuse."[5]

The writers of the report are concerned, with very good reason, that the label can be exploited by revisionists seeking to use state agencies to attack orthodox and historic Christian doctrine or ethics. This is evidently why some pressed for the law to "recognize Spiritual Abuse as a formal category of harm—particularly with children—and to add it to their current four-fold definition of abuse: physical, sexual, emotional abuse and neglect."[6] The report's writers question both the legal benefits of adding a fifth category as well as its impracticability. With reference to the claim that John Smyth's appalling physical abuses of boys at Iwerne camps[7] was linked to the doctrine of penal substitution, they note that "any idea that criminal prosecution of such abuse might turn on courtroom debate about the relative theological merits of one historic atonement model or another would be both undesirable and unworkable."[8]

The EA report does make a convincing case and, for the time being at least, seems to have been successful in preempting any calls to alter existing legislation. However, because this present volume is more concerned with the church's life and health than the legal frameworks within which religious organizations must operate, most (though not all) of this volume's contributors sense the wisdom of continued but sparing and precise use of "spiritual abuse" (as many working in this field insist on doing). As Michael Kruger points out in his 2022 book, it has a place despite its imperfections, simply because it brings into clear focus the gravity of what a Christian leader is doing. He draws on several writers in his extensive survey of the literature for corroboration. The crucial factor is that it highlights the abuser's exploitation of their ecclesiastical position or authority, and, by inference, their divine sanction to dominate, control, or manipulate a person, behavior described by one writer as "pious coercion."[9] That is what makes this so odious.

The problem comes, however, with defining its boundaries. Essential to precision is establishing clear and workable distinctions. Before we can proceed, however, it is important to recognize a cultural trend which adds further complexity, both because it muddies the waters for those trying to

---

5. Hilborn, "Reviewing the Discourse," 17.

6. Hilborn, "Reviewing the Discourse," 12, quoting Jayne Ozanne's proposal after the Bishop of Oxford's Tribunal Determination on the 2017 case of Revd Timothy Davis from Christ Church Abingdon.

7. See "Christian Camp Leader John Smyth."

8. Hilborn, "Reviewing the Discourse," 15.

9. Kruger, *Bully Pulpit*, 23–25.

navigate in the current climate and because it serves to buttress the prejudices of those contending that a concern for church power abuse is a capitulation to worldly agendas.

Safe spaces.

Greg Lukianoff and Jonathan Haidt caused considerable controversy when their book *The Coddling of the American Mind* was first published in 2018.[10] Lawyer and psychologist respectively, they were concerned about the increase in cancellations of unpopular speakers or groups on American campuses by those pejoratively deemed "snowflake students." Yet this represents a deeper trend, one motivated by the entirely laudable desire to protect and support students in a highly pressured environment. However, for all its good intentions, Lukianoff and Haidt are concerned that it is in fact counter-productive. They identify what they call the "three great untruths" of the contemporary scene:

- The Untruth of Fragility: what doesn't kill you makes you weaker
- The Untruth of Emotional Reasoning: Always trust your feelings
- The Untruth of Us versus Them: Life is a battle between good people and evil people.[11]

One outworking of this triad is the so-called "heckler's veto" whereby those that some deem unacceptable (for whatever reason) must be banned, even when fellow students might want to hear them.[12] This contributes to what the authors term the governing principle of "safetyism," the "culture or belief system in which safety has become a sacred value, which means that people become unwilling to make trade-offs demanded by other practical or moral concerns."[13] Citing the almost comical, extreme example of a primary school headteacher in East London who banned even the touching of snow one winter because "touching could lead to *snowballs*" which in turn might lead to a child's eye injury from a snowball containing grit. As they say, "That is the epitome of safetyism: if we can prevent one child from getting hurt, we should deprive all children of slightly risky play."[14]

---

10. Lukianoff and Haidt, *Coddling of the American Mind*.
11. Lukianoff and Haidt, *Coddling of the American Mind*, 4.
12. Lukianoff and Haidt, *Coddling of the American Mind*, 6.
13. Lukianoff and Haidt, *Coddling of the American Mind*, 30.
14. Lukianoff and Haidt, *Coddling of the American Mind*, 236.

One of the book's most significant insights is a lesson from psychology, from Cognitive Behavioral Therapy (CBT) in particular. They discern the campus "concept creep" of safety from the physical into the emotional realms. After all, the implication is surely that a professor wielding a weapon presents a far greater danger than if she uses an incorrect pronoun? Safetyism operates on the assumption that students are fragile. However, far from healing this fragility, safetyism inadvertently exacerbates it. Demanding the avoidance of triggers may actually make people mentally worse off. They take Post-Traumatic Stress Disorder (PTSD) as a case in point. This is "caused by an extraordinary and terrifying experience and the criteria for a traumatic event that warrants a diagnosis were (and are) strict."[15] It can only be caused by extreme experiences that are not regarded as normal. War or rape clearly qualify, while divorce and bereavement tend not to. But here is the important point: trigger avoidance is symptomatic of PTSD, not its cure. According to Richard McNally of Harvard's Department of Psychology, "trigger warnings are counter-therapeutic" whereas "evidence-based, cognitive-behavior therapies . . . [help students to] overcome PTSD. These therapies involve gradual, systematic exposure to traumatic memories until their capacity to trigger distress diminishes."[16]

Notice what this is *not* saying. McNally does not deny the reality of trauma, let alone of mental illness in general. Nor does he belittle the phenomenon of anxiety-causing triggers. Even less does he advocate a thoughtless license for anything that might be genuinely triggering for the wounded and vulnerable. He merely applies therapeutic wisdom and experience. It is not a laissez-faire approach to triggers but a methodical and contained process of help, support, and guidance designed to lead to recovery and acceptance. The goal is for particular circumstances to no longer function as triggers.

By extension, preventing exposure to different, difficult, or even obnoxious ideas is likely to be counterproductive. This is not an appeal for an absolutist free speech position but a corrective to widespread cultural assumptions. As someone who has battled with mental illness ever since a clinical diagnosis of PTSD in 2005, I know how profoundly destabilizing flashbacks and triggers are.[17] CBT was crucial in overcoming the immediate symptoms of my PTSD, so I can testify to the reality of what McNally describes. This does not prevent occasions in church life even now having a triggering effect. However, I am very clear that while the concern of this

---

15. Lukianoff and Haidt, *Coddling of the American Mind*, 25.
16. Lukianoff and Haidt, *Coddling of the American Mind*, 29.
17. Meynell, *When Darkness Seems*.

entire book is to call the church to be a safe environment for all including the most vulnerable, it is emphatically not driven by a "safetyist" mentality. The exposure of bullying and coercion is not the manifestation of some "snowflake" worldliness, therefore. It is driven by nothing less than the model and commands of the Lord of the church himself, as several of the book's contributors have demonstrated. A church is only said to be truly safe when it has fostered the kind of environment that gives members confidence to face difficult things, without fear of rejection, vitriol, or cruelty. A community that functions by pushing difficulty or darkness away hardly warrants the description safe. A safe church can only be nurtured by saturation in the gospel of grace because it is only at the foot of the cross that facing such darkness with hope is even possible.

That is what lies at the heart of Dietrich Bonhoeffer's inspiring vision for church life based on his experiences at the small, and under the Nazi regime illegal, training community at Finkenwalde.

> It is grace, nothing but grace, that we are allowed to live in community with Christian brethren.[18]
>
> It is a ministry of mercy, an ultimate offer of genuine fellowship, when we allow nothing but God's genuine fellowship, when we allow nothing but God's Word to stand between us, judging and succoring. Then it is not we who are judging; God alone judges, and God's judgment is helpful and healing.[19]
>
> In daily, earnest living with the Cross of Christ the Christian loses the spirit of human censoriousness on the one hand and weak indulgence on the other, and he receives the spirit of divine severity and divine love.[20]

But it is to how the distortions and egocentricism of human leadership harm "God's genuine fellowship" that we must now turn.

Critical Distinctions.

Andy Crouch has been involved in Christian parachurch ministry for many years and so has observed some of the challenges faced by believers in many different contexts. He describes spending time with Jayakumar Christian, then director of *World Vision India*, to witness how their attempts to tackle child slavery (often more euphemistically termed "bonded labor")

---

18. Bonhoeffer, *Life Together*, 10.
19. Bonhoeffer, *Life Together*, 83.
20. Bonhoeffer, *Life Together*, 95.

in southern India. Jayakumar made a passing comment which became transformative for Crouch's thinking. "'The poor are poor,' Jayakumar said to me, 'because someone else is trying to play God in their lives.'"[21] Crouch would use this metaphor for the title of the book he was working on. For our purposes here, it also functions as a helpful catchall for what we should call "spiritual abuse." "Playing God" evokes the sense of shock at the usurper, the horror at the illegitimacy and sheer presumption of those who wreak havoc in others' lives *in God's name*.

But while it is straightforward to show why it is a problem, establishing its boundaries is a thornier question. Unfortunately, there is not the space here to go into great detail, but Michael Kruger's recent book provides an excellent survey of both the key hallmarks of spiritual abuse and relational difficulties that ought not to come under its banner. So I offer here a brief summary of his insights. The heart of this abuse is the need to control others. This manifests in five ways:[22]

- *Hypercritical*: "a key characteristic of an abusive leader is that they lead through fault-finding." To the abuser's common defense that it is their job to identify people's sins, Kruger makes this trenchant comment. "But the victims of abuse know the difference between the gentle corrections of a loving shepherd and the oppressive fault-finding of an abuser."
- *Cruel*: abusive leaders seem to hurt people deliberately. "While some abusive pastors use 'fire' to hurt their victims, others use 'ice' they turn cold, quietly cutting off the person from the ministry of the church and from the relationships therein."
- *Threatening*: abusive leaders use threats as a form of control, so that victims comply out of fear. "Here's the point: It is not normal for people to have this sort of fear of their pastor. We need to let that sink in. If many people, across many years, express significant fear of a pastor, then something is very, very wrong."
- *Defensive*: all pastors get criticized, but the issue is how that gets handled. Criticism of "a spiritually abusive pastor bent on preserving his own authority" leads "in short [to] war. Abusive pastors are notoriously thin-skinned, seeing even the slightest bit of criticism as a threat to their power." Kruger continues: "The rich irony here is that the pastor who is unable to take criticism is often highly critical of everyone else."

---

21. Crouch, *Playing God*, 113.
22. Kruger, *Bully Pulpit*, 28–33.

- *Manipulative*: this occurs either through the deliberate use of malleable, partisan institutional structures or canny relational devices (such as flattery or selective trust).

Of course, every person in leadership fails from time to time. Each of us will be guilty of several, if not all, of these behaviors on occasion. We all must walk in perpetual humility when it comes to battling our sins. A sure mark that someone is not an abuser is a willingness, however reluctant, to evaluate accusations and come to true repentance. The issue is one of patterns, consistent and corroborated manifestations of these characteristics. Isolated incidents, concerning though they undoubtedly will be, are not in view. One final point before setting some boundaries here. Ken Blue produced an important book on caring for abuse survivors three decades ago, at a time when church leaders were far less aware of the issue than they are now. He makes an important caveat about the leader's intentions.

> Spiritual abusers are curiously naïve about the effects of the exploitation. They rarely intend to hurt their victims. They are usually so narcissistic, or so focused on some great thing they are doing for God, that they don't notice the wounds they are inflicting on their followers. So though I maintain that spiritual abuse is evil and dangerous and must be stopped, my definition of it leaves out the term intent to hurt.[23]

But it is crucial to identify where relationship difficulties, the stuff of normal community life the world over, end and spiritual abuse begins. For example, every relationship is subject to conflicts of one type or another, and these may well be constructive and even healthy. Kruger offers five more categories, therefore, to articulate relational problems which are not abusive per se.[24] This is important because they undoubtedly feel unpleasant to experience, and they may even *feel* abusive. But if, as Lukianoff and Haidt note, the notion that "feelings are everything" is a modern untruth, it is important to see where the clear water lies.

- Being Unfriendly: not all Christian leaders are warm, easygoing, or even able to remember names. "Their relational intelligence may be pretty low." But that does not make their behavior abusive.

- Intimidating Personality: projecting an air of confidence or competence can be intimidating, and many gifted people do so unthinkingly. Having an intimidating personality, however, is very different from

---

23. Blue, *Healing Spiritual Abuse*, 12.
24. Kruger, *Bully Pulpit*, 35–38.

"intentionally intimidating others through threats, attacks, and bullying." Only the latter is abusive.

- Not Getting Along: everyone finds some types of people difficult to get on with. Likewise, we will inevitably wind some others up the wrong way. That is normal community life. The experience of conflict in itself does not constitute abuse. But "if the lead pastor seems to be at the center of nearly every conflict, with a 'debris field' of broken relationships in his wake, then a more thorough investigation is warranted." Again, the issue is patterns of behavior.

- Accidentally Hurting Someone: this is a hard thing to face, especially when every piece of rope looks like a snake. But "The reality that some people can be overly sensitive, feeling hurt over every interaction and every exchange, can exacerbate these hurtful missteps. But being hurt is not, in itself, proof of abuse."

- Confronting People's Sins: most pastors would agree that this is one of the trickiest and most demanding aspects of ministry life. "Despite the claims of our postmodern culture, it is not harmful or abusive merely to uphold biblical standards of conflict in the lives of God's people." It was precisely this conviction that led to the EA's concern with legislating for spiritual abuse. The problem, as Kruger rightly notes from his own research, is "much abuse takes place precisely when a pastor is confronting sin." So, rather than avoiding the practice altogether, we should seek to do it with Christlike humility and love. *Abusus non tollit usum*: the potential for the abuse of a practice should not be used as a pretext for abolishing that practice. Post-blizzard primary headteachers take note.

Neither of these lists of characteristics is exhaustive. Many others have explored the issues with far greater expertise and depth.[25] This is by no means designed to make those who have suffered at the hands of leaders retreat into shame or denial about their experiences as if their perceptions were illegitimate or false. Far from it. There is evidently a need to work at repairing the relationship. Each of the second list's characteristics needs to be addressed and processed by leaders with humility and care, especially when such leaders have less emotional awareness than those on the receiving end of their words or actions. So, for example, it is not good enough for the leader to say, "I'm sorry you felt intimidated," as if it was solely the recipient's

---

25. Those that have been particularly helpful are McKnight and Barringer, *Church Called Tov*; Mullen, *Something's Not Right*; Langberg, *Suffering and the Heart of God*; Kruger, *Bully Pulpit*; DeGroat, *Narcissism*.

problem or fault. He or she must still take steps to understand causes and ways of improving the relationship. But all need care to avoid lumping every relational breakdown under the spiritual abuse banner. At the very least, it is vital to explore alternative explanations or categories for what has gone wrong, while never denying the possibility that spiritual abuse is the legitimate and necessary description.

For now, we will briefly explore what to do with complaints and desired outcomes.

2. On Receiving Complaints

Take it seriously.

Abuse survivors are reluctant to speak up for a host of reasons. They fear retaliation, particularly if the person they accuse wields great power. Perhaps they have seen dire consequences endured by previous testifiers. Or they assume nobody will believe them. They may even struggle to believe their own story themselves. But then abusers are often highly skilled in exploiting psychological weapons of which gaslighting is one of the most sinister and cruel.

So, it is essential to recognize that even broaching the subject will have been costly. The onus on the one listening is therefore immense. It is vital to take any such testimony with the utmost seriousness. Care must be taken to listen attentively and carefully, giving time and space for a person to open up. All the wisdom and best practice from the counseling realm must come into play here.

Furthermore, in the wake of the #MeToo exposure of widespread sexual abuse, another related hashtag slogan quickly became prominent during the process to confirm Brett Kavanaugh's seat on the US Supreme Court: #BelieveWomen.[26] Inevitably, such is the crudeness of hashtags and social media "debate," the phrase itself quickly became problematic. Some suggested that it conveyed a message of "guilty before proven innocent." That is certainly how those accused of abuses feel. While this is not the place to discuss the value (or its lack) of this form of discourse, it did elicit an important clarification that is relevant. The feminist columnist Judy Ellison Sady Doyle responded to many of the slogan's critics. Whatever the phrase means, she insisted that it "has never meant 'ignore facts'" and as such "does not actually come into conflict with fact-checking sources."[27]

---

26. See "Kavanaugh Hearing."
27. Doyle, "Despite What You May," para. 11.

Instead, its purpose, as far as such things are discernible, was to appeal for people not to "assume women as a gender are especially deceptive or vindictive, and recognize that false allegations are less common than real ones." It is a response to the all-too-frequent response to an individual's testimony that it is a malicious fiction. Of course, such a thing can occur as a recent British case grimly illustrates.[28] Yet, as veteran BBC America correspondent Katty Kay notes, one US study in 2010 found that only "2–10% of rape accusations . . . are proven to be fake," while official FBI researchers found that only 8% were "determined to be false after investigation."[29] Even while acknowledging that it is based on only two studies, that convergence is powerful. Ninety percent of accusations were *not* false.

Sexual abuse is not the same as spiritual abuse, of course. Comparable statistics are inevitably much harder to come by. But because of the peril and costs of making such accusations, it is surely reasonable to expect a similar weight in favor of the truthful, especially in cases when several people independently testify about their experiences. In fact, the whole point of #MeToo in the first place was to give courage to as-yet-unknown witnesses to speak out in order to corroborate survivors' testimonies.

So, when an accusation is made, it is incumbent on the one receiving it not to dismiss or belittle it, let alone conceal it. Believing the witness is not an invitation to ignore evidence. It may well be that there have been misunderstandings and errors of judgment, but a good process will establish those. Until that time, believing the survivor's story entails taking it seriously and following best practise. It does not mean that the testimony is automatically unquestionable. After all, as Kruger points out, "being hurt is not, in itself, proof of abuse."[30] But, when someone has clearly been hurt, he or she still needs pastoral care and love.

Triage and due process.

After a major disaster has left countless injuries and deaths, it is basic practice in emergency rooms to use a system of *triage*[31] whereby patients are separated on the basis of their injuries and life expectancy. Traditionally, there were three categories: likely to live without immediate treatment, unlikely to live with treatment, needs immediate treatment to live.

---

28. See "Eleanor Williams Sentencing."
29. "Truth about False Assault Accusations," paras. 3–5.
30. Kruger, *Bully Pulpit*, 36.
31. Derived from the French word *trier*, meaning "to sort or separate."

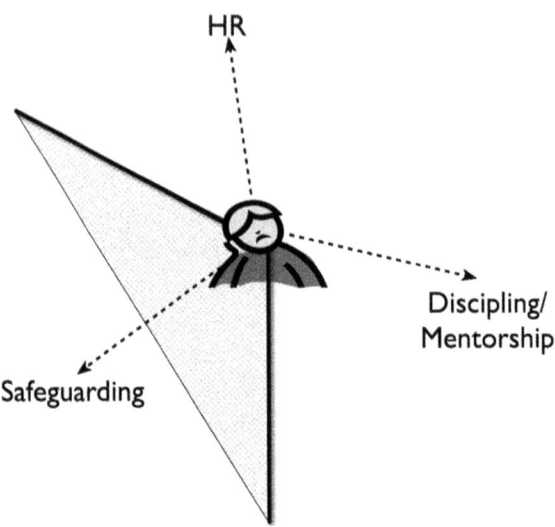

Circumstances may dictate different features and numbers of characteristics. But it is a helpful model for how we should process a witness who might come to us for support. We must quickly decide under which category a testimony should be handled. This is because an entirely appropriate response for one person could be unhelpful, and even highly damaging, for another.

- matters of Management/Human Resources
- matters of Christian Discipleship/Mentoring
- matters of Safeguarding

If someone is having problems with a colleague, or even a line manager, for example, then modern organizations and churches should have procedures in place for how this should be handled. If not, this must be rectified as soon as possible! The ideal is for the roots of the conflict are established, whether they derive from false expectations, mutual misunderstandings, a lack of job description clarity, or difficult behaviors and habits. These are regular occurrences in any organization with Christian institutions hardly immune. The hope, though, is that most of these have been anticipated by the institution's procedures. Responding to this category of complaint, then, is the most straightforward. It is a matter of following the institution's HR practice.

A complicating factor here is one common to churches and parachurch groups, namely the reliance on volunteers. This brings with it a range of particular dynamics and challenges, but there is no reason why these cannot be navigated well with good practices and thoughtful management.[32] Responsible leaders with a pastoral concern for the welfare of their people will ensure that these are handled well.

The second arena for potential conflict is often found within discipling relationships. As Marcus Honeysett's chapter explores, such relationships will invariably feature differences in age and experience between mentor and mentee. But because they lie outside formal institutional structures, his suggestions for best practice are valuable. Since such a relationship is bound to include discussing a mentee's lifestyle and behavior, it is vital that this is done well. Mentors need to search their own hearts to check that they are not driven by some ulterior motive in what they identify or highlight. As discussed in my chapter on the *Imago Dei*, it can never be the mentor's job to assume responsibility for another person's holiness or progress. That truly is to play God in their lives. Any discussion about a mentee's lifestyle must therefore be held in the context of a shared consciousness of divine grace revealed in the gospel, such that the mentor has no implicit claims to moral superiority. There should be no suggestion that the relationship is contingent on behavior, so that personal loyalty or obedience becomes the means of manipulated control. For as Kruger noted, it is at this point that a mentoring relationship is most vulnerable to abuses.

Yet, Christian discipleship has always been a matter of personal growth in spirituality and holiness. It is demanding. It can be painful. It will certainly be costly. It is not accidental, for example, that the apostle Paul sees the virtue of self-control as significant (it occurs five times in his letter to Titus alone). A good mentor will seek to be a prayerful and encouraging guide through all these challenges. Consequently, it may well entail hard and uncomfortable conversations. But these are by no means necessarily abusive but loving. The problem is that they can be exploited by abusers, which brings us to safeguarding.

The reason for clarity here is that when dealing with conflicts within HR or discipling relationships, it is natural to speak with the individuals concerned and even to hope for times of improved communication and even reconciliation. But in cases of abuse, it is essential that this does *not* take place, at least not in the short term and never without the survivor's consent freely granted. All the key resources on the subject are adamant and unanimous about this point, and yet it is one step which the naïve and uninformed might too often be inclined to take (out of a misapprehension of how grace should be worked out). This is why safeguarding best practice must be followed at this point. Again, if an institution or church lacks a

---

32. For example: Young and Malm, *Volunteer Effect*.

safeguarding policy, this must be rectified as soon as possible. Figuring out how to respond should not be left to the individual first receiving a testimony. The correct procedures should then provide a clear path towards establishing the truth with justice for survivors, protection for the innocently accused, and pastoral care for all.

One reason for following safeguarding protocols is to protect testifiers from the cruelties of what is sometimes referred to as DARVO. It is an acronym for a set of tactics commonly employed by abusers as a means of self-protection and deflection: Denial, Attack, Reverse Victim, and Offender. Of course, someone who is wrongly accused of something will deny it and rightly so. That is not in itself the sign of anything untoward. However, it gets more alarming when they proceed to attack the one making the charge—perhaps by seeking somehow to undermine their credibility or veracity, or by claiming to discern hidden motives—rather than dealing with the charge itself. Worst of all, abusers often attempt to portray themselves as the true victim and not the perpetrator, a reversal which loyal followers and advocates are always inclined to embrace. Again, it may well be that the accusations are indeed false and thus the one accused genuinely is the victim. However, it is essential to be alert to the tendency of abusers to exploit DARVO while remembering that the statistical likelihood of abuse accusations being false is low.

3. On Desired Outcomes

In conclusion, it is worth outlining in brief what the ideal outcomes from being presented with an abuse scenario.

Truth and *Love, not Truth* or *Love.*

Too often, truth and love are pitted against one another in churches as if the path of truth is somehow inimical to that of love. The former might be advocated by allies of survivors while the latter by those of the perpetrators. As John's famous prologue insists, Jesus was the embodiment and epitome of both (John 1:14).

But when there have been abuses, especially in circumstances that are less than clearcut or full of ambiguity, it might seem as if neither truth nor love is attainable. It will necessarily require due process and patience, cool heads and careful investigation. The difficulty is that this can take time. So this must be weighed against extending the agonies (for survivors and accused alike) far longer than they need to be. Whatever happens, though, both love and truth are needed. It is not loving to ignore, avoid, or conceal the truth. It is not truthful to offer a perpetrator love as if that is the only thing required at a given moment.

Repentance, not Revenge.

The scars caused by abuse are immense and the path to healing is long and difficult. A common motivation for survivors speaking out is the agonizing thought that others will continue to be vulnerable if they do not. They will rightly long for the truth to come out, for everyone's sake, the perpetrator included. For without acceptance of the truth, there can be no true repentance. Without repentance, reconciliation is impossible.

But the human heart, perhaps especially when wounded and scarred, is still prone to be as deceitful as the prophet Jeremiah warned (Jer 17:9). It would be natural and understandable for survivors' motives to be distorted; there should be no judgment by friends here. As fellow broken people, though, we must walk together in humility and trust in God's good purposes. It was not for nothing that God through Moses revealed, "It is mine to avenge; I will repay" (Deut 32:35). How well he understood why such injunctions were necessary. For victimhood is bound to elicit such desires. But they are invariably counterproductive and cause the psychological equivalent of self-harm. As Nelson Mandela was often quoted as saying, "Nurturing resentment is like drinking poison and hoping it will kill your enemies." So perpetrators' repentance is a godly desire; revenge against them is not.

It is notable that Ken Blue warned against degenerating into this kind of mentality when he first wrote about this, so that we do not "turn our concern with spiritual abuse into the Salem witch hunt of our time."[33] One of the great gifts of social media in recent years has been not simply to give survivors a voice but to enable them to find others with similar experiences. The #MeToo phenomenon was a powerful case in point. It is arguable that this is precisely what has tipped the balance of power in favor of those who once lacked it.[34] The shadow side to this shift has been the tendency of online crowds to stampede towards judgment and to shame those presumed to be guilty. While this might elicit an immediate sense of achievement (especially if following on from years of silence or marginalization), it tends neither to assist the long-term cause of survivors nor to bring about the repentance of the genuinely guilty. So perhaps a constant question for those

---

33. Blue, *Healing Spiritual Abuse*, 13.
34. Shirky, *Here Comes Everybody*, 148–60.

involved in seeking justice and truth is whether or not a cause of action makes repentance easier or harder.

Forgiveness, not necessarily trust.

What of forgiveness? Should the survivor be expected to forgive an abuser. This is a big question, and one that demands gentleness and sensitivity. It is certainly not for abuser's allies to lay burdens on survivors, still less to impose arbitrary timetables for when this is to be done. Naturally, within a Christian framework, forgiveness is the ideal goal, and we all need help and support to head towards it. But platitudes and thoughtless demands are not the way to get there. Timothy Keller has recently produced an excellent book that wrestles with the challenges of forgiveness with great sensitivity.[35]

One significant misunderstanding of forgiveness needs dealing with here, however. This is the idea that there is something Christian about quickly restoring leaders who have fallen in some way. Nobody is beyond redemption, certainly, and change is possible. But it has been a grim feature of many recent abuse cases on either side of the Atlantic that perpetrators have been rushed back into leadership positions without the true nature of their abuses being faced. This has been sometimes done in the name of the virtues of grace and forgiveness. However, forgiveness is not the same thing as being trustworthy. It may well be a significant contribution to the restoration of trustworthiness, but it should never be mistaken for being synonymous. Many checks and balances should be in place before someone can be trusted with pastoral responsibility again. In certain circumstances, that may never be possible. Not to face this reality is to do the experiences of survivors a profound disservice.

Fallen, not Devils.

Chuck DeGroat's excellent work *When Narcissism Comes to Church* stands out in the relevant literature as one of the few to give hope for those who themselves who are beset by narcissism. In his articulation of narcissism's effects on victims, he is unsparing. The devastation wrought is clear and heartbreaking. Those who have suffered will find great solace in his account from the reassurance he offers them; they were *not* going mad and what they endured clearly was wrong. But deGroat does not leave it there. He also probes what agonies lie concealed in the narcissist's heart and thus shows

---

35. Keller, *Forgive*.

great compassion to them as well. For example, he suggests that for a narcissist, "At his core, he is a scared little boy."[36]

As classic Christian theology has always insisted, human beings are made in God's image and yet also fallen. They do not cancel each other out. This is therefore true even of every abuser as well as ever survivor. The temptation to canonize victims and demonize perpetrators has always existed, but in the climate articulated by Lukianoff and Haidt, it has become as strong as it ever was. No one is as holy as it is possible to be; no one is as evil. Let us therefore take care to see everyone as the Lord does: beloved even when unlovely, redeemable even when offending.

CONCLUSION

It is striking that Matthew famously quotes from one of Isaiah's servant songs when explaining why crowds followed Jesus around, even though at this particular moment, he needs to withdraw from their incessant demands (Matt 12:15–21; quoting Isa 42:1–4). At first sight, Matthew uses the quotation to explain why Jesus instructs people to keep quiet about him. But it goes much further. What was it that would cause the "nations to put their hope," according to the prophet? Of several reasons, most pertinent for the purposes of this essay is his gentleness.

> A bruised reed he will not break,
> and a smoldering wick he will not snuff out,
> till he has brought justice through to victory. (Matt 12:20)

Because we are so far removed from the culture of Jesus's day, it is impossible to conceive of how countercultural this was. Yet it was surely one of his most compelling and magnetic characteristics. In a world of powers and authorities who lorded it over others for their own selfish ends, this must have been like cool fresh water to a parched desert traveler. How tragic, then, that those who speak and minister in this Lord's name fail to treat others as he did. It is our hope and prayer that this book contributes to a seismic shift in church culture, so that far from being shaped by worldly values, all those with responsibility for Christ's people love them as he does. The health of the body requires that bruised reeds are never broken and smoldering wicks never snuffed out.

---

36. DeGroat, *Narcissism*, 88.

BIBLIOGRAPHY

Blue, Ken. *Healing Spiritual Abuse: How to Break Free from Bad Church Experiences*. Downers Grove, IL: InterVarsity, 1993.

Bonhoeffer, Dietrich. *Life Together*. Translated by John W. Doberstein. London: SCM, 2005.

"Christian Camp Leader John Smyth Suspected of Abuse Dies." *BBC News*, August 12, 2018. https://www.bbc.co.uk/news/uk-england-hampshire-45161316.

Crouch, Andy. *Playing God: Redeeming the Gift of Power*. Downers Grove, IL: InterVarsity, 2013.

DeGroat, Chuck. *When Narcissism Comes to Church: Healing Your Community from Emotional and Spiritual Abuse*. Downers Grove, IL: InterVarsity, 2020.

Doyle, Jude Ellison Sady. "Despite What You May Have Heard, 'Believe Women' Has Never Meant 'Ignore Facts.'" *Elle*, November 29, 2017. https://www.elle.com/culture/career-politics/a13977980/me-too-movement-false-accusations-believe-women/.

"Eleanor Williams Sentencing: Men Tried to Take Own Lives over Rape Lies." *BBC News*, March 13, 2023. https://www.bbc.co.uk/news/uk-england-cumbria-64943465.

Hilborn, David. "Reviewing the Discourse of 'Spiritual Abuse.'" *Evangelical Alliance* (blog), n.d. https://www.eauk.org/resources/what-we-offer/reports/reviewing-the-discourse-of-spiritual-abuse.

"Kavanaugh Hearing: #BelieveWomen v #BackBrett." *BBC News*, September 27, 2018. https://www.bbc.co.uk/news/world-us-canada-45671920.

Keller, Timothy. *Forgive: Why Should I and How Can I?* New York: Viking, 2022.

Kruger, Michael J. *Bully Pulpit: Confronting the Problem of Spiritual Abuse in the Church*. Grand Rapids, MI: Zondervan, 2011.

Langberg, Diane. *Suffering and the Heart of God: How Trauma Destroys and Christ Restores*. Greensboro, NC: New Growth, 2015.

Lukianoff, Greg, and Jonathan Haidt. *The Coddling of the American Mind: How Good Intentions and Bad Ideas Are Setting up a Generation for Failure*. New York: Penguin, 2018.

McKnight, Scott, and Laura Barringer. *A Church Called Tov: Forming a Goodness Culture That Resists Abuses of Power and Promotes Healing*. Carol Stream, IL: Momentum, 2020.

Meynell, Mark. *When Darkness Seems My Closest Friend: Reflections on Life and Ministry with Depression*. London: InterVarsity, 2018.

Mullen, Wade. *Something's Not Right: Decoding the Hidden Tactics of Abuse and Feeling Yourself from Its Power*. Carol Stream, IL: Tyndale Momentum, 2020.

Mullin, Chris. "Dalai Lama Seeks Peking Accord." *The Guardian*, March 27, 1980.

Shirky, Clay. *Here Comes Everybody: The Power of Organizing without Organizations*. New York: Penguin, 2008.

"The Truth about False Assault Accusations by Women." *BBC News*, September 18, 2018. https://www.bbc.co.uk/news/world-us-canada-45565684.

Young, Jason, and Jonathan Malm. *The Volunteer Effect: How Your Church Can Find, Train, and Keep Volunteers Who Make a Difference*. Grand Rapids, MI: Baker, 2020.

Author Index

Acton, Lord (John Emerich Edward Dalberg-Acton), 66
Ailawadi, Sushila, 173
Alberry, Sam, 138
Angelici, Ruben, 25, 31
Appiah, Anthony, 89, 100
Aquinas, Thomas, 25, 31
Arendt, Hannah, 29–31
Aretaeus, 92
Aristotle, 73, 82
Armstrong, John H., 54, 59
Augustine of Hippo, 20, 31, 101–10
Austen, Jane, 86
Austin, Victor, 66, 82

Barclay, John, 83–84, 88, 100
Barringer, Laura, 227, 236
Barrs, Jerram, 133, 136
Bavinck, Herman, 48, 59
Bebbington, David, 89, 100
Beresford, Meka, 176, 184
Berlin, Isaiah, 155
Bettenson, Henry, 110
Blue, Ken, 52, 56–59, 226, 233, 236
Bockmuehl, 4
Bockmuehl, Markus, 4, 11, 16
Bonhoeffer, Dietrich, 73–74, 79, 82, 125, 127, 224, 236
Boulding, Maria, 199
Bourdieu, Pierre, 84–85, 100
Breshears, Gerry, 21, 31
Brown, Brené, 131, 136
Brueggemann, Walter, 76–77
Buckley, Jay H., 198

Burns, Bob, 186, 198
Burrell, David B., 23, 31

Carson, D. A., 129, 136
Chadwick, Henry, 110
Chapman, Tasha, 185–86
Charnock, Stephen, 24, 31
Chester, Tim, 123, 127
Christian, Jayakumar, 224–25
Clendenen, Ray E., 60
Collier, Peter, 100
Cooper, LaMar Eugene, 51, 60
Coupland, Douglas, 108, 110
Covey, Stephen, M. R. 195, 198
Crippen, Jeff, 48, 51, 60
Crouch, Andy, 186, 198, 224–25, 236
Cyril of Alexandria, 7–8, 11, 16

Dalai Lama, 218–19, 236
Davidson, Ivor J., 31
Davis, Rebecca, 48, 51, 60, 221
Dawkins, Richard, 69, 82
DeGroat, Chuck, 56–58, 60, 80, 82, 148–49, 157, 170, 172, 220, 227, 234–36
Dever, Mark, 145–46
Doberstein, John W., 82, 236
Douglass, Frederick, 68–69, 82
Doyle, Jude Ellison Sady, 228, 236
Driscoll, Mark, 17–23, 28, 31
Drummond, John J., 31
Duby, Steven J., 7, 9, 16

Edmondson, Amy C., 190, 195, 199

Eichmann, Adolf, 29
Emery, Gilles, 25, 31
Engelke, Matthew, 85, 100
Equiano, Olaudah, 68
Evans, C. Stephen, 6, 16

Fletcher, Jonathan, 124
Foner, Philip Sheldon, 82
Foucault, Michel, 101, 110
Frame, John, M., 48, 60
Freire, Paulo, 183-84, 186, 199

Gibson, Helen, 190, 199
Goebbels. Joseph, 70
Goldingay, John, 42, 46
Goldsmith, Belinda, 176, 184
Goleman, Daniel, 191, 199
Green, Christopher, 110, 147, 149, 157
Guinness, Os, 213, 217
Guthrie, Donald, 186

Haidt, Jonathan, 222-23, 226, 235-36
Hambrick, Brad, 130, 132, 134-36
Hansen, G. Walter, 4, 10-11, 16
Harnack, Adolf von, 26
Hauerwas, Stanley, 28
Hawthorne, Gerald F., 4, 9-11, 16
Haykin, Michael A. J., 89, 100
Hegel, Georg W.F., 26
Hilborn, David, 220-21, 236
Hill, Edmund, 20, 31
Hitler, Adolf, 63
Hofstede, Geert, 193, 199
Honeysett, Marcus, 158, 231
Hoover, Roy W., 10, 16
Hopkins, Nancy Myer, 180, 184
Hume, David, 26
Humphreys, Justin, 53, 60
Hybels, Bill, 124

Jamieson, R.B., 41, 49
Johnson, David W., 53, 60
Jones, Timothy Paul, 21, 31

Kakar, Sudhir, 177, 184
Kant, Immanuel, 26, 101, 109-10
Kavanaugh, Brett, 228, 236
Kay, Katty, 229

Keller, Timothy, 234, 236
Kgatle, 3, 16
Kgatle, Mookgo S., 3, 16
Kilby, Karen, 23, 31
Kohn, Jerome, 94, 100
Krauth, Lothar, 82
Kriete, Henry, 121-22, 124, 127
Kruger, Michael J., 221, 225-27, 229, 231, 236
Kruse, Colin G., 149, 157
Kubrick, Stanley, 72

Langberg, Diane, 131-32, 134-36, 186, 199, 227, 236
Leeman, Jonathan, 145
Levine, Amy-Jill, 93, 100
Lewis, C.S., 78, 82, 123, 127, 209, 217
Lukianoff, Greg, 222-23, 226, 235-36
Luther, Martin, 70

MacArthur, John, 28
Macaskill, Grant, 83, 94, 96, 100, 126, 208
Mackay, Norman, 59
Mackison, Nick, 47
Madan, Karuna, 176, 184
Malina, Bruce, 85, 100
Malm, Jonathan, 231, 236
Mandela, Nelson, 233
Mao Zedong, 218
Martin, Walter, 117-18, 127
Marx, Karl, 64
McCray, Alden C., 53, 60
McGuckin, John Anthony, 16
McKnight, Scott, 227, 236
McNally, Richard, 223
Mdingi, 3, 16
Mdingi, Hlulani, 3, 16
Merrill, Rebecca R., 195, 198
Meynell, Mark, 61, 70, 82, 126-27, 218, 223, 236
Michelson, Jared, 7-8, 17, 203
Middleton, J. Richard, 76-77, 82
Mullen, Wade, 227, 236
Mullin, Chris, 218-19, 236
Murphy, Francesca Aran, 31

Nietzsche, Friedrich, 62, 64

Norris, Robert, 67
Nouwen, Henri, 79–80, 82, 114

O'Donovan, Oliver, 105, 110
O'Neill, John Cochrane, 10, 16
Oakley, Lisa, 53, 60
Ottuh, 3, 16
Ottuh, John A., 3, 16
Ovey, Michael J., 155, 157
Ozanne, Jayne, 221

Pardue, Stephen, 6, 16
Parks, Rosa, 187
Peterson, Eugene H., 135, 137
Petry, Jonna, 19, 31
Phil, 4:2 5
Pieper, Josef, 70–71, 82
Piper, John, 31
Pitt, William, 67
Plantinga, Cornelius, 129–30, 137
Poggendorg-Kakar, Katharina, 177, 184
Putnam, Robert D., 175, 184

Regan, Richard J., 31
Ritschl, Albrecht, 26
Rotelle, John E., 31, 110
Rotten, Jonny, 120
Russell, Norman, 16

Sacagawea, 187, 198
Said, Edward W., 86, 100
Sancho, Ignatius, 68
Savile, Jimmy, 120
Sawyer, Pat, 63, 82
Schaeffer, Edith, 215
Schaeffer, Francis, 213, 215, 217
Sen, Amartya, 176
Shearer, Graham, 7, 101
Shenvi, Neil, 82
Shirky, Clay, 233, 236
Sievers, Joseph, 93, 100
Silva, Moises, 4, 16
Sinclair, Thomas A., 82
Sizemore, Blythe, 128

Smyth, John, 78, 221, 236
Sokolowski, Robert, 23, 31
Solzhenitsyn, Aleksandr Isaevich, 65, 82, 116–17, 127
Spinoza, Baruch, 26
Stalin, Josef, 63, 207
Stetzer, Ed, 28
Stewart-Kroeker, Sarah, 105, 110
Stirling, A. Mark, 3, 113, 161, 200, 214
Storkey, Elaine, 181, 184
Strauss, D.F., 26
Streep, Meryl, 120

Tanner, Kathryn, 23, 31
Taylor, Justin, 31
Taylor, Yuval, 82
Thompson, Curt, 131, 137
Tice, Rico, 65
Timmerman, Jens, 110
Timmis, Steve, 123–24, 127
Tomkins, Silvan, 131
Trump, Donald, 66

VanVonderen, Jeffrey, 53, 60
Vassa, Gustavus, 68
Vriend, John, 59

Ware, Bruce, 21, 31
Webster, John, 19–20, 31
Weinstein, Harvey, 120
Wilberforce, William, 67–68, 82
Williams, Eleanor, 229, 236
Williams, Rowan, 108, 110, 229, 236
Wittman, Tyler, 8, 16
Wookey, Steve, 115
Wright, Christopher J.H., 21, 28, 31–33, 35, 37, 40, 42–46

Xavier, M. Sreedevi, 178, 184

Yarbrough, Robert W., 149, 157
Young, Jason, 231, 236
Yousavzai, Malala, 187

Subject Index

abandonment, of Christian faith, 53
abandonment, feeling of by abuse
     victims, 134–35
abolition, of slavery, 67–68, 82
abortions, sex selective, 176
Abraham, 44
abuse, domestic, 179
abuse, of power, 3, 13–16, 18, 23, 27–
     30, 34, 40, 47–60, 64, 66–67,
     70–71, 74–75, 78, 82, 84, 96,
     100, 102, 109, 116, 125, 129–36,
     138–39, 147, 149, 154–55, 157–
     58, 161, 163–65, 167, 172–75,
     177–80, 182, 186–90, 193, 200,
     201, 203, 207–8, 211–13, 215–
     16, 219–22, 225–29, 231–34
abuse, pastoral, 23, 27–30, 47, 53, 55,
     59, 84, 102, 109, 129, 143, 165,
     182, 200, 216
abuse, sexual, 120, 173, 177, 220, 228–29
abuse, spiritual, 14, 51–57, 116, 225–
     29, 233
abuse, spiritual, discussion of
     terminology, 219–222
abuse, victims, 53, 55, 57, 58, 120,
     130–32, 134–36, 143, 146, 148,
     169, 177, 186, 219, 226, 228,
abusers, 47–49, 52–58, 60, 78, 130,
     132, 148, 155, 164, 220–21,
     225–26, 228, 231–32, 234–35
accountability, 27, 38–40, 53, 81, 122–
     24, 126, 131, 142, 145, 154,
     159, 162–65, 168–70, 183, 193,
     198, 201, 215, 218, 223, 233

accusation, 124, 128, 154, 202, 226,
     228–29, 232
achievement, 77, 233
addiction, 184
adultery, 49, 53–54, 80, 98, 116, 166,
     212
affliction, 42, 49, 68
agency, human, 74, 78, 91, 198
agendas, hidden/dark, 28, 63, 70, 75,
     147, 172, 193–94, 222
aggression, by leaders, 171
alienation, 131
allegations, 47, 132
allegations, false, 229
ambition, selfish, 6, 9, 11, 45
ambition, 34, 44–46, 201
anarchy, 155
anger, 58, 104, 157, 171, 195, 200, 202
Anglican, 47, 118, 148
anthropology, 85
anticlericalism, 141
anxiety, 17, 90, 99, 126, 128, 191–92,
     195, 223
apostasy, 36, 116
apprentice, 182
Arminian, 48
arrogance, 79, 121, 210
aseity, Divine, 55
atomization, 76
atonement, 55, 96, 221
attack, 123–24, 205, 221, 227, 232
attack, *ad hominem*, 202
attitude, human attitudes and unity,
     5–6, 9, 11

241

attitude, of Jesus, 3–4, 6–7, 10–11, 95, 174
attitude, sinful, 49, 108, 124, 180, 204
attitude, 3–7, 9–11, 16, 49, 95, 108, 123–24, 157, 174, 180, 204
attributes, of God, 7, 9, 26
authoritarian, 17–19, 27, 29, 32, 115, 138–46, 181–82
authority, 21, 27, 33–34, 44, 58, 62, 66, 69, 77, 156, 159–61, 163–65, 168, 172, 174, 182, 221
   apostolic, 15, 150
   biblical, 37, 72, 96–97
   ethical, 37
   of husbands and pastors, 21
   of Jesus, 12, 15, 216
   pastoral, 58, 74, 138–39, 141–46, 180, 203, 225
   positional, 13, 159
   religious, 34
avoidance, 34

banality, of evil, 29
Baptist, 47
Beatitudes, 113
belief, pastoral influence over, 187
beliefs, of Pharisaism, 94
beliefs, stated, 208
beliefs, underlying abuse, 178
believer(s), 3, 5–6, 12–14, 17, 23, 31, 44, 48, 56, 63, 67, 89, 94, 104, 116–19, 121–22, 126, 128–29, 131–34, 137, 148, 151, 157, 173–75, 180, 182–83, 204, 219, 224, 228, 236
beloved, 14, 22, 28–29, 68, 141, 182, 235
benevolence, 10, 24, 29, 75, 85, 88, 148, 186, 212, 214
bereavement, 223
betrayal, 39, 50–51, 53, 55, 115, 130, 204, 211
blacklisted books, 208
blame, 64, 104, 130–31, 171, 176–77, 198, 219–20
blameless, 90, 93
blessing, 3, 12, 75, 121, 123–24, 182, 186, 188–89, 201–4, 206, 212, 214–15

blindspots, 62–63, 104
boundaries, 58, 79, 81–82, 86–87, 89, 95–98, 161, 166, 208–9, 221, 225–26
bribery, 37, 39–40
bride, of, 28
brokenness, 128–29, 131, 133, 135–37, 186
brothers, 53, 134, 141, 144, 151–53, 174, 176, 189–90, 192, 213
bullying, 18, 47, 125, 138–41, 148, 151, 154–55, 182, 190, 224, 227
burnout, 57

calling, 21, 28, 36, 45, 143, 170, 190, 194
Calvinist, 48
capital, symbolic, 78, 83–85, 90, 94, 100, 117, 208
capital, symbolic, accrual, 84, 86, 95, 208–9, 212
caste, 175
casualties, of misuse of, 53, 116
celebrity, 53, 119, 121
censor, self-, 171
censoriousness, 224
Centralization, of power and, 35, 153
character, 117, 140, 146, 152–53, 155, 162, 168, 171, 190, 202, 204–5, 208, 216
character, Christian, 119
character, God's, 4–5, 7–10, 13, 15, 37, 40, 144, 200, 201, 205,
characteristics, 42, 86, 154, 225
characteristics, performed, 86
charm, 52, 130, 154
Christ, 3–23, 28, 31, 51–52, 54–55, 58–59, 63, 70–71, 78, 80–81, 84, 91–92, 94–95, 99–100, 118–19, 121, 125, 131–32, 134, 136, 141–44, 146, 158–59, 181–82, 185, 189–93, 198, 204–9, 211–14, 221, 224, 235–36, see also union, with Christ
blood of, 55
body of, 14, 189, 190, 204, 206, 213, 214
example of, 6, 7, 51, 58

SUBJECT INDEX

gaining, 92
identification with Yahweh, 7
image of, 21
as king, 21, 23
knowledge of, 91, 209
mindset of, 3–23, 95
pattern of self-giving, 9, 14, 15, 95, 99
peacemaking work, 5, 14, 204
presence of, 94
as single acting subject, 7n5
three offices of, 20 (see also *Munus Triplex*)
as true shepherd, 52, 142, 144
"warrior," 18, 19
Christendom, 36
Christianity, 18–19, 62–63, 65, 80, 82
Christians, 28, 31, 48, 62, 74, 80, 83, 90, 101, 121, 129, 134, 142, 148–49, 151–52, 156, 164, 178
christlikeness, 77, 129, 146, 210, 227
christology, 6–7, 16, 18, 21
church, 3, 5, 8, 18–19, 21, 23, 27–31, 36–38, 41, 45–50, 52–60, 63, 70–73, 79–84, 87, 94–95, 97, 99–100, 109, 115–19, 121–36, 138–40, 142–57, 159–66, 168–69, 172–74, 178–82, 184–92, 194–95, 197–216, 220–27, 230–32, 234–36
  as capital economy, 99
  discipline, 58, 81, 139
  emergent, 18
  membership, 54, 152
  and mission, 28
  planting movement, 121
  safe, 224
  seeker-friendly, 18
  "success" in, 212, 213
  unity, 5
circumcision, 91, 94–95, 139, 142, 150, 184
clergy, 72, 117–18, 162, 180, 187, 191, 198
coaching, 208
codependency, 27, 29–30, 161
coercion, 75–77, 101, 141, 143, 145, 171, 221, 224

cognitive therapy, (CBT), 223
collaboration, 95, 150–51, 156, 187, 192, 196
collectivism, 86
collegiality, 159, 167–69
collusion, 36, 210
command, 4, 6, 9, 12–14, 16, 37–38, 57, 103, 105, 107, 141, 224
command, right of, 170
commandment, 4, 15, 49, 191, 200
commodification, 18, 91
commodity, 92, 96, 175
communication, 69, 71, 160, 190–93, 195, 197, 231
communion, 13–14, 208
communism, 76
community, 21, 26, 33, 35–36, 44–45, 49–52, 54, 60, 70, 73, 76, 82, 85–86, 90, 123, 127, 130, 144, 150, 153, 157, 169–70, 174–75, 181–84, 186, 207, 209, 212, 218, 224, 226–27, 236
compassion, 40, 56, 105–6, 134, 235
competence, 87, 168, 216, 226
competition, 85, 95, 97, 119, 144, 204, 206, 214
competitiveness, 90, 95, 98, 119, 174, 190–91, 203–4
complacency, 75, 113, 201
complaints, 128, 228, 230
complementarianism, 181
compulsion, 139–41
concealment, 55, 70, 78, 170, 211, 219–20, 229, 233
confidence, 55, 83, 91, 96, 113, 118, 123, 132, 168, 175, 195, 204, 224, 226
conflict, 34, 159, 162, 195, 226, 231
conformity, 208–9, 212
confrontation, 17, 22, 49, 55, 227, 236
confrontational, 18, 22–23
congregation, 27–30, 45, 54, 57–58, 106–7, 116–17, 119, 123, 141, 143, 153, 173, 189, 192, 203, 210–12, 215–16
congregational, 123, 153
conscience, 79, 81, 143, 161, 205
consent, 53, 141, 231

SUBJECT INDEX

consequences, of sin, 49, 53, 55
consequences, of misuse of, 52–53, 77, 130
contemplation (of good), 106
contentment (in God), 14
control, 73–74, 77, 79–80, 104, 114, 125, 147, 153, 158, 166, 168–70, 177, 179, 185, 191, 193, 198, 214, 221, 225
control, Bible as tool of, 53, 57
control, self-control, 231
controlling, 78, 143, 156, 170
conversion, 20
cool/coolness, 85, 108
corruption, 34, 36, 38–39, 48–50, 66, 124, 129–31, 170, 174, 187
counsel, directive, 203
counseling, 53, 128, 175, 177, 228
countercultural, 38, 46, 185, 235
courage, 57, 135, 148, 190, 193, 195, 202, 229
covenant, 33, 35, 49, 51–52, 182, 186
cover up, 55, 116, 135, 154, 160
createdness, 68
creation, 8–9, 20, 26, 64, 73–74, 107, 109, 129, 185–86, 189
Creator, 21, 23, 73, 75–76, 78, 97, 105, 107, 180, 195
creature, 8, 13, 20–24, 27–30, 67–68, 73–76, 104
creatureliness, 24
creaturely, 14, 22, 29, 78, 106
credibility, 159, 161, 187, 232
crime, 20, 175–77
critical, 29, 45, 63–65, 73, 82, 110, 113, 124, 161, 216, 224–25
critical theory, 48, 63–65, 73, 82, 142
criticism, 26–29, 35, 85, 97, 120–22, 124, 152, 166, 201–6, 208–9, 215, 225
critique, 21, 26, 206, 209
cross, of, 4–5, 7, 9–12, 14, 16, 72, 119, 125–26, 132, 204, 216, 224
Crowded House, The, 121, 123–24, 127
cruelty, 29, 65, 224–25, 228, 232
cult, 34, 115, 117–19, 121, 123, 125, 127, 150, 152–53
cultish, 151, 209

culture, 61, 63, 65, 70, 75, 78–79, 85–86, 89–90, 93, 100, 120–21, 124–25, 140, 142, 144, 148, 154, 156, 166, 174–77, 179–81, 185–86, 188–93, 195, 197, 199, 201–3, 218–23, 227, 235–36
culture, of Israel, 40
culture, Western, 72, 135, 149, 189, 191, 193
culture, narcissistic, 149
culture, organizational, 201, 202
culture, patriarchal, 174, 176, 177
culture, postmodern, 227

damage, 44, 50–52, 55, 57, 115–16, 130, 148–50, 161, 171, 177, 185, 191, 198, 203, 211, 230
danger, 18–19, 23, 51–52, 57, 63, 65–66, 75, 83, 96–97, 102, 128, 144, 149, 165, 167, 172, 174, 176, 181, 184, 201, 210, 212, 223, 226
DARVO, 232
deacons, 152–53
decentralization, of, 34–35
deception, 77–78, 166, 210
decision making, 35, 80, 88, 123, 127, 143, 145, 152, 161, 168–71, 181, 185, 192, 194–97, 204–6
defensiveness, 11, 13, 21, 34, 37, 41, 46, 56, 62, 69, 87, 97, 163, 168, 170, 195, 202–3, 215, 225
deflection, 45, 130, 232
deity, 9–11, 33, 175
democracy, 34, 220
dependency, 166, 170
depravity, 48, 57
depression, 128, 236
diagnosis, 3, 50, 56, 59, 64, 80, 201–3, 207, 216, 223
dignity, 69–71, 132, 134–35, 180, 190
disagreement, 20, 25, 117, 123, 156, 168, 181, 202, 207–8
disappointment, 105, 116, 156, 171, 176, 204–5
disapproval, 45, 205
discernment, 154, 191–92

SUBJECT INDEX

disciple, 4, 12, 57, 74, 122, 126, 154, 158, 160–61, 163, 166, 181, 204
discipleship, 22, 28, 46, 75, 77–79, 125, 127, 137, 145–46, 158–61, 163, 165, 167–68, 191, 194, 208, 216, 230–31
discipline, 23, 55, 58, 73, 78, 81, 106, 139, 150, 164, 180
disempowerment, 171
disillusionment, 53, 59, 105, 116
disloyalty, 123–24, 168
disobedience, 123–24, 155, 179
disorientation, 130–32, 136
disqualification, by sin, 54, 144
dissent and dissension, 18, 74, 113, 127
dissonance, 47, 207
disunity, 96, 204
diversity, 28, 35, 56, 76, 93, 187, 189, 194–95
divinity, divine, 7–8, 10–11, 16, 67–68, 79, 81, 116, 148
division, 34, 95, 98, 113, 198
divorce, 57, 223
docetism, 91
doctrine, 7, 16, 18–21, 23–24, 26, 30–31, 48, 50, 67–69, 89, 94, 118, 143, 154–56, 200, 221
domination, 30, 58, 71, 73–74, 98, 123, 145, 151, 153, 164, 168, 170, 173, 175–76, 178, 186, 193, 214, 221
domineering, 18, 139–43, 145–46, 155–56, 158
dominion, 50
doubt, 41, 59, 74, 78–81, 143, 148, 205
dynamics, 20, 26, 49–50, 73, 75, 77, 81, 83–87, 89–91, 93, 95–99, 101, 122, 159–60, 166, 192, 198, 207–9, 214, 220, 230
dysfunction, 153, 201, 213

economic, inequality, 189
economics, in OT, 33–37
economics, of symbolic capital, 87–88, 92
economy, of gift, 99–100, 199
education, 61, 82, 175–76, 209
efficacy, of the cross, 5, 204

efficiency, 21, 23, 193, 213
egalitarianism, 181
ego, 131, 146, 153, 211
egocentricism, 151, 224
elders, 19, 35, 41, 43, 52, 74, 81, 116, 123, 126, 130, 145, 148–49, 152–55, 194
eldership, plural, 142, 145
emergent, 17–18, 67
emotion, 29, 50, 60, 82, 131, 157, 165–67, 179, 191, 195, 197, 205, 211, 220–23, 227, 236
empathy, 56, 185, 188, 191, 197
empowerment, 12–13, 52–53, 64, 145, 161, 185, 187, 189, 191, 193–95, 197, 199
encouragement, 22, 55, 146, 187
enemies, 14, 22, 72, 116, 129, 185, 233
Enlightenment, The, 26, 62–63, 75–76, 78
EQ, 191, 197
equality, Christ's with God, 3–4, 6–12, 16, 69, 95, 189
equipping, 48, 214
error, 18–20, 77, 108, 118–19, 154, 156, 229
eschaton, 14, 28
ethics, 9, 18, 33, 35, 37, 41, 46, 62, 89, 98, 110, 221
ethnicity, 61, 91, 175
evangelical, 21, 26, 47–48, 53, 62, 84, 87, 90, 93–95, 99, 107, 115–16, 121, 148, 155, 165, 220, 236
evangelicalism, 18–21, 47, 62, 89, 98, 100, 213
evangelicals, 18–19, 21, 26, 66, 69, 84, 89, 94
evangelism, 18, 133, 136, 152, 207
evil, 22, 29, 47–48, 50, 52–53, 57, 59, 65, 70, 116, 129, 131–32, 135–36, 150, 155, 178, 180–83, 189, 222, 226, 235
example, Jesus', 4–6, 9, 12, 57, 58, 204
example, pastoral, to the flock, 139–41, 145–46, 163, 211
example, Paul's leadership, 15
excuses, 117, 148, 191, 202, 208, 210, 216

exhortation, 5, 58, 139
expendability, of people, 79
expertise, 96, 227
exploitation, 11–13, 48–51, 56–57, 59, 72, 80, 144, 164, 171, 173–74, 176–77, 183, 221, 226, 228, 231–32
exposure, 47, 52, 55, 64, 66, 72, 75, 88, 90, 99, 120, 138, 151, 154, 175, 215, 220, 223–24, 228

factions, 95, 98
failure, 30, 57, 63–64, 77, 124–25, 171, 207, 211, 215, 236
faith, of the weaker brother, 53–54, 143
faith, damage caused by abuse, 115, 143, 205
faithful, 14, 46, 54, 81, 94, 129, 131, 144, 153, 155, 181, 197
faithfulness, 41, 51, 57, 133, 181
fantasies, 106
Father, God the, 4, 6–7, 13–14, 21–22, 25, 28, 31, 58, 102, 109–10, 134
fauxnerability, 170, 172
favoritism, 171
fear, 126, 131, 175, 178, 191, 193, 197, 202, 204, 225
fear, of God, 183
fear, of reputational damage, 55, 171,
feedback, 191, 194, 197–98, 202–3, 206
feelings, 108, 116, 131, 168, 193, 197, 201, 227
fellowship, 7–8, 13–14, 81, 122, 124, 127, 150, 156, 175, 194, 224
finances/financial, 30, 50, 52, 57, 59, 68, 175, 214–15
flashbacks, 223
flattery, 15, 71, 204, 226
flourishing, 27, 66, 76, 82, 129, 154, 185–87, 189, 191–93, 195, 197, 199
follower(s), 26, 70, 99, 131, 156, 226, 232
force, 67, 72, 75, 80, 92, 141, 143, 145–46, 219
forcefulness, 143, 146
forgiveness, 58, 62, 125, 129, 178, 181, 187, 197, 234, 236

formation, spiritual, 31, 161
fragility, 222–23
fraud, 47, 50, 52, 156
freedom, 23, 31, 33–34, 53, 59, 68, 73–74, 76, 78–79, 81, 105, 131–32, 141, 161, 173, 176, 178, 184, 198, 203, 223, 236
fruit, 5–6, 52, 77, 155, 189, 208
fruitfulness, 185–86, 190, 198
frustration, 120, 145, 171, 197, 219
fullness, 7–9, 11
fullness, in, 13

garbage, 92
gaslighting, 148, 228
gender, 151, 175–77, 181, 189–91, 193–95, 214, 229
generosity, 9, 22, 24, 26, 75–76, 109, 204, 206
gentleness, 15, 19, 23, 79, 136, 141, 146, 155, 160, 176, 225, 234–35
gift, 8, 24, 52, 59, 69, 72, 84, 88, 92, 99–100, 109, 162, 186, 198, 208, 236
gifts and giftedness, 28, 39, 41, 43–44, 52, 88, 119, 121, 129, 140, 161, 168, 171, 187, 189–90, 206, 210, 213–14, 216, 226, 233
givenness, of human nature, 69, 73
glory, 4, 6–7, 15, 45, 78, 82, 110, 123, 127, 130, 133–34, 209, 216–17
godliness, 120, 181, 190, 205–6, 233
goodness, 24, 91, 102, 104–7, 109–10, 141, 236
Gospel, 15, 18, 21, 46, 55, 62–63, 65, 72, 74, 77, 79, 82–84, 90, 94–95, 98–100, 115–16, 118–19, 121, 125–27, 130, 149, 154, 159–60, 166, 169, 187–88, 200, 203–4, 211, 216, 224, 231
gossip, 123–24, 148
governance, 142
grace, 9, 14, 64, 77–78, 83–84, 90, 100, 117, 122, 125–26, 132, 153, 159, 186, 190, 204, 211, 224, 231, 234
gracious, 5, 14, 76, 136, 183, 201
graceless, 54, 77

SUBJECT INDEX

greed, 38, 40, 99, 141
grief, 103–4, 108, 135–36, 139, 177
grievance, 136
growth, 13–15, 27–28, 44, 74, 77, 122,
    136, 144, 159–61, 163, 167,
    198–99, 201, 208, 211–12, 231,
    236
guilt, 48, 175

happiness, 24, 75–76, 102–3, 106, 113,
    132, 142, 156
harassment, 125, 190
harm, 9, 50, 53–56, 129, 131, 136,
    148–49, 186, 198, 202, 220–21,
    224, 233
harmful, 192, 200, 220, 227
harpagmos, 10–11, 16
harshness, 51, 64, 79, 173, 201
healing, 51–53, 56, 58–60, 82, 103,
    129, 133, 135–36, 157, 188,
    190, 196, 198, 223–24, 226,
    233, 236
heaven, 4, 6, 22, 113, 174
Hellenization thesis, 26
heresy, 91, 116, 156
hierarchy, 21, 33–35, 85, 123–24, 153,
    177, 180
hierocracy, 36
holiness, 7, 25, 28, 37, 41–42, 46, 75,
    78–79, 102, 118, 126, 129, 189,
    191–92, 201, 211, 231, 235
honesty, 30, 39, 55, 57–58, 79, 88, 122,
    124, 127, 191, 195–97, 203,
    211–12
honor, 31, 70, 85–86, 88, 133–35, 144,
    153, 178–79, 189–90, 197
hostility, of culture, 62
household, 34–35, 41, 177, 179, 186
hubris, 77, 210
humanity, 5, 7–8, 14, 21–23, 48, 61,
    67–68, 76, 101, 103, 180, 183,
    200, 204
new humanity, 5, 14, 204
humiliation, 64, 76, 124, 131, 179–80
humility, 4, 6–13, 15–16, 19, 38, 41–43,
    46, 80, 96, 99–100, 120, 128,
    134, 145, 154, 185, 189, 193,
    202, 204, 210–11, 215–16,
    226–27, 233
hurt, 130–31, 133–34, 197, 205, 222,
    225–27, 229
hyperawareness, 193
hypercritical, 225
hypermasculinity, 18
hypersensitivity, 171
hypersexualization, 189
hypocrisy, 48, 64, 66

idealism, 58–59, 62
idealistic, 30, 55
idealogues, 207–8
identity, 7–8, 11, 20–21, 28–29, 31,
    74–76, 83–87, 89–90, 93–100,
    177, 189, 191, 195, 197, 206,
    208, 218
ideology, 62, 207–8
idolatry, 44, 46, 83, 94, 105, 107–8,
    110, 206, 215
idolatry, institutional, 28, 206, 215,
    226, 231
image, 9, 13, 21, 23, 27, 33, 61–63, 65,
    67, 69–71, 73–77, 79, 81–82,
    84, 96, 103, 109, 133, 162, 173,
    180, 186, 189, 231, 235
imbalances, 50–51, 53, 130, 160–62,
    165, 174–75, 180
imitation, of Christ and of God, 3–5,
    13–14, 20–24, 30, 37, 134, 163,
    182
imitation, of Paul, 99
imitators, 14, 182
immorality, 45, 117, 147, 166
incarnation, 7–11, 55, 91, 125, 154
incest, 177
individualism, 76, 191
inefficiency, 206
inequalities, 180, 187–90, 193
infanticide, 175
infidelity, 144
influence, 13, 18, 36, 54, 74, 79–80, 101,
    144, 150, 157, 160–61, 170, 172,
    180, 186–87, 192–93, 205
injustice, 36, 40, 64, 176, 178, 180, 183,
    187–90, 192–93

insecurity, 14, 66, 74, 96, 126, 168, 202, 204–5
integrity, 27, 38–40, 120, 168, 183
intelligence, emotional, 27, 64, 96, 100
intersectional, 89
intimacy, 44, 52, 56, 80, 114, 182
intimidation, 138, 141, 145, 164, 168, 171, 226–27
isolation, 54, 124, 152, 171, 209–12, 226
isolationism, 151
Israel, 7, 27, 32–41, 44, 46, 51, 54, 135
Israelite, 32–38, 183

jealousy, 42–44, 46
Jesus, 3–4, 6–7, 9, 12, 15–19, 21–23, 26–28, 32, 41, 49, 54, 57–59, 61–62, 79–80, 82, 87, 90–92, 105, 113–14, 118–19, 125, 127, 132, 136, 142, 144, 146, 150–51, 154–55, 158–60, 163, 174, 179, 181, 184, 187, 200, 204, 207, 211, 213, 216, 232, 235
joy, 5, 25, 81, 99, 107–9, 132, 154, 159, 175, 187, 190, 206
Judaism, 87, 93
judgement, 18, 22, 24, 48, 53, 100, 117, 127, 166, 168, 171, 192, 224, 229, 233
justice, 33, 35, 40–41, 57, 60, 62, 64, 90, 113, 129, 134, 181, 189, 232, 234–35

kenosis, 3, 6, 8–9, 16
kindness, 22, 64, 105, 109, 157, 200–201
king, 18–21, 23, 27, 34, 36, 38–39, 41, 80, 182
kingdom, 28–29, 36, 57, 113, 117–18, 122, 127, 163, 181, 186, 206, 214
kings, 21, 23, 28, 31, 33–34, 38–39, 51, 80, 174
kingship, 21, 33–34, 53
kinship, 34–35
knowledge, 26, 91–92, 126, 140, 199, 215

L'Abri, 215
lament, 189
law, 33, 36, 38, 49, 51, 57, 69, 87, 90, 92–94, 122, 134, 140, 166, 220–21
lawgiver, 33
laws, 32, 176, 184
lawyer, 128, 222
leaders, 3–4, 13–15, 18, 21, 23, 27, 29, 35–39, 41–48, 51–54, 56–59, 63, 65–66, 72, 74, 77–78, 81, 83, 96–97, 99–100, 109, 115–17, 119–24, 126, 130, 141–46, 150–55, 160–67, 169–72, 180, 182, 185–86, 188–92, 194–95, 197–98, 200–217, 220–21, 225–27, 231, 234, 236
leadership, 3, 8, 10, 14–16, 18, 20, 31–32, 34–35, 37–42, 44–46, 49, 51–53, 56–59, 69, 74, 76–77, 80–81, 83–89, 91, 93–99, 103, 106, 114–15, 118–25, 127–28, 139–46, 148, 150–56, 161, 168–70, 173–74, 176, 178, 180–83, 185–91, 193–95, 198–200, 202, 204, 206, 208, 211, 213, 215, 222–27, 234
learning, 73, 98, 121, 123–27, 186, 191, 194, 196, 199, 215
leavers, 205, 208
legalism, 54, 57, 77–78, 83–84, 90, 93–94
liberals, 18, 26
libertarianism, 76
liberty, 75–76, 78
license, 22, 78, 102, 223
lies, 7, 15, 34, 37, 39, 56, 62, 64, 71, 74, 89–91, 100, 132, 134, 149, 171, 184, 224, 226, 236
Lord, 4, 6–7, 22–23, 32–34, 36–39, 41, 43–44, 46, 51–52, 56, 59, 66, 80, 91, 95, 106, 115, 129, 132–36, 142–44, 149–50, 158–60, 189, 204–5, 209, 211–12, 224, 235
love, 5, 9–10, 12–15, 19, 22, 25, 27–30, 41, 52, 58, 61–62, 66, 69, 80, 102–10, 114, 127–28, 133–35,

140–41, 144, 146–49, 151, 153, 155–59, 181–83, 185, 191, 201, 204, 224, 227, 229, 232–33, 235
loved, 14–15, 28, 102–4, 108–9, 123, 134, 150, 153–56, 182
lovelessness, 155
loving, 12–14, 22, 25–26, 62, 101, 103–6, 108, 110, 147, 149, 151, 153, 155, 157, 169, 181–84, 205, 225, 231, 233
loyalty, 108, 147, 150, 153, 156, 169, 231–32
Lutheran, 48
lying, 71, 128

malpractice, ministerial, 53
manipulation, 15, 56, 60, 70–71, 73, 77–79, 97, 154, 161, 166, 170, 172, 195, 197–98, 204–5, 214, 221, 226, 231
marginalization, 97–98, 124, 177, 183, 203, 207, 233
marriage, 45, 57, 163, 177–78, 182, 194
Marxism, 63
maturity, 77, 152, 158, 161, 167, 189, 193, 201, 211, 213
mediator, 205
meekness, 18, 42, 170, 204
meetings, 69, 74, 128, 133, 138, 145, 147, 154, 192–95, 197–98
mega 122, 145
members, 27–28, 51, 71–72, 85, 87, 89, 93, 97, 116, 118, 121–25, 127, 142, 147, 149–51, 160, 162–63, 169, 173, 187, 194, 197, 201, 204, 206, 209, 211–14, 224
membership, 54, 86–87, 123, 125, 139, 152, 208
mentee, 158, 161–62, 167, 172, 231
mentor, 79, 158–67, 169, 171, 189, 191, 231
mentoring, 158–68, 172, 210, 230–31
mercy, 41, 57, 128, 132, 224
messy, 206–8
metaphysics, 16, 26, 101, 110
methodology, 75, 78, 207–8
micromanagement, 18

mindset, of Christ, 3–5, 7, 9, 11, 13, 15, 47, 173, 176, 178, 180, 213
ministers, 23, 53, 55, 67, 70, 115–16, 118–20, 154, 166, 168, 198, 210–11, 215–16, 235
ministries, 84, 97, 115, 121, 124, 139, 189, 194, 204
ministry, 15, 18–23, 30, 41, 44, 53–54, 71, 75, 77–79, 81, 98, 116–19, 124, 129, 134–35, 138, 140–41, 143, 147, 153, 157, 159–63, 165–66, 169–70, 174, 185–94, 197–98, 201–2, 204, 208, 211, 213–14, 224–25, 227, 236
misconduct, 59, 139
misogyny, 180
misrepresentation, 4, 8, 15, 87, 93, 200–201, 208, 216
mission, 27–29, 45, 78, 152–53, 159, 162, 168, 170–71, 185–86, 189
missional, 5, 30, 207–8, 210
missionaries, 149, 151–52
missions, of the Son and Spirit in time, 24
mistreatment, 52, 102
misunderstanding, 16, 48, 55, 141, 171, 198, 200, 211, 216, 229–30, 234
misuse, 3–4, 13, 49–50, 53, 153, 161, 165, 201–2, 204, 207, 211, 216
MMA, 23
model, 4, 18–19, 22–23, 30, 41, 45, 51, 55, 58, 61, 76, 99, 121, 139–40, 151, 163, 183, 188–89, 191, 196–97, 211, 221, 224, 230
modeling, 23, 37, 154, 160, 211
modernist, 62, 69, 213
modernity, 26, 213
modesty, 10, 16, 38
monarchy, 35–36, 38
morphē, 95
Moses, 21, 32, 36, 41–46, 64, 200–201, 233
motivation, 66, 75, 203, 212, 233
motives, 77, 231–33
Munus Triplex, 21, 31
murder, 49–50, 53, 65, 67, 116

naïveté, 47–49, 53, 56, 58–59, 75, 164, 226, 231
narcissism, 56–58, 60, 80, 82, 148–49, 152, 157, 176, 220, 226–27, 234–36
nature, 8–9, 20–21, 23–26, 29, 37, 48, 52, 64, 69, 74, 102, 104, 177, 220, 234
natures, 26
NDAs, 171
negotiation, 150, 186, 192, 198, 218
neighbor, 33, 61, 65, 67, 69–70, 73, 77–78, 81–82, 104–6, 108–9, 133, 185, 187, 191
nepotism, 171
newcomers, 209

obedience, 4, 7, 12, 16, 27–30, 32, 84, 90–93, 124, 134–35, 137, 141, 146, 180, 231
objectification, of women, 189
offenders, 180, 232
opposition, 10, 35, 171, 214
oppression, 33–34, 36, 39, 41, 58, 64, 76, 130, 174, 176–78, 183–84, 186–87, 199, 225
oppressors, 40, 64–65, 130, 183–84
ordination, 23, 54, 58, 118
organization, 28, 45, 54, 72, 159–60, 162–65, 168–71, 181, 187–88, 191, 195, 197, 199–204, 206, 210, 212, 214–15, 220–21, 230, 236
Orientalism, 86, 100
orthodoxy, 8, 16–19, 52, 64, 155–56, 216, 221
outcomes, 75, 134, 162, 188, 197, 212–13, 228, 232
outsiders, 81, 85, 121, 179, 195
overdependence, on leaders, 126
overseers, 126, 152–53
oversight, 139–40, 159, 167, 169–70

para28, 210, 224, 230
paradigm, of, 4
parenting, spiritual, 159
parents, 22, 173, 188, 212
partiality, 37, 49

participation, 5, 25, 28–29, 35, 76, 95, 99, 158–60, 189, 194, 197
partnership, 74, 180, 190, 194
passion, 9, 19
pastor, 27, 29–30, 45, 53–54, 57–59, 72, 101, 138–43, 145–47, 153–54, 173, 179–80, 187–88, 192, 194, 203, 212–13, 215, 225, 227
pastors, 19–23, 27–30, 41, 47, 53–54, 57, 72, 101–2, 109, 130, 138–40, 142–45, 147–49, 153, 157, 180, 185, 187–89, 191, 193–95, 197–99, 215, 220, 225, 227
patience, 50, 55, 63, 74, 134, 159, 192, 232
patriarchy, 174–80, 184
patronage, 161, 171, 214
pattern, Jesus', of self-giving, 4, 6, 9, 13–15, 182
patterns, of abuse, 55, 147, 182
patterns, of discipleship, 75
patterns, of leadership in OT Israel, 32, 35
peace, 49, 132, 136, 157
peacemaking, 5, 14, 204
pedestals, putting ministers on, 116, 119, 211–12
peers, 96, 161, 164
perfectionism, 212
perfections, of God, 25
performance, of obedience, 84
performance, of roles and identities, 85, 89–90, 93–96, 98–99, 208
performance, of characteristics, 86, 89, 96
performative characteristics, 87, 94
perpetrators, 49, 55, 65, 149, 176, 178, 232–35
persecution, 22, 129, 159
perseverance, 12, 140, 219
personality, 21, 56, 60, 69, 78, 98, 119–20, 123, 138, 143, 145–46, 148, 152, 156, 161, 172, 187, 226
Pharisaism, 49, 54, 57–58, 87, 90, 93–94, 98, 100
philosophers, 26, 62, 70, 84
philosophy, 26–27, 62, 83, 107
piety, 94

SUBJECT INDEX

pitfalls, 57, 107
platform, 47, 58, 156–57, 214
platitudes, 234
plurality, in leadership, 35, 142, 145, 153–54, 159, 170
policies, 68, 162, 165–66, 169, 232
politics, 16, 33–37, 39–40, 51, 61, 63–65, 69, 71, 82, 95, 116–17, 147, 174, 184, 186, 189, 198, 218–19, 236
popularity, 3, 97, 109, 120, 148, 162
populist, 156
postmodern, 31, 69, 227
poverty, 41, 59, 124, 174, 180, 183, 192, 225
power, 3–4, 9–13, 15–16, 18, 31, 33–36, 38, 40–46, 49–53, 58, 60–82, 84, 88, 90–91, 97, 100–103, 109–10, 114, 116, 127, 130–33, 141, 144, 147, 149, 151, 154–55, 159–67, 169, 172, 174–76, 178, 180, 182–202, 204, 206–7, 209, 212, 214–16, 220, 222, 225, 228–29, 233, 236
    as a Zero-sum Game, 144
    as human capacity, 186
    centralized, 35
    Christ's attitude to, 3, 10–12, 58
    corrupts, 66
    dispersed within Israel, 33
    dynamics, 49, 50, 81, 101, 159, 166, 192, 220
    economic, 34,
    exercised by religious leaders, 36
    formal, 159, 187
    and freedom, 73
    God's, 174
    greed for, 141
    human hubs, 34
    imbalances, 50–51, 53, 130, 160–62, 164–65, 180, 187–88, 198
    informal, relational, 96, 150, 159–61, 163, 167, 172, 187–88, 193, 220
    misuse of, 3–4, 9, 13, 15–16, 18, 33–34, 36, 40, 49–51, 64–65, 70, 74, 78, 84, 97, 101–2, 116, 130, 147, 154–55, 164–65, 167, 172, 174
    male abuse of women, 175, 180, 182, 190, 200–202, 204, 206–7, 209, 212, 214–16, 222
    and money, 214
    of, 132
    of the Imago Dei, 61
    of the resurrection, 133
    of the Spirit, 43–44
    paradigm for use of, 4
    pastoral, 101, 131, 180, 200
    political, 35–36, 71
    power distance, 193
    powerplay, 151, 174
    relationships and identity, 84
    relative, subject to Yahweh, 33
    right use of, 13, 40, 45–46, 76, 110, 185–86, 192–93
    seeing, 186
    separation of powers, 34
    and social wealth, 175
    temptation of, 80, 114
    to enable self-giving, 12
    use of human, 69–70
    varying amounts of, 187
    will to, 64
    without ambition, 44
    without jealousy, 43
    without pride, 42
powerlessness, 68, 80, 135, 162, 188, 193
praxis, 64, 77
prayer, 14, 22, 53, 118–19, 132, 135, 151–52, 163–64, 183, 185, 189–90, 192–93, 202–3, 231, 235
preachers, 65, 124
preaching, 21, 58, 65, 72, 74, 77, 81, 106, 119, 121, 125, 138, 145, 153, 194, 202, 206–7, 209–11
predation, 52
predators, 47, 120
prerogatives, 10, 46
Presbyterian, 47, 153
Presbytery, 153
presence, 5, 39, 43, 46, 50, 52, 54, 58–59, 94, 97, 139, 145, 155, 189, 215–16

pressure, 90, 96–98, 116, 134–35, 139, 166, 185, 190, 193, 197, 211–12, 222
pride, 17, 22, 42, 46, 113, 204, 208, 210
priesthood, 36, 174
priests, 20–21, 31, 34, 36, 40, 135, 183
privation, 50
privilege, 11–12, 35, 43, 63–64, 66, 68–69, 72, 80, 82, 123–24, 160, 174
professional, 29–30, 156, 167–68
program, 20, 28, 117, 194, 207–8, 213
programmatic, 208
promise, 18, 43–44, 190, 200, 207
propaganda, 72, 135
property, 86, 92, 179–80
prophets, 20–21, 31, 34–37, 39, 43, 135, 233, 235
prosecution, criminal, 220–21
prosperity, material, 107
protection, 9, 11, 23, 34, 36, 40, 44, 48, 53, 55, 58, 71, 128, 144, 154, 162, 164–66, 168, 170, 191, 219, 222, 232
providence, 64
psychology, 3, 53, 90, 187, 192, 199, 220, 222–23, 228, 233
PTSD, 128, 132, 223
pugnaciousness, 22
pulpits, 72, 74, 116, 215, 221, 225–27, 229, 236
punishment, 78, 99, 156, 177, 207–9
Puritans, 24, 47
purity, 172, 183

qualities, 5, 37, 41, 79, 83–84, 86–87, 89, 91, 93, 98, 187, 216
questions, 81, 124, 168, 180, 203, 208, 220
quickfix, 72

rape, 50, 173, 176–79, 183–84, 223, 229, 236
rationalization, 79, 178, 201, 210
realism, 59, 62
rebellion, 45, 49, 129
rebuke, 12, 79, 108, 204
reconciliation, 5, 31, 58, 130, 134, 181, 204, 231, 233

recovery, 19, 58, 181, 223
redemption, 12–13, 29, 40, 76, 97, 129, 134–35, 149, 174–75, 185–86, 189–90, 198–99, 234–36
reductionism, 3, 63, 65, 71–72, 207
reformation, 26, 50
reformed, 17–18, 23, 59, 94
relational, 5, 23, 40, 159–61, 167, 172, 187–88, 191, 194, 225–26, 228
relations, 21, 23, 25
relationships, 5, 12–14, 21, 30, 33, 37, 44, 50, 52–53, 75, 77, 80, 84, 87, 90, 94, 107, 114, 119, 122–23, 128, 130–31, 141, 144, 149, 158–69, 172, 174, 180–82, 187, 191, 197, 205, 210, 225–28, 231
religion, 33, 56, 62, 80, 84, 125, 129, 218, 220
religious, 33–34, 36–37, 40, 54–55, 86, 93, 220–21
repentance, 84, 125, 160, 189, 197, 215–16, 226, 233–34
reputation, 53–55, 71, 85, 93, 98–99, 121–22, 171, 202, 211
resilience, 167
respect, 11, 30, 42, 71, 85, 144, 161, 167, 169, 186–87, 189, 191, 193, 195–97, 211
respected, 91, 116–17, 120, 122–23, 146, 156, 180, 197–98
restitution, 64
restoration, 9, 13, 18, 23, 53–54, 103, 121–22, 134–35, 182–84, 234
results, 8, 20, 23, 77, 98, 124, 131, 134, 140, 160, 191, 196, 201, 207–8, 218–19
resurrection, 133
revenge, 149, 177, 233
rhetoric, 76, 96
righteousness, 7, 40, 49, 83–84, 90–95, 209, 212–13
rights, 3, 10, 12, 33, 41, 69, 75, 113, 177–80
rubbish, 91–92, 209, 213
rulers, 62, 142
rules, 16, 57, 142, 174, 184–85, 191–92, 197, 209

sacrifice, 7, 10, 14, 27, 29, 36, 55–57, 59, 169, 182, 207
safeguarding, 81, 165, 230–32
safety, 159, 189, 199, 222–23
safetyism, 222–24
salvation, 5–7, 20, 26, 48, 59, 83–84, 88, 90, 118
sanctification, 78, 189, 207–8
sanctifier, 79
sarcasm, 79, 81
satisfaction, 104, 108–9, 190, 203
satisfied, 7, 157, 201
Savior, 7, 115, 180
Scripture, 8, 15–16, 21–22, 26, 37, 47, 49–50, 53, 55, 57–58, 63, 76, 93, 96–98, 118, 125, 133, 135, 139, 142–43, 166, 185, 215
scrutiny, 40, 62, 159, 162–63, 165–67, 169
secrecy, 151, 170
secularism, 17, 42, 120, 142, 158, 164, 185, 197, 220
security, 14, 27, 30, 206
self, 16
self-critical, 29
self-destructive, 64
self-giving, 3, 13
selfish, 3, 6, 9, 11–12, 15, 25, 45, 113, 201, 235
selfishness, 28, 66, 76
self-righteous, 91, 175
sensitivity, 89, 101, 133, 181, 227, 234
sermons, 117, 202, 210, 216
servant, 3–4, 7, 11, 16, 41–42, 45, 58, 95–96, 124, 134, 144, 163, 174, 181, 235
servanthood, 9, 95
servant-leader, 42
service, humble, of others, 3, 10, 11, 12, 13, 16, 96, 144, 185
service, Jesus', 58
service, of God, 76, 79, 94
services, 27, 87, 94, 124, 138
servitude, 58, 77, 144
sex, 20, 38, 120, 151, 165–66, 176–77, 184
sexuality, 61, 180, 184

shame, 75, 81, 85–86, 92, 122, 124, 131–32, 136–37, 139–41, 175–77, 197–98, 211, 227, 233
shepherd, 52, 139–40, 142
shepherding, 144, 155, 163, 189
shepherds, 15, 51–52, 54, 56, 99, 126, 142, 153, 155, 158, 163, 207, 216, 225
signposts, people as to God's goodness, 109
signs, 26, 44, 66, 102, 122, 167, 172, 200–203, 205–11, 213, 215, 217
silencing, 55, 64, 72, 74, 127, 135, 171, 196, 207, 233
sin, 13, 22–23, 47–51, 53–55, 57–59, 64–66, 70, 78–79, 84, 92, 94, 106, 116, 125, 129–32, 137, 139, 143, 148, 155, 162–63, 178, 180, 183, 186–87, 191, 200–201, 204, 206–8, 211, 225–27
Sinai, 44
sinfulness, 47–50, 70, 73, 104, 124, 186, 201, 204
skepticism, 63
skills, 132, 160, 175, 191, 194
slavery, 40, 59, 67–69, 73, 76, 80, 82, 141, 144, 182, 224
societies, 50, 66, 86, 176, 185, 189, 198
society, 33–35, 37, 40, 51, 64, 86, 89, 93, 108, 137, 175, 177, 179–80, 187, 190, 198
sociology, 33, 37, 62, 83, 85, 100
Solomon, 38, 116
Son, God the, 7, 9, 11–12, 14, 21–25, 28, 31, 41, 51, 55, 73, 102, 109–10, 133, 158–59, 175, 177, 184
sonship, 25
soul, 15, 48, 72, 103–6, 109, 130–33, 137, 141
sovereignty, 33, 51, 73, 129, 216, 218
speakers, 119, 209–10, 222
spin, 72, 123, 130
Spirit, Holy, 5, 7, 13–14, 21, 24–25, 28, 41–44, 46, 52, 77, 79, 102, 109–10, 126, 129, 135, 141, 143, 189, 195, 214
spirit, human, 134, 162, 224

spiritual, 14, 19–20, 29–30, 36, 40–41, 43–44, 51–60, 80, 82, 101, 106, 116, 121, 133, 144, 157, 159–61, 163, 178, 180, 208, 211–12, 219–21, 225–29, 233, 236
spirituality, 143, 231
spouses, 57, 105, 166, 182–83, 194
standards, 37–40, 113, 125, 176, 212, 220, 227
status, 11, 19, 43–44, 61, 82–83, 85, 87–88, 91–92, 94, 96–97, 113, 121, 124, 169, 172, 175, 194–95, 203, 209
stereotypes, gender, 189, 214
stewardship, 59, 174, 186, 193
strategic, 82
strategies, 18, 97, 140, 181, 202, 207
structures, 33–35, 54, 122–23, 129–30, 142, 153, 160–63, 167, 169–70, 172, 187, 196, 200, 226, 231
style, leadership, 16, 18, 20, 22, 32, 58
subcultures, 89
subjugation, 177
submission, 30–31, 39–40, 58, 76, 128, 141, 158, 178, 182, 216
subordination, 21, 175
substitution, penal, 221
subtlety, of power abuse, 201
subversion, 84, 170–71, 208–9
success, 27, 65, 72, 109, 113, 119–20, 134, 139–40, 157, 181, 191, 201, 204, 206–9, 211–13, 221
success measures, achievable, 212
suffering, 10, 42, 54, 59, 65, 68, 91, 121, 131–36, 159, 177–80, 186, 188–89, 204, 219, 227, 234, 236
suicide, 177, 211
supervision, 160–61, 163, 167
supervisors, 128, 162–64
suppression, of dissent, 18
survivors, 132, 135–36, 219, 226, 228–29, 231–35
suspicion, 63, 87, 89, 91, 122, 148, 192, 213, 219–20
symbiosis, 30, 155
sympathy, 67–68, 175

symptoms, 60, 71, 128, 200–201, 203, 205, 207, 209, 211, 213, 215, 217, 223
systemic, 52, 54–55, 192
systems, 34–35, 57, 127, 153, 170, 179, 183, 200–201, 203, 205, 207–9, 211, 213, 215–17, 222, 229

talents, 57, 187, 189, 198
taproot, of abuse, 14
teachability, 79, 160, 162, 215
teachers, 96–97, 102, 118–19, 147–48, 152, 154–55, 210
teaching, 13, 26, 36, 47, 49–50, 54, 57, 78, 97, 101–2, 110, 117–19, 123, 142, 151–56, 158–59, 181, 203–4, 206, 209–10
teams, 72, 74, 79, 145, 153, 156, 160, 162–63, 169, 190, 192, 195, 197–99, 219
teamwork, 190–91
technique, 213
temptation, 12–13, 22, 27, 29, 38, 40, 44–45, 64, 70, 72, 78–80, 114, 117, 119, 129, 131, 135, 166, 169, 191–92, 211–12, 214–15, 235
terminus, 103
testimonies, 57, 68, 97, 100, 229
testimony, 20, 23, 47, 219, 228–30, 232
thanksgiving, 99, 190
theocracy, 33, 36
theology, 16, 18–20, 24–26, 31, 42, 46, 48, 60–61, 64, 110, 180, 184, 190, 204, 215, 220, 235
theorists, 84
therapies, 223
threatening, 225
threats, 9, 13, 35, 74, 78, 80, 90, 107, 114, 123, 141, 164, 171, 225, 227
throne, 40, 132, 174
totalitarianism, 31, 63, 71
toxicity, 18, 40, 75, 97, 126, 140, 197, 209
tradition, 18, 22–23, 26–27, 29, 35, 84, 89, 118–19, 175–76, 178–79, 229

training, 65, 74, 117–18, 128, 160, 162–63, 169, 189, 194, 207, 216, 224, 236
transaction, 87
transcendence, 8, 19, 27
transference, 171
transformation, 64, 79–80
transformative, 78, 225
transparency, 22, 40, 55, 159–60, 162, 165–66, 168, 172, 198
trauma, 132–34, 136, 184, 203, 206, 223, 236
triage, 229
tribalism, 28, 34, 36, 44, 74, 91, 94, 113, 117, 187, 214
triggering, 133, 223
Trinity, 7–8, 13–14, 16–17, 19–27, 29–31, 102–3, 105, 108–9
trust, 39, 50–51, 72, 76, 79–80, 82, 130, 133–34, 155, 160–62, 167–68, 172, 187–88, 191–98, 201, 205–6, 208, 211, 219, 222, 226, 233–34
trustworthiness, 159, 234
truth, 18–21, 42, 54–55, 59, 62–64, 66, 70–74, 77, 94, 99, 102, 116, 118–20, 122, 125–26, 129, 135–36, 150, 154, 181, 183, 197, 201, 229, 232–34, 236
truthfulness, 31, 70–71, 229, 233
typology, 31
tyranny, 34, 76, 126, 155

unequal (relationships), 180, 220
unfriendly, 226
ungodliness, 73, 116, 203, 205
unhealthy, 78, 161, 167, 200–203, 205, 207, 209–11, 213, 215, 217
unholy, 48, 51, 60
uniformity, 76, 208
union, with, 5–6, 9, 11, 16, 75, 92, 94, 100, 158, 208
united, to, 5
united, 5, 8, 13–15, 23, 99
unity, 5, 190
unmasking (false brothers), 60, 152
usurper, 225
usurping (God's authority), 77

utopia, 207

values, 30, 81, 87–89, 93, 96–98, 161, 163, 172, 181, 199, 235
vengeance, 22
vicar, 138, 163
vice, 28, 30
victimhood, 64–65, 193, 233
victims, 12, 49, 52–53, 55, 57–58, 64–65, 116, 130–32, 134–35, 139, 148–49, 162, 171, 177, 180, 219–20, 225–26, 232, 234–35
violence, 21, 23, 74, 155, 176–77, 184
virtue, 22, 42, 98, 106, 139, 175, 178, 180, 183, 231, 234
visionary, 58, 206
volunteers, 188, 190, 198–99, 230–31, 236
vows, 23, 54
vulnerability, 36, 41, 48, 50, 53, 56–57, 62, 64–65, 96–97, 126, 131, 155, 166, 170, 172, 174, 178–79, 182–83, 185–86, 197, 211, 220, 223–24, 231, 233

warnings, 52, 66, 108, 122, 126, 140, 223
warriors, 18–19, 23
weakness, 42, 50–51, 53–54, 64, 71, 74, 80–81, 106, 143, 155, 178–79, 184, 211, 215, 222, 224
wealth, 35–36, 38, 61, 82, 86, 89, 175
weapons, 38, 57, 131, 223, 228
whistleblowers, 47, 164, 169
wickedness, 48, 68, 134
widows, 36, 40, 54, 59, 180
wife, 18, 24, 116, 175, 177, 190
winsome, 27, 52
wisdom, 37, 48, 79, 102, 139, 163, 165–67, 188, 193, 203, 221, 223, 228
witness, 39, 58, 118, 122, 212, 219, 224, 229–30
wokeness, 63
woman, 21, 31, 50, 173, 175, 177–80, 187, 192, 195–96
women, 38, 64, 98, 131, 165–67, 174–82, 184–99, 214, 229, 236

worldliness, 71, 78, 81, 142, 169, 222, 224, 235
worldview, 173
worry, 184, 203–4
worship, 8, 17, 33, 69, 76, 78, 119, 175, 180, 183
wounds, 102, 131–34, 136, 196, 219, 223, 226, 233

wrath, 22, 44, 179–80
Wrathful, 22

Yahweh, 6–7, 33–34, 36–37, 40–41, 76

Zeal, 94

Scripture Index

Genesis
1:26	50
3:5	22
3:16	50

Exodus
18	21
32	44
8:6	53
8:13	53
8:15	53
16:48–50	183
20:7	200

Leviticus
11–14	36
18	32
19	32, 37
4:20—23:28	55
10:10–11	36
10:11	21
11:44–45	49
18:1–5	32, 37
19:2	49
19:33–34	41
20:7	49
25:23	33
25:35–38	41

Numbers
14	44
11	42–43
11–14	41
1:47–53	36
11:16–17	43
11:24–25	43
11:21–22	43
12:3	42
12:7–8	44
14:10–12	44
20:2–13	200
20:12	201
35:1–5	36

Deuteronomy
16:18—18:22	34
9:23–29	44
10:17–19	41
15:12–15	41
17:14–20	33, 38
17:16–17	38
17:18, 19	51
17:20	51
24:19–22	41
28:15–68	51
32:35	233
33:10	36
10:12	37

Joshua
5:14	34
13:14	36
18:7	36
21:1–42	36

Judges
8:22—9:57	35

1 Samuel
3:12	116
8:1–20	34
8:3	40
12:1–5	39
13:14	116
23:16	158, 164

1 Kings
21	34
11:4–6	116
12:25–33	36
21:7	34

1 Chronicles
29:17	38

2 Chronicles
15:3	21
17:7	21
19:4–7	34
19:4–11	35

Job
13:15	59

Ezra
7:6	21

Nehemiah
8:7–9	21

Psalms
5, 10, 17	39
27:4	106
33:5	40
34:18–22	134
89:14	40
99:4	40
130:7	135
11:7	40

Proverbs
3:34	42
8:15	50
8:15, 16	50
16:19	42
18:17	147
31:8–9	41

Ecclesiastes
4:1	130

Isaiah
14	22
45	4, 6–7, 9–10
14:14	22
42:1–4	235
44:28	51
45:5	6
45:6	6
45:14	6
45:18	6
45:21	6
45:22–25	7
53:3–5	136
61:8	40
63:10–14	41

Jeremiah
2:8	51
2:13	182
10:21	51
14:2	95
15:9	95
17:5	103
17:9	233
18:8	21
20:1–6	36
23:1–6	51
25:34–38	51
31:34	52

Lamentations
3:18	132

3:19–24	133	10:37	62
		18:11	49
Ezekiel		18:26–27	62
34	14–15, 51–52, 54	20:47	54
7:26	21	21:2	59
22:29–31	183	22:27	144
34:1–5	51–52		
34:5	54	**John**	
36:25–27	52	1:5	55
		1:14	232
Micah		13:5	174
3:11	21	16:33	136
5:4–5	51		
6:8	41	**Acts**	
		1:14	151
Zechariah		1:15, 16	151
11:4–17	51	2:29, 37	151
		3:17, 22	151
Malachi		11:19–30	152
1:2	182	13:1–3	152
1:3	182	14:23	153
1:9	183	14:24–28	152
2:4–7	36	18:18, 27	152
3:2	183	20:28–3	126
		20:29	52
		21:7, 17	152
Matthew			
5:2–12	113	**Romans**	
5:43–45	22	5:12	48
5:48	22	12:3–8	190
9:36	54, 58	12:10	144
12:15–21	235	12:19–20	22
12:20	235	13:1, 2, 4	50
23:4	57	14:1	143
23:15	54	14:23	143
23:23	49, 57	15:16	21
Mark		**1 Corinthians**	
6:34	54	1–4	98
10:42	142	2:1–5	211
10:45	58, 174	2:2	119
		3:9	59
Luke		6:9	58
9:49–50	204	8:11	53
10:25, 29	61	10:12–13	129

1 Corinthians (continued)

12:4–18	190
13:2	140
13:8–9, 14	141
14:37	141
16:11–12	151
16:12	58

2 Corinthians

1:24	159
8:23	151
11:26	152

Galatians

2:4	152
2:20	134
6:2	134

Ephesians

2:1	14
2:1–3	14
2:12	14
2:13–14	5
2:14–15	14
2:15	5, 14
2:18	13, 14
2:22	5
4:1–2	204
4:1–16	190
4:11	153
4:11–16	214
5:1–2	14, 182
5:22–33	182
2:11–22	204

Philippians

2	3, 5, 95
3	83, 88, 209, 213
1:1	153
1:25–26	159
2:1	5
2:1–2	5
2:1–11	4
2:2	5, 95
2:3	58
2:3–4	6
2:5	3–6, 9, 12, 95–96
2:5–11	3, 4–5, 12, 96, 174
2:7	8, 95, 174
2:6–8	6
2:6–11	3
2:7	174
2:9	6
2:9–11	6
2:12–18	6
3:1–2	94–95
3:1–16	84, 90
3:4	83, 91
3:4–6	84
3:4–16	83–84
3:7	91
3:9	92
3:10	133
3:12	92
3:17	99
4:2	5, 95

1 Thessalonians

2:3–8	15
5:12	141, 144

1 Timothy

3:2–3	155
5:17	153

2 Timothy

3:10	159

Titus

2	167
1:1	144
1:5–9	153
2:11–15	78

Philemon

16	141

Hebrews

2:11, 12, 17	151

2:17	55	**3 John**	
3:1, 12	151	1	150
3:1–6	41	1–3, 5	150
3:13	148	2, 5, 11, 14	151
4:16	132	2–4, 5–8	151
12:2	132	3	150
12:17	182	3, 5, 10	150–51
13:7	146	3, 14b	151
13:7, 17	153	4	154
13:17	141	5–8	150–51
		6, 9	150
James		8	152
1:17	28	9–10	151, 157
2:9	49	9–10a	150
2:10	49	10	150–51
2:11	49	11	150, 155
3:1	53–54	12, 14	151
		12	150
1 Peter		13	157
1:6	49		
5:2	141	**Jude**	
5:2–3	139–40	1:12	52
5:3	145		
		Revelation	
1 John		1:8	50
1:5–7	55	2:20–23	155
1:8–10	129	4:8	50
2:19	154	5:6	174
2:22–23	155	11:17	50
3:4	49	15:3	50
4:2–3	154	16:7	50
4:19–21	155	19:6	50
5:3	155	21:4	136
5:16	53	21:22	50

2 John

7, 9   154

Milton Keynes UK
Ingram Content Group UK Ltd.
UKHW020045121023
430368UK00011B/179